# MANAGING RISK

*For Susan, Nancy and Richard*

# Managing Risk

How to work successfully with risk

IAN M. JOHNSTONE-BRYDEN
*Rayzarb Associates*

# Avebury

Aldershot • Brookfield USA • Hong Kong • Singapore • Sydney

Published by
Avebury
Ashgate Publishing Limited
Gower House
Croft Road
Aldershot
Hants GU11 3HR
England

Ashgate Publishing Company
Old Post Road
Brookfield
Vermont 05036
USA

**British Library Cataloguing in Publication Data**

Johnstone-Bryden, Ian M.
   Managing Risk: How to Work Successfully
   with Risk

ISBN 1 85972 255 5

**Library of Congress Catalog Card Number:** 95-79002

Printed and bound in Great Britain by
Athenaeum Press Ltd, Gateshead, Tyne & Wear

# Contents

# Author's note

Risk is frequently introduced by communication and the limits of natural language. This results from inconsistent use of words and terms, misunderstanding of words used, and offence caused by use of particular words and terms. The wider the audience, the greater the potential for risk.

In writing a book which covers the full range of risk management, a number of niches are covered, such as crime prevention, health and safety, and quality control. Each niche has generated its own jargon and one of the worst areas is in Information Technology. To further complicate matters, a term used freely in one niche area may also be used with equal freedom in another niche, but to mean something very different. As far as possible, jargon terms have been avoided throughout this text. Where it has been necessary to use a particular specialised word, its meaning has been described at least at the first point of use.

One particular area of risk today is the use of words which imply gender. The structure of English gives a writer limited choice in this matter, and maximum potential to offend some readers. The writer either has to select one gender, or to produce a confusing and unnecessarily long document where every point contains an explanation of equality. This book uses the male pronoun in the interests of economy and has standardised on the male gender throughout the text only in the interests of continuity. The writer has not intended to favour one gender above the other, and asks the reader to treat all uses of gender as full equality without preference.

# Acknowledgements

I would like to thank all those who taught me and debated risk management with me. I am grateful for all that I learnt from them and the inspiration they gave me. In particular, I am indebted to Stan Cordell for inviting me to join the Visiting Faculty of the Cranfield Institute of Technology and the opportunity which it gave me to learn and to share experience. I would like to thank my colleagues in the ISiS Consortium for their helpful suggestions during the preparation of this work. In particular, for their encouragement and debating, I would like to thank Leroy Lacy, Randy Brown, Mike Rose, and Scott Howard. I would also like to thank Jonathan Wood for his knowledge and lively debate on the subjects of government efficiency and the introduction of legislation. Finally, I would like to thank those colleagues who have served with me on working parties and shared their views and experience at seminars and conferences.

# Foreword

This foreword will start out like most found at the beginning of books with the statement that, "this book is a book that needed to be written". In this case, the statement is really true. This book addresses the subject of risk management and gives focus to the entire process of computer security in the context of the enterprise, and specifically addresses the relationship of the information processing activity with the enterprise need for security and privacy played against investment required and the level of importance of the information being protected.

I have been in the computer security business since its inception in the early days of mainframe and timeshared super computers in the US Department of Defense. At that time we were but a few computer scientists who all used the same computer and shared resources based on informal agreements not to disturb each others data. It was clear at that time, as the population of users on the computer became large, some form of information security would be required. We first began to enforce privacy mechanisms by segregating users by access times, where all the users of the system with similar needs to know used the system at the same time. It didn't take long for all those whose time slot came at 02:00 in the morning to begin to complain. We computer scientists in the operating system group began to develop software mechanisms to separate information and granulate access to information based on users attributes. Because this branch of system development was directed by the DOD, it focused heavily on non disclosure as opposed to data integrity and non denial of service. Since this effort was headed by us technologists it tended towards the algorithmically sophisticated and did not necessarily address all aspects of the relative importance of the information being protected. It clearly did not access other sources of loss of the information, such as errors and omissions or theft of information using other means.

As time has progressed, the science of information security has matured and become a more robust endeavor, we have developed many more mechanisms to enhance security, integrity and privacy but we have done this with out much focus on how this work fits into the overall information processing goals of the entire enterprise. As I have worked in the field, I have done so without much guidance based on the amount of loss that can result from a failure. We, down in the IT shops, have invested tremendous sums of money and effort to make sure that it was impossible for a failure of any of our systems to cause a compromise in the information processed by systems that we support, while the copier just outside the shop door is a large bandwidth path out of the company. The IT industry in general has conducted fragmented and inefficient efforts to protect information processed by the enterprise. We continue to take the "the hole won't be on my side of the boat" approach to information security, which is clearly the most expensive in the cost of effort and money approach to the problem.

Now that we in the computer science industry have networked most computers in the world, the concept of protecting information and controlling access to that information has become a popular topic. I have noted that just about every aspect of the information technology security industry has been addressed in print except for the concept of risk. You can find all about the mechanisms and techniques to protect information and granulate access to information, but there is still not much published about how to go about the process of integrating this technology into an overall approach to the task of protecting information within the enterprise as a whole. Ian's book is the definitive source for the manager of an enterprise information system to control all aspects of the information processing system to assure that the information is protected while it is allowed to flow freely through out the enterprise to the individuals who need the information to make daily decisions. This book directs the reader to the areas where effort must be invested to make sure that all members of the information processing team are working in concert to assure the widest dissemination of information while protecting that information to the level that it needs to be protected and no more. If the guidelines in this book are followed, the implementor can be assured that the information processed is protected and that the investment in protecting that information is reasonable

I am pleased to find that Ian has taken the time to write this book and am sorry that the book that should have been the first publication has come out at the tail end of the process. I would recommend that the information practitioner read Ian's book, and then go back and re-read all the other literature that has been collected with the concepts gained from Ian's book as a guide. Following that course, the total investment in security and integrity will be much lower and the overall security of the system will be much more consistent. Read on and I think you will find the book well written and will provide valuable information about how to view the entire process of information security and risk management.

Leroy Lacy
President Armadillo Systems
Ben Lomond
California
United States of America

# Introduction

*Managing Risk* examines the subjects of risk analysis, risk reduction, and risk management as a comprehensive subject across an enterprise. The principles apply equally to all sizes and types of enterprise. Most organizations still deal with aspects of risk piecemeal, with very few enterprises charging one individual with the ultimate responsibility for managing risk across the enterprise, resulting in unmoderated risk and unnecessary costly duplication of effort.

Human nature is optimistic, We prefer to think that risk only affects other people. It can be difficult to decide the probability and impact of any particular risk, encouraging the strong temptation not to invest precious funds in countermeasures which we hope will never be needed. When we do take risk seriously, it is often just after we have suffered from fire, theft, or accident, and by then it may be too late to act.

Historically, enterprises have attempted to address areas of risk in isolation. Today, even the smallest enterprises automate processes making it impossible to reliably divide operations. Quality management relates to health and safety issues, fire protection can conflict with crime protection, every activity involves personnel, and we increasingly rely on complex computer networks. Effective risk management must span all of these areas.

*Managing Risk* shows how risks can be identified and reduced economically and effectively, before serious damage occurs.

Chapter One defines risk and security, providing examples of how the use of terms affects the process of controlling risk. Terms in common use are explained and related to each other within the framework of risk.

Chapter Two examines the use of enterprise and risk policies in successful risk management. Methodologies are examined, establishing the need for dynamic policies to test threats and solutions.

Chapter Three examines the process of risk analysis, necessary to the production of enterprise and risk policies. The methods of evaluating risks are discussed and compared with common enterprise practice.

Chapter Four examines the part which people and legislation play in the expansion and reduction of risk. It shows how people contribute to the generation of risk, why their needs and behaviour must be considered, and how this may be achieved.

Chapter Five examines risks which affect enterprise sites and describes methods of reducing and managing risk within the area of a site.

Chapter Six continues the examination of a site, considering the special and different requirements of buildings within a site. Risk reduction methods are described, in relation to area site protection.

Chapter Seven reviews the challenges presented by facilities shared with other enterprises and with the general public. Examples are provided of the different technology and approaches and the need to balance protection with the operational requirements of enterprises.

Chapter Eight follows the examination of risk management at fixed installations, by reviewing the different needs of mobile facilities. It examines the reasons for mobility and the new technologies which are changing the patterns of mobility and resultant risks.

Chapter Nine examines the way in which the use of information is introducing social and economic change with major changes to risks. It identifies why information systems are making enterprise wide risk management essential and not only desirable, through their bridging of traditional divisions in the work place.

Chapter Ten examines the ways in which information risks may be successfully managed. The dramatic growth of computer based systems and international networks is examined in its relationship with risk development. The national and international security criteria are examined against the background of the commercial development of computer and communications equipment.

Chapter Eleven discusses some of the changes which may be introduced by the Information Revolution and how these will affect risk management. In particular, the social and economic possibilities are explored. It concludes that there will be revolutionary change, that a number of possible courses are open, and that this change will have a strong impact on the way in which risk develops and may be managed.

# 1 Definition of risk and security

*Security* conjures up different images for different people. In general, it produces images of policemen, barbed wire fences, locks, and weapons. The Oxford English Dictionary defines *security* as, "condition of being secure". It defines *secure* as, "feeling no care, or apprehension; without care; careless; free from care, apprehension, anxiety, or alarm; overconfident; free from risk; having a safe prospect".

By definition, *security* is a subjective feeling and is not an objective statement. This may explain why security, as a subject, is emotive and frequently irrational. It raises expectations which cannot be satisfied completely. It often encourages people and organizations to embark upon a course of actions which result in a false sense of security. This condition may be considerably more dangerous.

Total security is a state which no one is ever likely to achieve, or maintain. The enterprise which fits the very best locks to doors and windows may still become a victim of burglary. The best that can be achieved is a greatly reduced risk of attack. Over a period of time, it will be necessary to upgrade the equipment to maintain the same level of protection. The enterprise will also have to employ a number of other devices and techniques to adequately reinforce the locks. Most enterprises inadequately protect their assets, but some greatly over protect. Almost all fail to frequently review the level of protection which they have provided, or to take the necessary steps to upgrade the protection. In the process, the enterprise may spend money to protect against theft, when the major risks may be in other areas, such as fire. The only way to avoid this is to look at all *risks*, rather than just one type of risk.

Large organizations may spend considerable sums of money on buying security devices, but they are often providing an even lower level of protection, proportionately, than that provided by small enterprises. The

3

protection which is provided is often less effectively employed. In many cases, the protection is also poorly applied because the risk calculations are incorrect.

Even small enterprises may have a number of people to consider, working in different parts of a building. It is very easy for equipment to be misused, or even disabled, by a worker through lack of thought or training. Sometimes, inappropriate equipment is installed because the person buying it failed to understand the nature of some processes involved in the organization. The larger the organization, the greater the risks. An important factor in risk expansion is poor communication. This develops through divisionalization of the workforce and, in the largest enterprise, a lack of identity with the organization and its assets.

As long as we regard objects in a proprietorial manner, there will be theft Ownership promotes envy and, in addition to theft, there will be vandalism to consider. Risks of this nature may be a very small proportion of the range of threats that any enterprise may have to consider. A larger problem is often caused by thoughtless actions and lack of training. There are also threats which result from unidentified equipment failure. Unless adequate protection is provided, these threats will cause businesses to fail and even result in personal injury and loss of life.

In view of the severe consequences which may result from inadequate protection, why do we not take security seriously?

There are three major reasons for our failure.

One reason is that we are eternal optimists. Fire, burglary, murder and disasters never happen to us - *until they do*. Many risks often seem very remote possibilities and, generally, most people prefer not to dwell on the less pleasant aspects of life. The best protected person, or organization, is usually the person who has either suffered directly, or has a close contact who has. This can result in a desire to over protect against the recent known risk, ignoring a wider range of more significant threats.

The second reason for failure is a narrow view of *risk*. In larger organizations, this may be compounded by having a number of people who have a formal *risk management* responsibility for a part of the organization's operations. This can result in some unnecessary duplication of effort, whilst fatal gaps are left in the defences. Most *security* effort goes into countering perceived external threats. Attention also tends to dwell on threats which result from deliberate aggressive actions. This is a consequence of the use of the word *security*, rather than the term *risk management*.

The third reason for failure is financial. Risk Management costs money. This cost is generated by; risk analysis study; solution acquisition costs; implementation costs, and; running costs.

Cost of acquisition may be substantial, not least because the developers of devices are required to invest heavily in research and development to maintain the effectiveness of their products.

Implementation costs may be significant, because they should include the training of personnel to correctly use the devices, in addition to the cost of purchasing, installing and commissioning the protective systems. Adequate training is essential, because without it the system is unlikely to produce the full expected level of protection.

Running costs may vary considerably. Some devices do not require extensive test and maintenance procedures, while other devices do. Most counter measures demand frequent review to ensure that the threat has not changed and that the perceived level of protection is being maintained. Some devices, particularly those employed in information technology systems, may reduce the performance of production systems, requiring additional equipment, and/or manpower.

The total costs may be very significant. Taking into account the optimistic nature of most people, this provides every opportunity to avoid acquiring adequate protection, either by not making a purchase, or by implementing a reduced solution. The latter situation is always the most dangerous because the deficiencies may not be recognized.

Cost of provision is not the only financial issue. There may be an additional cost. In any enterprise, a risk may already be recognized. Public knowledge of that failure may be very embarrassing and result in loss of customer confidence. Fear of this risk has been the reason why some organizations continue to operate a system with known flaws. A full review of the original problem may identify a number of other unknown problems, but the temptation is to ignore the problem operationally and build the forecast losses into the business costs. This course of action has been taken by a number of organizations, such as banks and credit card companies, who have ignored system design faults and known fraud which is permitted by these defects. It is a form of risk reduction, because the problem is passed on to other enterprises but, once this is realized by the new victims, they may retaliate in a variety of ways which introduce much greater risk.

In some cases, enterprises see a risk, particularly risk of injury or death, and want to reduce this risk. They are deterred because they believe that this may put them at a trading disadvantage and hope that legislation will be introduced to ensure that their competitors have to carry a similar cost. Vehicle manufacturers frequently take this position and continue to build vehicles which are known to contain serious safety risks. This attitude can present risks to the manufacturers in that actions may be brought by customers for damages, and there have been cases when one manufacturer has introduced safety features and turned this to positive marketing advantage.

It could be said that the three frequent reasons for not protecting assets are only excuses for inaction. When viewed from outside this is true but, to the people involved, they appear to represent valid reasons.

An external risk analyst will usually identify a number of security deficiencies, even in the best run organizations. In some organizations, these deficiencies may be very obvious and serious. It may be true that the organization's managers are too close to the problems to recognize them. It may also be true that the consultant has a specialist experience of risk analysis, and there is little benefit in hiring a specialist who does not have a better knowledge of the specialist subject than the client. Usually though, the risk analyst will take a less restricted view of the subject. The core difficulty is the interpretation of what *security* and *risk* are.

The European Harmonized Criteria for Information Technology Security has been produced by the combined efforts of four countries; the United Kingdom; the Netherlands; Germany, and; France. As is often the case in multi-national co-operation, language is of particular importance. In preparing the early stages of the criteria, the use of particular words was carefully discussed. As a result of this discussion, three words were selected to describe specific areas of Information Technology security; *Assurance; Integrity; Availability*. Although the representatives were interested in Information Technology security, the terms which they chose apply equally to any risk assessment.

*Assurance* means the level of confidence resulting from the ability of the counter measure to reduce risk. This is frequently the only measurement applied to security issues. Measurement becomes more accurate as the potential risks are more clearly defined, because it only estimates the ability of a counter measure to deal with an identified threat. Threats are rarely constant. They can diminish, or grow, over time. They may also be increased, or removed, as a new threat develops. As a result, a level of confidence can only be developed by a comprehensive review of potential risks, and maintained by subsequent reviews.

*Integrity* may be considerably more important to most organizations. While *Assurance* is more concerned with countering aggression, *Integrity* is concerned with the dependability of the counter measures and the subjects which they protect. As a simple example, a sophisticated lock which offers theoretically high assurance against attack may be difficult to use and may offer low integrity because it becomes too much trouble to use. In reality, it should also be regarded as having low assurance because its design defects reduce the probability that it will be used, and therefore that it will be performing the intended duty.

*Availability* is also very important. In the example of the lock, the device intended to defeat a criminal may more frequently defeat the authorized users. If the lock design prevents it being opened easily, the authorized user will be prevented from gaining access. This is the aspect of security which is often overlooked. It would be relatively simple, and inexpensive, to make a car thief proof by encasing it in concrete. This could provide a very high assurance against the risk of theft, but would provide limited integrity and zero availability. Reliable security must enable the authorized user to employ the resource for the purpose it was intended to be used for.

By using *Assurance, Integrity* and *Availability* to define *Security*, it is possible to provide security which works. Any attempt to interpret security as *denial* is likely to be flawed because it is likely to deny the resource to authorized users. It is therefore essential to decide what an *Authorized User* is.

The *authorized user* is a person who has an identified and approved need to access a resource. Military security has long used two measures. Data subjects have been classified according to their sensitivity. This is important when security is designed to safeguard secrets because a secret becomes available to progressively more people over a period of time, until it eventually becomes general public knowledge. It is therefore important to know where knowledge of a subject is at any given point on the path from secret to public information. There is little point in expending effort to guard a subject which no longer needs guarding. It could be argued that a secret ceases to be a secret once it is known to more than one person. The military have therefore employed the *need-to-know* principle to identify *authorized users*. This is designed to maintain a given level of security for as long a period as necessary, by reducing the number of people who can gain access to the information.

It might be thought that this approach is a unique requirement of the military which does not apply to other types of enterprise. This is not so. A thief will only try to enter premises if he thinks there is something worth stealing. Therefore, an enterprise which advertises wealth is advertising that it is a worthy target. An example of this could be the mounting of alarm bell housings in a prominent place at the front of a building. The intention is to deter. Often, the reality is that the enterprise is advertising that it has something worth protecting. In addition, the alarm bell housing will usually prominently display the name of the supplier. A professional criminal then knows what type of devices have been installed and what steps he has to take to counter the counter measures.

7

In the days when most workers were paid each week in cash, payroll robbery was common. The employment of a security vehicle advertised the method of transport and the size of the payroll. A serious robber could then plan to counter the defences. Well intentioned protective measures often present more difficulties for the people who need to access the resource than they do for the aggressor.

The principles applied to reduce the risk of attack by spies and thieves can also be applied to any other risks. Many accidents occur because an unauthorized and untrained person attempts to operate equipment. Equally, some accidents occur because equipment is claimed to be safe, when only a proportion of potential risks have been catered for and a false sense of security is generated by the safety claims.

The identification of the *authorized user* therefore has two particular points of importance. It should ensure that only people who have a verified need to access are allowed access privileges, to maintain a given level of security for as long as necessary, or possible, and it should ensure that protective systems do not unnecessarily impede those people who do have an acknowledged need to access. It may also be necessary to permit an authorized user to assign access privileges to a deputy to act for him during periods of absence. This means that the achievement of *risk reduction* requires an understanding of the resource, how it is used, and what part it plays in the overall operation.

*Risk reduction* is the process of taking account of the identified risks, and their relative importance, followed by steps to reduce them to an acceptable level. In a building, systems which give the most effective protection against burglars may introduce new risks in the event of fire and may be considered unacceptably unsightly. An acceptable reduction of risk may be achieved by using different countermeasures.

Therefore, an essential early step in reducing risk is to build a *Risk Policy*. The risk policy must identify the potential threats and identify the ways in which they may be eliminated, or reduced to an acceptable level. However, it is unwise to develop a risk policy in isolation, although this is frequently the way that many of us proceed. The first step should be to produce an *Enterprise Policy*.

The *Enterprise Policy* identifies the objective of the enterprise and the actions and resources which are necessary to achieve that objective. Within the actions and resources *risk* should be addressed. Every enterprise has a principal goal, even if most people do not take time to clearly identify that goal. Without identification of our true *objective*, it is very difficult to know whether we are wisely using any time or resources.

Once the principal *objective* has been identified, it is possible to start the planning process. To meet any *objective*, it will be necessary to identify a

8

number of *tasks*. A *task* may involve the building and operation of a factory, or the purchase of an asset. Each task will involve a number of *processes*, necessary to the successful completion of the task. Each *process* will require a number of *tools* and resources. In a more complex environment, it may be necessary to divide a process into a number of subprocesses. Within this environment, risk management may be a process, a subprocess, or a tool. The *Risk Policy* therefore appears to start some way down the *Enterprise Policy*, but the information which is required to build the enterprise policy will contain some highly sensitive data and will itself require protection.

The *Risk Policy* deals with threats and countermeasures. It should therefore not be restricted to theft, fraud and other aggressive acts. Equally, it should not deal solely with external threats, because these may be a lesser problem than internal threats. This is frequently the reason why larger organizations fail to provide themselves with adequate security. It is not uncommon for a number of people to each have responsibility for security issues and be located in different departments, reporting to different managers and directors.

This results in two situations which increase risk. Lack of communications is usually a major problem. A greater problem is that risk countermeasures are often evaluated financially in isolation. This means that a security officer will present a proposal for funding without the ability to relate the financial and operational impact on the processes, tasks and objective of the organization. The decision maker has a similar problem, being provided with only part of the information needed to make a reliable decision.

This results in the cost of the protective measures being viewed as an overhead which does not provide a return financially. The reality may be that the costs of risk reduction are a very small percentage of the cost of the risk itself if it is allowed to go unchecked. The probability of those losses may be great and lead to even more significant losses. For example, seven out of every ten companies which suffer a major fire close down within twelve months of the incident. These fires may have been caused by a wide variety of agents, from deliberate arson to equipment failure. Similarly, 90% of all companies which suffer a major computer failure go out of business within eighteen months of the incident. The reasons for failure may be even more diverse than those which apply to fire and, in some cases, will be a secondary result, or the primary cause, of the fire. In both cases, human error may play an important part.

*Probability* is an important factor in enterprise and risk management. If it is considered that one risk is very likely to result in an incident, it has a high probability factor. This can prove difficult to calculate. A frequent approach is to study statistics produced by some respected authority. Given weight of the statistical claims, which have been regularly published, the cost of protection may be seen to be a very small proportion of the cost of not providing it, in simple financial terms. This is only a part of the total picture. Serious security breaches may result in injury, and even death. These results cannot be measured solely in financial terms, and there may be additional consequential costs.

The enterprise policy which contains a risk policy provides the comprehensive approach across the enterprise. This overcomes the communications problems which result from departmentalization.

The key component of the risk policy is therefore risk analysis. Although security, as a subject, may be subjective and emotive, risk analysis is capable of precise expression. However, this expression can take several forms. A typical risk analysis may be informally and imprecisely expressed in *natural language*. The difficulty of using a natural language is that it is open to interpretation. The author may understand exactly what he perceives as a risk and exactly how it will be reduced, but a reader could form a very different impression. Techniques originally developed to assist the design and implementation of computer based systems are increasingly employed to reduce the scope for interpretation.

*Structured methods* are perhaps easiest to understand in that they are methodologies which employ natural language. By combining graphics and text in a logical order, structured methods can be understood by a wide range of people. Because they impose an order, they allow errors to be identified more rapidly, which was why they were introduced to assist computer software development where a large number of steps are required to build a computer programme. They also make it easier to amend later. As structured methods already exist as software applications, in a form which can be developed into an expert system, they have much to offer those building enterprise and risk policies.

An alternative is *formal methods* which use a mathematical language. There is a school of thought, particularly strong in academia, which maintains that formal methods are the only unequivocal way of expressing a requirement, or describing a process. The disadvantage of using *formal methods* is that they are less widely understood. It is also debatable that they provide the level of accuracy claimed for them. Research into the use of *formal methods* in evaluation of computer security products has identified the need to add natural language to provide adequate description.

The failure to provide adequate security could therefore be defined as the result of inadequate risk analysis. This again calls for an understanding of the enterprise objectives. It also requires a method of estimating threats. This may be an intelligent understanding of risks which has been developed by experience and takes account of local information, or it may be the result

10

of specific research. A simple written plan may provide an adequate risk policy for the individual, but a large organization may produce a series of procedure manuals according to a methodology and the result may be stored electronically within a computer system.

The larger the enterprise, the more complex and demanding the risk policy and the more formal the risk analysis. A range of risk analysis techniques are available and will probably be computerized. They should, in any event, form part of enterprise modelling. The more complex the situation, the greater the resources required to develop the risk policy. It is also probable that a large organization will benefit from employing specialist consultants to assist both in the production of the policy and in the periodic audit of the countermeasures. However, the responsibility cannot be sub-contracted and forgotten. The habit of producing a simple written summary is as valuable to the head of a major multinational company, as it is for the individual. The primary value is that it encourages the user to develop the habit of thinking about risk as a natural and integral part of his activities. It also ensures that any policy produced by subordinates, or consultants, can be tested with some authority.

Security should therefore be more completely defined under the headings of assurance, integrity and availability. Rather than being a state of total peace of mind, security should mean that risks have been reduced to an acceptable level. A risk policy is essential to record the steps taken to achieve this position and their relationship to other vital processes in achieving a set objective. Having produced a risk policy, it must be reviewed and updated to maintain its relevance. No policy is effective unless it is capable of being tested.

No risk policy has any real value unless it is *enforced*. Enforcement may comprise two investigative activities; response to an alarm, and; routine random checks. Therefore, the risk policy will include details of the steps which should be taken to enforce its requirements. Equally, one person, or department, should have the ultimate responsibility for enforcement, but enjoy the active support of every manager in carrying out local enforcement and observance down to the smallest work groups.

Inadequate levels of authority can make effective enforcement unattainable. As with any system of laws, success is only achieved in an environment where no one is above the law. A common reason for failure of risk management is that the person tasked with the responsibility does not have the seniority, or access to a supportive superior, to ensure that every employee can be brought to account. It is not unusual in a commercial enterprise to find that senior managers use their positions to ignore those aspects of the risk policy which do not suit them. The risk manager feels unable to take issue with a colleague who enjoys a senior rank, most often

11

because he is threatened with sanctions, such as reduced career prospects if he attempts to enforce rules which are unpopular with a superior. That is not so much a failure of the risk manager as a failure of the corporate culture and the irresponsible behaviour of superiors. Effective risk management requires courage and persistence and any person who is concerned with his popularity is not going to be able to perform his duties. Although it may be common in some enterprises for a senior person to abuse his rank and threaten a junior tasked with policing the risk policy, it is much more common for the pressures to be perceived rather than actual. It is a duty for senior personnel to be seen to obey the rules and to lead by example so that this situation does not develop.

# 2 The enterprise and risk policies

The risk policy has a number of objectives. It sets out the risks which have been identified and analyses their potential and probable impact. It identifies the possible countermeasures and analyses their impact. It sets out procedures and training requirements. It establishes a framework which can be reviewed and tested.

The starting point should be an enterprise model and policy. This is a major and essential exercise for a large organization. It is equally important for the smallest enterprise, but may be produced quickly in a simplified form. It could be argued that an organization is only the sum of a number of individuals and therefore it will operate more efficiently if each worker has his own personal plan. Planning and preparation plays an important part in the life of an individual just as much as it does for a company.

If the risk policy is the starting point, a number of significant factors will have been assumed, or ignored. This means that the risk policy is likely to be seriously flawed. As a result, countermeasures may be incomplete, inappropriate, or both. It is most unlikely that security will be provided in a cost effective manner. It is probable that a false sense of security will be established, increasing risk, rather than reducing it. There is also the probability that security will be treated as an isolated entity.

A crude example of this situation could be a club, or a dance hall. There have been a number of serious fires in public buildings of this type around the world and, sadly, there will be many more. The building is usually subject to some form of inspection by a public authority and is required to conform to a number of minimum standards in terms of safety and hygiene. Because a relatively large number of people will be present in the building during its use, and many of them may be unfamiliar with the building, most countries mandate fire alarm systems and adequate exit routes with emergency lighting to ensure that rapid evacuation is possible in an emergency. Many exit routes will be fitted with fire escape doors, designed to secure the exit against the outside. Panic bolts are fitted to enable the doors to open easily from the inside under the pressure of bodies trying to escape. This is very important when large numbers of people are flowing down a relatively narrow passageway because anything which slows the traffic will increase the risk of people being trampled in the stampede.

A common risk to clubs and dance halls is people avoiding the entrance fee. One person pays the entrance fee and then opens a fire exit to let friends enter free. This can be a major problem for a business which operates on low profit margins. A simple low cost solution is to chain and lock the exit doors.

The financial problem is solved but, in so doing, the operator has created a major new risk. Even after many fires in buildings of this type, and consequent loss of life, operators continue to adopt this practice. It may be difficult to believe, but some operators genuinely do not understand the danger which they have created. However, most who take this action do so as a financial expediency. The alternative is to patrol exit doors, or fit special remote controlled locks. Fitting chains is cheaper and easier, - *until there is a fire!*

A major fire is likely to result in loss of life, and the emergency services will be hampered in their efforts to fight it. The operators may be prosecuted and the building closed down. The operator will be unable to meet the original company objective to make money from operating the facility, as a result of not producing an adequate risk policy.

An enterprise plan enables all aspects of the enterprise be viewed in relation to each other. A planning approach of this kind is often referred to as a *Top Down View*, or a *Gods Eye View*. This implies that only one view is taken, from the top of the enterprise. To be effective, an enterprise plan should identify a primary objective first and then move on to the identification of Tasks, Processes, Sub-processes and Tools and this also provides a view across the enterprise. The plan should be flexible and permit a series of views to be taken from a number of points as part of the testing process. The plan may deal with a major enterprise, or a single individual. It is easier to look first at planning for the individual because this reduces complexity.

The majority of people exist and work without any formal planning framework. It is therefore very easy to progress through life without any clear idea of direction. The result is likely to be one of unfulfilled potential, whilst resources will have been applied expediently without producing maximum benefit. Some people find it very easy to plan, but most fail to see the benefit of devoting a small amount of time to planning to gain productive time. Essentially, it is an issue of life, against quality of life. A person who fails to obtain best value for himself is less likely to obtain best value for an employer, because we carry attitudes between work and leisure. Many enterprises do not adequately plan because there is no planning culture within the work force.

The simplest enterprise policy may be based on a time and activity management system. This is not a diary, which is only a record of events against a timetable. Diary information is adequate to show what time the next meeting will take place, and contain some essential details about the meeting, but planning requires a wider picture to be presented, covering a number of months and a wider range of information. It is also necessary to retrieve information and a diary can only be indexed by date, which may not be the best reference for an information search.

A time and activity management system should relate events, actions and meetings to a planning framework and will include a diary facility. A number of organizations and individuals have promoted their own methods of managing time and activities. Each shares core principles, but uses a different packaging. Which philosophy is chosen is less important than choosing one, but it is important to chose a system which can be followed into the future. A considerable sum of money can be spent on buying time and activity management systems and training, only to follow the system for a short time and then discard it. This is very similar to diet and exercise systems. The only ones which work are the ones which an individual can relate to and develop into a habit. There are so many systems to chose from because they have each been designed and tested by individuals and reflect the variation between people, although most systems share common concepts and differ more by detail.

The first stage is to identify the primary objective. This objective should be testable. An objective which is *to make a return on investment*, or *to be wealthy*, cannot be tested. It must contain qualification of time and value. Therefore, it could be *to make a return of £X against an expenditure of £Y, over a period of Z months*, or *to make, for an investment of £X, £1,000,000 by a specified date.*

Having identified the prime objective, a number of tasks will have to be performed to make the objective achievable. It is desirable to avoid setting a large number of tasks because this will make the plan difficult to manage. Different proprietary time and activity management systems have different views on how many tasks should be set. A good maximum number is nine, because the average human brain is able to handle nine tasks simultaneously. The brain delegates and packages tasks. A new skill may occupy most of the conscious brain during the learning phase. As the learning process continues, the new skill is built into a *chunk* and, when it is needed, the brain treats it as a single process unless it detects an abnormal

15

situation. Therefore, a plan is most effective if it conforms to the same patterns.

It might be considered unimportant to condense activity to nine primary tasks, particularly if the time and activity management system is run on computer equipment. The benefit of reducing the plan in this way is that it more readily becomes an automatic habit. Any system of documents becomes less likely to be carried as it grows in size and weight. A package which can be put into a pocket, or comfortably carried in the hand, is much more likely to be used. There should also be no need to constantly refer to the system for information on primary tasks, only for fine detail of processes and for information recording.

In principle, the basic requirements are the same for an individual as they are for the largest enterprise, but there will be some important differences. We are all primarily self-centred. That does not mean that we are prepared to admit this selfishness to others, or even to ourselves. In the opinion polls taken before elections, this may be graphically demonstrated. When the pollster asks if the interviewee is in favour of increased public spending on some socially worthy enterprise, the answer is invariably affirmative. However, the money has to be found through increased taxation and although the political party advocating social spending is ahead in the opinion polls, the party committed to reduced spending and taxation is the one to win at the election.

Each individual views life from a personal perspective and enterprises are no different. A corporate view usually assumes that life for each employee centres around the company. Some employees may live for the enterprise, but most will see work more as a way of being free to do other things, which are more important to them, in the remaining available time outside work. This is the point at which some time management systems fail, because they do not encourage, or allow, for the employee to express his own needs in his personal time planning system. This can extend to the point where some organizations consider an employee disloyal if he even considers his own needs first. The majority of enterprises would also be horrified if they found an employee who was considering life beyond the organization. This attitude may be practical for a slave owner but, in a free society, employees can, and do, move employment, and enterprises may need to change staff to take advantage of changing opportunities.

This means that any successful time management system should not just allow an employee to include his personal planning, but positively encourage it and respect the employee's right to privacy and ownership of personal data. If this approach is taken, an enterprise can encourage a planning culture and objective achievement in its work force. This will positively benefit the enterprise because the habit will not just be one which an employee tries to put on with his work clothes, but will become his life habit.

Individuals are motivated by many things and money, in a pure sense, is very rarely one of them. Unfortunately many enterprises believe that financial reward and penalty is sufficient motivation under all circumstances. This creates major risks for the enterprise. It should not matter to an enterprise if a particular employee regards his current work as a stepping stone to a different future. What does matter is that he works as effectively as possible during his employment. It can be argued that an enterprise will benefit by training employees beyond the requirements of their current work and perhaps beyond the requirements of the enterprise today. An employee will be most effective if he is happy in his work and happy with his progress in life. That means that he should always feel a challenge, because otherwise he will either become complacent or bored, presenting increased risk for the enterprise.

Sometimes this approach will be difficult, or impossible, because of the way in which an organization rewards employees financially. A practice most common in public service enterprises is to increase pay each time that the employee gains a new qualification. As each job grade has a pay scale, this may not be a major problem until the employee reaches the end of the pay scale, although some would question the merits of paying two people different amounts to perform the same duties, when the only difference was the number of qualifications held. A greater problem arises when the employee has gained sufficient qualifications to justify re-grading, but where no vacancy exists at the higher grade. As a result, personnel managers in such enterprises may restrict the amount and type of training provided to employees. That can produce just as much increased risk because employees will not feel a challenge, perform duties in an uninterested and automatic way. This has often been the mark of the bureaucrat.

Creating a challenge culture means that training must be personal. Everyone has a different learning rate and responds individually to situations. The result is that personnel training must equip every employee with the skills needed to perform the assigned tasks and also to develop his potential. There may very well be a point at which the employee must move to another enterprise to continue this development and satisfaction with life. An enterprise should not regard this as a threat for two important reasons. A well trained and motivated employee will work to optimum performance. If a positive attitude is taken by an enterprise to any employee looking beyond the enterprise for his career, there will be no dangerous period when the employee becomes frustrated and resentful. There may also be a later benefit. An employee, who feels that an employer respects and values him and is genuinely interested in his well being, will never be reluctant to return to the company at a later date. There may be a time in the future when that employee can make a significant contribution again.

Part of the rigid and selfish enterprise attitudes date back to the early days of the industrial revolution, when manpower was regarded as another resource to be owned and exploited. There were exceptions then when some enterprises built model towns for their workers and built facilities for the workers' families, but even here the motivation was often selfish, seeking to control the work force. The dramatic changes which are being introduced by the communications revolution are creating a new job mobility. Many established working practices may change and it could become normal for much of the work force to hold several jobs with different enterprises at any one time. There are signs that the labour market in many developed countries is moving in this direction. It produces new opportunities and new challenges, making reliable planning even more essential.

Before looking at time management in an enterprise, we should look at an example of the individual. The example below could just as easily have been written around a more mundane scenario, but the case study shows a relatively complex set of conditions without the added complexity of a number of employees and multiple sites.

An individual might produce a personal plan which identifies a primary objective to make £X by a specified date, so that he can take five years to sail round the world. The true objective is not making the money, but fulfilling an ambition to sail around the world. Generating £X by the specified date is an important Task. During the period, time will have to be devoted to creating the required money to fund the enterprise, learning how to sail a boat and meeting social obligations.

The Task to generate the money needs to be broken down into a number of Processes, and even Sub-processes. It is possible that one person's principal objective might require less than nine tasks, but the tasks should be checked to ensure that a number of naturally individual tasks have not been grouped under a single heading.

To follow the analogy above, *learning to sail* is a task which has to be completed by a target date. It will involve a number of processes. One process may be to identify, and list by priority, all the subjects which must be mastered and how they can be learned. Some skills can be learnt as theory in a class room, or by studying books and other reference material. There will be a need to practice the skills and learn those which can only come from sailing a boat under instruction. It may be desirable to obtain formal qualifications, or it may be a mandatory requirement in order to obtain insurance and be permitted to sail in certain areas. There will also be the need to sail, without an instructor, to prepare for what may be a long and lonely voyage. It is not unknown for a person to dream about sailing alone around the world and spend considerable effort in preparation, only to find that he cannot cope with the loneliness of single-handed sailing.

Having identified the processes, and inserted testable features, it will be necessary to identify the Tools required to perform the processes. These will be required at stages and generate the need to allocate funds to purchase the tools. This may identify the need for additional processes. For example, it may be necessary to visit a series of boat shows to examine the available tools and make the best selection. Some tools will be obvious, such as the need to have navigation instruments before starting a navigation course. The course syllabus may list the minimum required, together with a list of useful non-essential tools. Other tools may be identified as part of the exercise of testing the plan, or from practical experience as skills develop. Risk analysis will form an integral part of processes and tools.

At this point we have established a workable personal plan. It may have been necessary to reach a compromise in a number of areas. For example, the primary objective may not be possible without finding a new job, either because there is a need to generate more funds, or because it is necessary to make more time available for training and preparation. Alternatively, it might be necessary to make changes to the training and preparation programme to fit around the demands of work.

So far, we have not dealt specifically with risks and the plan which we have produced cannot have included all circumstances and factors which will influence its execution. Therefore, having established the plan, it is most unlikely to remain unchanged. A number of factors might force a revision of the target date; because all funding may not be available by the original target; sickness may have delayed a number of processes; or additional tasks/processes may have been identified.

Under the worst conditions, the objective may prove unattainable and a major rethink may be required. However careful the planning, the unexpected will occur. There will be setbacks and there may also be unforeseen advances. If the plan is inflexible and incapable of frequent review and modification it is seriously defective. Therefore, however good the initial planning, the quality of the exercise will depend on constant monitoring and adjustment. It then follows that the initial plan should include specific points at which a review is carried out and the minimum extent of that review. For example, time should be budgeted each day to a review of the immediate period ahead.

The personal plan has a direct relationship with the employer and his enterprise policy. Any employee who has set himself this type of objective is unlikely to respond well to any obstruction. If both the employee and the employer feel able to share information positively, both can benefit enormously. It may be possible to adjust work duties to better match the time requirements for the trip preparation. Any flexible support by the employer is likely to maintain the employee's motivation and productivity.

In far too many enterprises a negative approach is taken and the employee's plans would be viewed as a threat. The best that this attitude would produce is a demotivated employee, the probability is that the employee would look for alternative employment, and the worst result would be that a resentful employee would find a suitably negative way is expressing his resentment.

Taking the principles of the personal plan to build a plan for a major organization is only a question of scale. The people responsible for managing the enterprise should also have a personal plan, which should include the high level actions in the work related sections of their business plans. This may seem an obvious approach, but very few organizations carry out consistent planning in this way. Periodically, most organizations are motivated to spend time on training and systems to correct this lack of planning. In most cases, the programme falls into disuse, sometimes very quickly.

The reasons for this may be complex, but they can be reduced to three basic areas. Firstly, a major reason for failure is that only a part of the organization receives training and time/activity management systems. Secondly, little, or no, follow up work is carried out. Thirdly, insufficient thought goes into selecting a system which the enterprise and its personnel can relate to, resulting in a system which requires major changes in behaviour. It could be said that this distils down to a single reason, *crisis management.*

From the individual, to the largest organization, crisis management is often the reality of day-to-day activity. It is all too easy to slip into the habit of reacting to situations which could have been predicted and dealt with much more effectively on a planned approach. Crisis management is seductive because it generates the need for frantic activity. It is very easy to convince ourselves that activity equates to productive endeavour. It is also very easy to attempt to correct a situation by taking action in response to one crisis, and then move to the next crisis without finding out if the action just taken was effective and appropriate. If the problem has gone away for a while, we are relieved and assume that we were effective.

This is often the temporary motivation for taking time and activity management training in an attempt to correct some obvious and recent problems, or in response to a suspicion that there is *room for improvement.* Having completed a short training course, and received some planning material, possibly in impressive leather folders, or some other *executive toy,* the problem is solved. However, the people who have just completed the training do not implement all that they have been taught. Other pressures distract them from maintaining what they have implemented and, very soon, few of them are using the system in any way. The problem returns and develops until someone decides that it is time to buy some more training. Very frequently, that training comes from a new provider because someone assumes that the original training failed through poor provision. Both providers probably have equally good packages, but neither package will work unless the user has the determination to monitor, use and develop the system to meet his specific requirements.

In the early stages, there may be considerable merit in devising a training program which starts with formal training away from the work place. During this period, each student builds an initial plan without any distractions. Having completed the first stage, each student returns to work but has a number of days allocated over a period to review the developing plan away from the work place as refresher training. This approach has been used by some organizations and has proved so successful that each employee has time allocated each month to planning at a site away from the work place. As the planning process has developed into a good habit, the organization has discovered that natural work groups do not necessarily equate to the work groups described in the original organization chart. This has resulted in the redrawing of the organization chart.

Individuals can buy their own training if their current employers do not have the foresight to arrange training for their staff. There are several time management specialists who run short courses, sometimes in the evenings, or at weekends. However, even if this type of training is not available, there are several excellent books which cover the subject.

Many organizations do not seem to recognize that a happy, motivated workforce will produce a better result. All too frequently, measurement of happiness and motivation is estimated without regard to the feelings of individuals and groups. This is most frequently a condition in a large organization because it is less common for this type of enterprise to ask its personnel what they want, or how they feel. It is also common for employers to consider that time management training is only necessary for salesmen and senior managers.

Any organization is only as strong as its people. Financial power and machinery are of limited value if there is no one to apply them intelligently. Any achievement can be quickly dissipated by incompetent management and unwilling workers. Any government which becomes insensitive to the people it serves will fail, however much effort is directed to controlling the people. Equally, no company can survive if it cannot carry its workforce with it. The only variable factor is the time which such an organization can survive. Perhaps the most amazing aspect is that people and organizations actually expend so much effort negatively, to persist in propping up a failing structure, when a planned positive approach could reverse the situation and benefit everyone who is touched by the enterprise.

A major risk is created by self important insensitivity. Unfortunately, this is very difficult to deal with because it is an almost inevitable consequence of status, which is in turn an almost inevitable product of corporatism. This endemic condition makes sound planning difficult and seeks to restrict the process to a *chosen few*. It explains in part why a company may restrict time and activity management to narrow areas of its personnel. Enterprise planning works best when all personnel are directly involved, motivated to support the process, and contribute positively to it. Given that this highly desirable state is so rare, how can we change the situation?

Time and activity management is like a language. If a number of systems and methodologies are used in a single organization, there is minimum potential for success. The first step is to choose a system. From the many systems available, each has some benefits which the others lack, but all follow a broadly similar concept. Some are systems which offer no training courses, while others are basically training courses which also provide a system. Many are designed to appeal to the company executive and offer expensive symbols of status, which may have limited practical value. It is necessary to decide what the objective is.

The first step is to produce an enterprise policy which will identify the primary objective of the enterprise and, from that, identify the most efficient methods of achieving the objective. To develop an enterprise policy, it is necessary to introduce a common time and activity management system across the enterprise, to assist during the development of the initial enterprise plan, and then to support the maintenance of the plan. Within this approach, every member of the enterprise should receive the same basic level of training and use the same system. However, there should be scope for personalisation. If a single standard is applied and enforced, it is likely to be based on the lowest common denominator and be very *grey* and unappealing. To encourage a person to use something, there should be scope for pride in procession, giving a sense of involvement and value. This may not be related to any existing status system.

The answer may be the selection of a supplier who has a strong training base, supported by a physical product which has a number of variations. The training process may automatically start to build the basis of an enterprise policy. A methodology training package of the type sold to Sales Directors for their salesmen may not be at all suitable.

The employment of a time and activity management system could provide everything which the individual requires for his own personal enterprise plan. A good system will consist of a method of binding information, contained on preprinted forms, and stored in cross referenced sections. It should be sufficiently compact to be comfortably portable, because it will only remain effective if it is used frequently and updated.

It is now possible to obtain a system which is computer based, to operate on small portable machines, such as Notebook PCs. This may not be as suitable as the traditional paper systems. It is likely to cost much more than the paper system and may be both slower, and more difficult to use. This performance deficit results from the type of data which is most frequently added and the places where this addition is probably taking place. A pencil written note can be added very quickly to any part of the system and removed, or amended, very easily. A computer usually requires a stable surface to rest the machine and has to be switched on and set up before use. This means that frequent, but irregular, use of the system from different locations favours the paper and pencil over the computer.

It may also be necessary to employ different media across an organization. Part of the crisis management culture is a belief that new technology solves all problems. People working from fixed locations are more likely to use some form of computer as part of their work and this may make a computerized system more desirable. Some personnel may be engaged in activities where a computer based system produces a range of benefits. However, it is highly likely that many workers are better served by pencil and paper.

The computer based system has advantages in processing and updating. Although data entry may be slower and less convenient, the system could update a series of records from a single entry. The computer is also able to prompt the user to take a series of steps and can prevent the attempt to miss out important steps. It can advise, remind and alarm. This may be of less benefit to the individual using a system for personal reasons. A user who is one member of a group may gain significantly from using a computer based system because it could be used to provide communication with the other members of the group and with other groups. This may enable the reliable automation of tasks and reduce the workload on individuals. It may also reduce errors by requiring some standardization across a number of individuals. The greatest benefit of a computerized system may be its ability to provide multiple choice for data search and retrieval. The user may not always remember how, or where, information was stored, and may not realize how one activity has modified another. In this situation, the computer provides the means to locate data more easily and quickly, and can flag all activities which have been affected by one event.

The main weakness of a computerized system may be lack of flexibility and reliability. A piece of paper and a pencil is very flexible because it allows any shape to be recorded and errors can be easily erased. It provides an environment which does not restrain creativity. This could be very important in planning because it enables an individual to think outside the confines of a box created by someone else. The availability of pen based computers may provide a solution in that they are able to combine the best points of both approaches. They are still constrained by the need for a power supply which is the common technical weakness of the portable computer. The availability of voice operated computers may prove even more significant because, as their technology develops, they will be small enough to wear and could operate through a headset. This would make them effective in conditions where no other system would be practical.

The probability is that the computerized system will become, progressively, the first choice for most people. The reduction in size and cost, and the improvements in battery performance, continue to reduce the disadvantages. Changes in communications patterns will also influence the choice. Electronic communication has steadily been replacing written communication since the introduction of the telegraph in the Nineteenth Century. The process is now well established in business and government communication practices. It is beginning to extend from the workplace into the home. In the process, this will blur the divisions between home and work. In turn, it produces the greatest challenge and opportunity to planners and individuals.

The growth of corporatism has caused people to think of work and home as two distinctly separate places and groups of activity. In the early days of the Industrial Revolution of the Eighteenth and Nineteenth Centuries, the new industrial processes demanded new buildings to house them and accelerated the growth of urban areas. The late Twentieth Century has seen changes in both telecommunications and production technologies which make it practical for increasing numbers of people to work from their homes. This requires new disciplines, introduces new risks into the domestic environment and makes it essential to have a personal enterprise plan. It may influence the method of operating the plan and make a computer based system more desirable.

The more sophisticated the personal requirement, the less likely it is that a traditional time and activity management system will satisfy all the needs of the individual. The work group will certainly require greater sophistication and the need will grow with the size and complexity of the enterprise. The principles will be very similar, so where does enterprise planning depart from time and activity management?

Although companies may buy time management systems for a workforce, they are essentially a number of personal systems which have been bought in bulk. Enterprise planning is a corporate system which includes individuals. It is only effective if it identifies the objective, the tasks, and the relationship of resources. If the enterprise consists of a number of people, their relationships must be established in terms of the goal achievement. Their activities should be planned in relation to tasks and time. As part of the resources available, the people are directly part of the enterprise plan, but not the full extent of the identified resources. The planning and management of their activities against disposable time is actual rather than simulated, and forms part of the tactical execution of the tasks to achieve the goal. The enterprise plan takes a strategic view of the whole and should provide a modelling capability.

If an enterprise plan exists, it identifies what processes are needed to achieve the goal and it will include time as part of the target setting and testing facilities, but it cannot assume full responsibility for setting the goals of individuals, allocating time, and managing the process.

There are two reasons why the enterprise plan cannot assume full responsibility. Firstly, each individual will only dedicate part of their disposable time to the enterprise and therefore they must be responsible for managing the time which is available for other activities. Secondly, a rigid group plan will not be responsive to the myriad variables which are presented to the people every day.

The individual should therefore be able to set his own activity levels within the broad framework of the enterprise plan. Therefore, the enterprise plan should calculate the need for manpower and the actual manpower available. It should also identify the effectiveness of the available manpower in completing the tasks. It therefore has to produce estimates of output for all processes, including people as tools, or resources. It is most efficient when it can report actual output against estimates as the work activity proceeds. In this ideal situation, it would be possible to adjust processes for optimum output as a continuing activity. The nearest that we are likely to get to this ideal is in a simulator where we can control activities and events which are normally outside our control. A time and activity management system would not include simulation, but an enterprise policy should have an associated modelling system to provide simulation. As more information becomes available to compare actual performance against projected performance, the system could identify trends and relationships which would allow future projections to be much more accurate.

In a very small enterprise, with less than four people, a personal time and activity management system can also be the basis for the enterprise policy, with little expansion and modification. The maintenance of the system should provide both a review and modification of the policy. The system should become a habit. To be effective, the system would have to include information which the owner considers sensitive. This may present a security threat and, for this reason, many people who use systems of this type only carry part of the system with them. If it is contained in a portable computer it is more likely to be a complete system, but a paper system becomes heavy as it develops, encouraging the owner to archive information and sections, making the system less immediate and less effective.

When the enterprise consists of a number of people, the time and activity management system is separated from the enterprise policy, but it also represents a sub-section of the policy and combines a personal subset enterprise policy. The challenge lies in maintaining communication. The longer a personal system is divorced from the enterprise model, the less closely it is likely to conform to it, because the individual is neither contributing to the development of the policy, nor observing subsequent changes in it. It may be a physical barrier, when one person has no method of communicating as a result of local conditions, or result from the difficulty in achieving the best balance between central control and individual freedom. Some level of central control is a basic requirement of any enterprise which involves a number of people, but many workers are very resistant to control and supervision. This is sometimes put forward as an excuse for not having an enterprise model and may explain why some enterprises produce a basic plan and then never update it.

It is possible that one person could produce a complete enterprise policy. It becomes progressively less likely that this will result in an effective plan as the size of the enterprise grows. It is unlikely that one person could reliably maintain the plan unless the enterprise was very small. The reason for this is that policy maintenance would become all consuming and one person would have severe difficulty in maintaining a level of communication to include the experiences of all personnel. So the question is, - how to encourage everyone to communicate freely?

Fear and doubt are the main restrictions on communication. This may be well-founded concern. Some enterprises are managed in an aggressive and confrontational manner. The culture demands scapegoats. This is very unhealthy, because a worker may make a mistake and then try to cover it up. Eventually, the error will surface and become much more serious and difficult to correct. In some enterprises, the process may extend to the extreme where an intolerant and insensitive manager is only told what his staff think he wants to be told. This situation is a disaster waiting to happen.

To produce and maintain a sound enterprise policy, there must be an environment where information is honest, accurate and current. This means that no one should be penalized for bringing bad news, or making mistakes. It is important that mistakes are avoided and not repeated when they do occur. Many attempts at producing enterprise policies founder because the basic information is not accurate. In an established organization, this is often a result of fear and suspicion caused by poor communication. Most people fear change and therefore a management must communicate the reasons for carrying out the research necessary to produce an enterprise policy. If this is not done, a work force is likely to suspect that the exercise will result in staffing reductions and provide a less than enthusiastic response. The potential problem increases with the size of the enterprise.

A small enterprise should have the advantage of short lines of communications. A small number of people can easily meet to discuss the challenges which face them. They may not always agree, but they have the opportunity to debate and to reach a consensus. It is probable that they will already have some form of enterprise policy which is not formally documented and the production of a formal system may require little more than documenting what already takes place. A large organization will not usually have this advantage because it will be divided into a number of units, which may be subdivided further. This division may have been appropriate at some time in the past, but may no longer be an efficient structure.

In a manufacturing company, a board of directors may accept areas of responsibility for marketing, sales, manufacturing, field engineering, administration and finance. This sets the basic divisions of the company and a structure extends below each director. These structures may represent logical functional groupings, but not represent the real work groups needed to run the operation. It is not unusual to find that the theoretical relationships do not correspond to the actual relationships.

In some enterprises this does not present a significant problem because enthusiastic and dedicated staff work flexibly to deal with the day-to-day needs of the enterprise. In many enterprises this is not the case. It is very easy for a culture to grow in each division, which makes it a separate tribal grouping and establishes a *them and us* environment where divisions work together reluctantly and with ill grace. This can be particularly severe if the directors do not work well together at a personal level, because the friction can easily spread down through their respective departments. In most cases, there will not be a single individual at board level who has ultimate responsibility for risk management. It is also likely that the management of risk, in the management tier below board level, is divided in an arbitrary way across a number of people who do not freely communicate with each other.

The enterprise policy will consist of three phases and it is important that the objectives of each phase are communicated to all personnel ahead of start dates. It is equally important to communicate progress and win the support of all personnel. The first phase will be an information gathering process, requiring enthusiastic support and active participation. To achieve success, the process should take place in an unrestricted atmosphere. This can be very difficult to achieve where defensive tribal attitudes are well established. It can also be very easy to convey the impression that the exercise is aimed at cost cutting. This will not produce reliable base information because staff will be selective in what information they pass.

At the end of the first phase, it will be necessary to evaluate the information and begin building a policy structure. It is probable that the research phase will have produced some surprises and some conflicting information. The second phase will therefore consist of evaluation and checking. It is important that the staff understand how the programme is progressing and how important their contribution is, so that they understand the key contribution which they make to the process.

The third phase will follow with the development of a full enterprise policy. At this stage, a new picture of the enterprise will be presented and it may be very different from the organization which people thought they were part of. This new environment may be a formal acknowledgement of the reality, or it may result in major changes. Great care is needed to ensure that personnel are able to adapt and relate to the new situation.

The process of building an enterprise policy will extend over a period of time. The ideal situation is to complete the work quickly. This may not be possible, even for a small organization. The first phase should be completed as rapidly as possible by using automation tools and external consultants to speed the work. The longer it takes to assemble the basic information, the less accurate it will be because, by the time the last information is collected, it may be seriously out of date. This is where good preparatory work repays the effort. Willing participants, who understand the objective of the work, will produce reliable and complete information. They will also help, rather than hinder, the second and third phases of the program.

Only the management team can decide what the primary objective of the enterprise is. This obvious task can be remarkably difficult. A public body will have been established originally to provide a specific service, such as community health care. A commercial organization may have been set up to exploit a particular unique design for a plastic container. Both organizations would claim to fully understand their primary objective but, over a period of time, circumstances change.

An original clear goal is modified over time as new duties and interests are added. The plastic container manufacturer will have expanded his range of containers to meet customer demand and have diversified into other types of packaging materials. The public body may have changed in a more subtle manner. Unlike the commercial organization, a public body can be highly resistant to customer demand and yet survive. Community health care might be a good example.

Health care is an emotive issue in many countries and is generally controlled, or provided, by government agencies. The demand for health care services is probably infinite. As the medical skills develop, people who would otherwise have died from a condition may now be treated, only to develop other conditions which require treatment during their extended life. Medical procedures inevitably become more complex and costly, while the size of the organization grows in terms of total funding requirement and personnel. As with any organization, it will diversify into new, but broadly related areas. It can also become insensitive to customer demand. The human desire to extend life fuels growth which in other markets might be controlled more strenuously by simple financial considerations.

In enterprise policy terms, health care could be expressed as a goal to defeat all illness, repair all injury and extend every human life indefinitely. This would not be an adequate primary objective because it is incapable of testing, not least because *indefinitely* is not a measurable quantity. If health care is provided by a government agency, funding will be allocated annually. There will also be a division of duties between a number of authorities which might be carried out on the basis of duties and/or geography. Each authority then becomes an organization in its own right with a management team which enjoys considerable autonomy within the constraints of the allocated budget. That management team has to have an agreed goal against which to establish tasks and allocate resources. In this respect, health care organizations are no different from any other enterprise. Where they do differ from a commercial organization is in their insulation from their customers.

A particular health authority may have a heavy demand which it cannot satisfy, because it is unable to recover funding directly from the customers wanting treatment, and it is unable to gain any increased funding from its government treasury. Alternatively, a service for which there is no longer a real demand may continue to be provided because there is established funding. Neither situation is likely to continue indefinitely because public pressure will build up until some action is taken. A commercial enterprise in a similar situation would be able to meet demand curves more rapidly because it would be able to collect the funding directly and could not afford to maintain a service which is no longer subscribed by customer demand. In this crude example, the authority could claim that it would like to be able to respond more rapidly to patient need, but is denied adequate funding. There is an added challenge in that a range of services must be on standby for a demand which cannot be fully identified. If an emergency arises, be it an accident, natural disaster, or new virus, the public expect to be treated and there will not be time to create new facilities. A similar challenge faces police and military organizations which have to plan and provision for

29

events which they hope will never happen. In turn, the same applies to any risk countermeasures.

A community health care program may impact the primary goal in rather more subtle ways. Until some point, family units cared for their young, sick and old, turning to external agencies only when they had exhausted their own resources. The main requirement for health care was therefore confined to the dispensing of treatments over relatively short periods. Serious conditions required the patient to be housed in a hospital. In poorer countries, the family may travel with the patient and camp beside the hospital, providing food and other non-medical support for their sick relative. This system seems to work remarkably well because it reduces the demand on resources which have to be provided by the hospital and it keeps the patient close to familiar contacts. There are indications that this close family contact has a beneficial effect on the patient. After receiving treatment, the patient may continue to require special care. Where the family unit is strong, or where an extended family exists, this care is provided in the community. In many developed countries, this care is not available in the community and the patient has to remain in hospital because it is not safe to allow him to return home. How much this adds to the cost of health care is difficult to quantify, but it is likely to be considerable.

Health care in wealthy countries has therefore followed a different path to institutional control. In many countries, the original goal of service to the people has been subverted into service to the staff. This has generally resulted from the tasks becoming the goal setters, rather than the means to achieve the goal. It is unlikely that any health care authority deliberately set benefits to the staff as the primary goal. What has happened is that the attempted achievement of the primary goal has resulted in the development of complex tasks, structures and resources which are no longer under the full control of the management. Crisis management has become the standard management method of the enterprise. In the process, more families are encouraged to place their aged relatives into institutions run by the health care authorities, placing severe moral, social and financial pressures on the oldest enterprise, the family unit. Increasing numbers of children are taken out of the family unit and placed into institutional care. All this well intentioned effort has created a situation which is almost totally opposed to the original goal of health care authorities.

This condition is not confined to public authorities. Any activity, where the supplier has control over the customer, is prone to the same failures. Nineteenth Century political thinkers, such as Karl Marx, believed that it was a result of private control of capital and that the only answer was control of property by the state. Twentieth Century political thinkers, such as Margaret Thatcher, believe that it was a result of state control and that the answer was to privatize public services and submit to market forces. History may well prove both groups wrong. Sound management and reliable communications are the only answer. The first step is the identification of the goal and the development of the enterprise policy. That policy must then be maintained and developed, demanding continuing reliable communication.

One form of enterprise policy which has become popular in commercial organizations is the *Mission Statement*. This wondrous device is communicated to customers and staff and is proudly displayed in the companies' buildings. Most mission statements consist of one or two paragraphs. The most comprehensive may cover an entire page. Some organizations state that their mission statement is the primary corporate goal and the heart of their enterprise policy. Dangerously, some enterprises believe that this is the case. Certainly, considerable sums of money and management time are devoted to the production of a Corporate Mission Statement.

In reality, a Corporate Mission Statement is a marketing device. It originally had two objectives. One objective was to convince a customer that the company was the most important and capable supplier of a type of product and, by implication, no other company was worthy of his custom. The second objective was to convince staff that they were working for a caring employer who cosseted them and overpaid them. Neither objective forms an enterprise policy and might disguise a very different policy.

A typical Corporate Mission Statement might be summarized; " The Ajax Widget Corporation will become the dominant supplier of widgets World Wide. This will be achieved through the relentless pursuit of quality and an unequalled service to our customers. This is possible through the total commitment of our dedicated work force, which is trained to the highest possible standards and rewarded for 'doing it right first time'. We will invest heavily in the future to maintain our unique position as the pioneer of this exciting technology".

The reality behind the mission statement might be that the Ajax Widget Corporation was an early manufacturer of widgets, who has failed to keep up with developments, is faced with decreasing share of a market, and does not know what to do about it. Their staff may be poorly paid and motivated, whilst virtually no money is invested in improved production machinery and technology development. The mission statement might be the management's belief in the situation, but it is not even remotely an enterprise policy.

Some organizations treat the risk policy in a similar way. A recent incident can generate a few fine words on a sheet of paper, but no planned action. There is a worrying trend in commercial organizations to paper the walls of their reception areas with framed policy statements and compliance certificates. If an organization has achieved particular standards, or set itself specific goals, there is no reason why it should not be proud to tell staff, customers and suppliers all about it. In that case, it would be a very satisfying trend. Unfortunately, many enterprises regard the collection of certificates as the goal and feel obliged to print Corporate Mission Statements because a competitor has already done so. The most concerning factor is that there may be little, or nothing, behind the piece of paper. There is no benefit in operating a process for the sake of operating it. There is also little benefit in establishing a quality control system which is then ignored. Equally, there is no benefit in introducing a quality standard which becomes an excuse for rigid and dangerous bureaucracy, where the system is used not to control quality, but to protect the inefficient.

A well prepared enterprise policy, for even a relatively small organization, may run into several volumes. As it details all aspects of the enterprise, very few people need access to all parts of the policy. Equally, any enterprise policy which is adequately detailed is a valuable and sensitive asset which should be protected. It should also contain a series of overviews and these may have much more impact and be faster to read if they are in graphical form. A careful selection, or subset, of these documents may be suitable for inclusion in marketing literature and display in public areas.

In producing an enterprise policy, there are a number of reasons why external consultants should be particularly effective. Certainly, they should have an advantage in that their speciality is in analysing enterprises, rather than running them on a day to day basis. They are experienced because they see many different enterprises and observe the many different ways of tackling similar problems. Very often, their major strength is that they have not been conditioned to believe that a particular method is the only way of doing something and that the method continues to serve the enterprise well. They are also outside any established corporate politics.

The ability of an external consultant to observe from outside with fresh eyes is therefore an advantage, as is his experience in carrying out analytical studies of enterprises. Very often, a management team will bring in consultants because they do not have the time to attempt the work themselves and, on occasion, they abdicate responsibility to a consultant for unpopular decisions. There is a risk inherent in using external consultants.

It is naturally important that a manager satisfies himself that an external consultant will be reliable and discrete, maintaining a strict confidentiality at all times, both inside the enterprise and outside it. This is not usually too difficult because consultants generally gain work through reputation and expect to provide some proof of their capabilities. The hidden threat lies in how they are employed and relate to the management. The enterprise policy, which is built during this exercise, will have to be dynamic to match the many changes which will occur after its production. The management of the enterprise therefore needs to understand how the first policy was produced so that they can amend it when this proves necessary. They could, and periodically should, bring external consultants back to carry out independent checks of the policy. However, they should take responsibility for driving the process, and not pass it to a consultant. At no stage should a management team pass executive responsibility to a consultant. Firstly, a consultant cannot assume ultimate responsibility for decisions because, unlike the enterprise management team, he is not accountable directly to stock holders, or voters. Secondly, his skills are in identifying what the current situation is, what are the needs, and then recommending a number of courses of action. The management team must accept the responsibility and decide which options to take.

The management team and the external consultant must therefore work closely together to produce the enterprise policy. During this period, the management team should be learning how to maintain the policy and model potential changes. Some of this work can be aided by computer based systems. A variety of engines, languages and methodologies are available for the purpose and many of them are remarkably inexpensive. As with time and activity management systems, there is considerable choice and each system has its special advantages. However, systems readily available are not expert systems and therefore require the user to develop a range of skills. Some available systems are very user unfriendly and require a high level of skill. It may prove practical to engage consultants to carry out the initial work using a selection of computer based tools and provide training in their operation. This approach would build a base for future self operation and reduce the work required should the consultants be brought back later to check the enterprise policy. Such an approach would additionally include the building of some operational skills into the systems and provide the means for developing an expert system.

The ideal situation would be to develop a computer aided enterprise policy with a full range of modelling facilities. A system of this nature would enable a small management team to model changes and then produce a complete set of documentation for the selected changes. Strategically, it would be an excellent investment, but many organizations would have difficulty in finding the funds to execute the program in one attempt. The probability is that a largely manual enterprise policy will become progressively more automated over a period of time.

At the end of the third phase, the enterprise policy should consist of a series of procedural books with cross referencing and over views. The complete set would be restricted to a small group of people. Each department, or work group, would have its own policy book and each member of staff might have a personal book, or fact sheet. A member of the senior management team should have specific responsibility for risk management. In some enterprises it might prove desirable to set up a risk management department. This person, or department, would be the custodian of the risk policy.

Where the enterprise policy covers all aspects of the enterprise in a series of procedural instruction books issued to departments, the risk policy would run across the departments. Working on a need to know principle, the security responsibilities of each department and each member of staff would be part of the manual for that group, or person. Therefore, every member of staff would have a reference document which covered code of conduct, safety, quality, integrity, availability, and protection, as it applied to them. Each person would then know what was expected of them and what security systems related to their area of work. They would also know how the security interests related to their dealings with other work groups and external agents. If they did not need to operate a particular system, they would not need to know how it worked, or who operated it. However, some aspects of risk reduction should be known to most people.

Safety and quality are two areas where a widespread knowledge could enhance the operation. Obviously location of fire extinguishers and first aid kits should be widely advertised. Safety guards on machinery are obvious, although there may not be any merit in widely advertising how to open them. However, someone other than the machine operator should know how to open a guard in case the operator becomes trapped through a fault. In small enterprises, production machinery may be serviced, or at least cleaned, by the operator. In large factories a maintenance crew may be responsible for carrying out all servicing and cleaning of machines. Whichever system is in use will determine who is trained to do what in relation to which machinery.

Fire alarm systems must be capable of easy operation by people who may not be calm and there must be adequate displays of essential information, such as where escape routes and assembly areas are located. Therefore, as with other safety systems, some aspects of the fire alarm should be widely advertised and practised, while other aspects, such as how to deactivate the system, are closely controlled.

A part of the risk policy should include personnel selection and vetting. This is often a neglected area and no system will be 100% effective. Even the most comprehensive selection systems, run for very sensitive areas of government activity, have been breached by opposing security organizations. This means that a risk policy must assume that personnel selection may fail to eliminate all people who could present a security risk, but every effort should be made to ensure that it is as effective as practical.

The potential failure rate will have an effect on the availability of information on the risk policy and access to security related systems. For example, a retail store may introduce a number of systems to stop, or identify, fraud which is a result of collusion between a member of staff and a customer. There is a beneficial deterrent effect in informing all personnel that steps have been taken to prevent this type of crime, but it would be a mistake to identify the precise steps taken. If a potential perpetrator knows what counter measurers are in operation, he may be able to find a method of avoiding them. Equally, if access to the systems is not carefully controlled, the perpetrator may be able to subvert the system and remove evidence of the incident.

In a large organization, an enterprise policy can bring all the aspects of risk analysis and countermeasures together. Without a mechanism for central overview and control, it is very easy for the person responsible for theft prevention to introduce a technology, or procedure, which adversely affects the work of the safety officer, or the quality control manager. It is also very easy to duplicate effort without any increased benefit. For example, a uniformed security officer may be responsible for providing guard personnel and surveillance systems. The user of a personal computer in an office may decide to buy security products to protect his computer. A higher, or more appropriate, method of protection might be to make some minor changes in the guarding system. It is also possible that this may be a more cost effective solution.

The only reliable and cost effective way to reduce enterprise risk is to build an enterprise policy which contains a risk policy and then ensure that the resulting system is frequently checked and improved to meet changes in risk. Although the basic principles of enterprise and risk management apply to every type and size of enterprise, each system will be unique to each enterprise. Only by identifying risks and their relationships to the business of the enterprise can we hope to reduce those risks successfully.

# 3 Risk analysis and reduction

In the first phase of preparing an enterprise policy, a number of risks will have been identified. As part of the process of developing the enterprise policy, these risks will be analysed and a program of risk reduction will be put into operation. As time goes by, a number of new risks will emerge and some may reduce, or even cease to exist. This continuing change will result from a range of factors, some external, but many will be internal. The only guaranteed factor will be change.

From the individual up to the largest enterprise, there will be a vast array of risks which will potentially threaten. It will not be possible to provide a complete counter to every threat and it may not be practical to comprehensively counter any individual threat. It is therefore important to calculate the threat probability presented by each risk and produce a priority listing. This is inevitably a subjective assessment to some degree. The degree of subjectivity can be reduced by applying a formal method of assessment.

An individual will carry out an automatic, and largely subconscious, risk analysis which may be very subjective. If the house next door is burglarized, this may encourage the individual to purchase new locks, a burglar alarm, and take other obvious measures to reduce the perceived threat. A series of reports, in the local newspapers, of muggings at a nearby shopping centre may encourage the individual to take special care, perhaps even to the extent of avoiding the shopping centre. Some people are driven by fear of risks to take extreme measures. This could result in a heavily restricted life style. In the process, risk will not have been eliminated. It may be that one set of risks have been replaced by another set. The new risks could represent a much greater actual threat.

If the response to reported muggings at a shopping centre results in the individual avoiding the location, it will still be necessary to shop somewhere. The fact that the muggings have attracted attention may have eliminated the problem at that location, because counter measures have already been taken. These counter measures may include increased police patrols and improved lighting. The new environment will not stop mugging, but it may move the problem to another shopping area which does not have adequate counter measurers. The individual who has responded to the threat by shopping elsewhere may have moved with the muggers and may have generated increased risk because the threat is still there, but not the perception of the threat.

A similar situation may result from urban terrorism. The objectives of the terrorist are to win publicity and frighten the population into acceding to some unreasonable demands which cannot be achieved through democratic debate and agreement. To achieve these objectives, the terrorist attacks targets which are least able to defend themselves. There is no complete defence against threats of this type because the small numbers of terrorists have a wide choice of potential targets. Giving in to the terrorists' demands is also unlikely to remove the threat because, as one demand is conceded, additional demands will be put forward. Experience shows that terrorists become addicted to their life style and the only effective counter is to starve them of publicity and increase the risks to them. This presents a dilemma for a democratic open government. It is unable to effectively prohibit publicity of terrorist outrages, and the news media has shown itself to be incapable of self regulation. In fact, the news media appears to need disasters as much as the terrorist is driven to cause them. The public are naturally reluctant to travel to an area where they risk being blown up. The terrorist is therefore winning. If this situation continues, the risk increases because the terrorist is encouraged to continue and to expand his campaign. He will also win if a government is driven to introducing oppressive measures, because another objective is to destabilize the government by making it unpopular.

A democratic government is left with limited choices. A significant increase in spending on policing measures, to reduce the terrorist threat, will take money from other areas of government spending, or result in increased taxation. Neither situation is welcome, or desirable, but all governments take some action of this nature. This results from subjective and emotional judgement in response to public concern generated by emotional, and often inaccurate, news reporting. A greater proportion of resources may be devoted to a vain attempt to halt terrorist bombings in cities, than is devoted to reducing death and injury caused by motor accidents and fire. A terrorist bomb exploding in a city, or being found and defused in time, will be a major item on national news. A fatal road accident, or injury in the home, is unlikely to achieve the same level of news coverage. Probably, any coverage will be restricted to a few lines in a low circulation local newspaper.

However, the risk to the individual from road and domestic accidents will be considerably greater than those resulting from terrorist actions.

The impact of the news media on risk analysis is frequently to distort the process. If risk analysis depends on news, and responds only to that, it will be both a superficial and a reactive process. Inevitably, news is only available after the event has begun. If the event does not directly affect the enterprise, it may provide information which should be included in the analysis process. If it does directly affect the enterprise, it is may be too late to consider because it may already have inflicted fatal damage.

The public also have a part to play in actively defeating threats such as terrorism. No police force is able to dedicate the resources necessary for the prevention of terrorism. The news media have more resources to advertise the terrorist than police agencies command for all policing duties. Therefore, a police force needs all the help it can get. Unfortunately, police forces have some communications difficulties with the public.

The British policeman was internationally famous for his good natured common sense, courtesy and reliability, to the extent that a book by a Jewish refugee from Nazi Germany was titled "And the Policeman Smiled", because the refugee had never before experienced a policeman who was there to cheerfully serve rather than to grimly control. British police should therefore have the best prospect of reliable communication with the public. At the other extreme, some police forces revel in the projected image of storm troopers, and may expect a less enthusiastic relationship with the public.

Even the British police experience difficulties in dealing with the public. There are two reasons for this situation. Firstly, the law adversely affects a higher proportion of the population than it did only twenty years ago. In particular, the police are responsible for enforcing road traffic regulations and this puts them into direct adverse contact with an increasing number of people. As a result of human nature people always value law when it is applied to someone else, but often feel outrage when it is applied to them. It does not matter whether the police are used for traffic duties because they are there, or because traffic offences are regarded in the same light as murder and burglary. To the average traffic law offender, he has only committed a minor indiscretion and objects to being treated as a common criminal. He associates the police with the traffic law and comes to regard them as the enemy. People caught breaking other laws may make similar distinctions. Unfortunately, this disrupts communication between the police and the public. As most of the adult population may potentially come into contact with the police through traffic law breaches, this is a growing problem. It may be that the British government introduces a separate organization to deal with road traffic laws. This has already occurred to a limited extent with the introduction of Traffic Wardens to police parking regulations and minor motoring infringements. There is evidence that this has improved the public regard for the policeman in towns and could help to improve communication between the criminal police and the public, although it might not improve driving standards. As the risks to the individual from crime and terrorism may be much lower than those from road accidents, there is a danger that the reduction of risk in one area could result in an increased overall risk by increasing risk in another area. This is an example of the difficulties which result from perceptions of *security*. The work of a police agency in reducing road traffic risk is as important as the work carried out to reduce other risks such as burglary.

The temptation is sometimes there for the legislature and policing agencies to go soft on some crimes, or to ignore some offences in the interests of *economic* policing. This can also increase risks dangerously in several ways. Once a particular offence is decriminalized, pressure is exerted by special interests groups to remove other offences from the statute books. As the process continues, it becomes increasingly difficult to defend and justify outlawing a wide range of human activities. Before an offence is actually removed from legal control, people will begin to ignore the law and it ceases to be effective, so increasing pressure for that removal. Treating some offences as uneconomic to address has a very similar knock on effect and encourages increased lawlessness and reduced regard by the general public for legislation and the police.

The other barrier to communications between the police and the public results from changing methods of policing. These changes have been forced largely for financial reasons, although they may have initially attracted attention because of perceived operational benefits. The conditions relate to policing in most countries, but the British police provide a good analysis example because of their traditions of close relations with the public and the traditions of service rather than control.

Until the 1950s, the British police relied on foot patrols and their organization had remained largely unchanged since the establishment of the first police force. Each police force was controlled by a Watch Committee which was a local authority tracing its origins back hundreds of years. The local community was able to develop pride in their *own* policemen. Each policeman was a respected member of the community in which he served and did not need to carry arms to perform his duties. He was familiar to all the people who lived and worked in the area he patrolled and a bond developed between them.

As a source of help and advice, he was respected and relied upon and the local people would speak freely with him. His main method of communication, while on patrol, with colleagues was the police whistle and

40

this meant that patrols had to be organized so that an officer needing help was within whistle range of at least one other officer. The public could be relied upon to help him in most areas. Even in deprived areas, where it is now assumed that a lack of money is a justification for crime, the policeman could usually rely on the local people to help him. He also dispensed justice in limited form. A boy stealing from a shop might receive a light blow and some sound advice, rather than being taken to the police cells and then to the courts. This behaviour is now socially unacceptable and a policeman taking such action is likely to find himself in court.

When the whistle was augmented by the telephone, this did not change policing significantly, because the telephone was housed in a police telephone box with a flashing light to indicate an incoming message. Several foot patrols converged on the telephone box so that one policeman would be able to reach the telephone very soon after the light started to flash. The telephone boxes also provided an emergency phone service for the public and a method whereby a policeman could quietly summon help .

The policing system changed with the introduction of the car and the radiotelephone. These new technologies enabled a single policeman to cover a much larger area and be in instant contact with a control room. There was also the opportunity for a number of policemen to travel together for mutual support. First response to a call for help might be slower but, instead of response being limited to one man on foot, the new systems enabled an appropriate response to the emergency, and radio communication meant that additional support could be called for if necessary. By most measurements, mobile radio equipped police have been a great success and financially more efficient. Many of the risks faced by policemen appeared to have been reduced. In reality, personal risk to policemen has increased and, even in Britain, policemen now routinely wear body armour and are starting to routinely carry firearms. This has also increased risk for citizens and enterprises because the risk of injury through bombing and shooting has increased. One factor often ignored is the danger police firearms may pose to the police and to the public. A police officer has a limited field of fire in a public place, but the criminal probably does not mind if his bullets strike anybody in the area. This places the policeman at a severe disadvantage because, by carrying arms, he encourages the armed criminal to shoot at him, but his ability to return fire safely is restricted. The policeman may kill or injure a member of the public by accident during a shooting, and there is an even higher probability that the criminal will hit a member of the public.

These changes present a challenge for the risk analyst. The risk of bombs and guns has been present for hundreds of years, but suddenly the percentage increase in incidents has risen alarmingly. However, the probability factor is still extremely low. Even a high risk area, such as Italy,

Spain or Northern Ireland, which have suffered regular terrorist outrages, has a relatively low probability per head of population. Some parts of these countries have never suffered an incident. A risk analyst working in an area where such events are a daily occurrence cannot afford to ignore them. If he is working in an incident free oasis, it becomes a more difficult matter. Experience shows that parts of North Ireland have never suffered from bombing, during a twenty year period of terrorist activity in the region, but one day a bomb is placed and does terrible damage. Some of this damage would have been avoided had the population taken similar measures to those which are a natural way of life for people living only a few miles away, but who have experienced many such assaults.

When cities, such as London, have been targeted by terrorists, enterprises in the area have discovered the hard way that a low probability risk can be very damaging when it does become an actual incident. The consequences are much more widespread than direct physical damage from the explosion. Those buildings which have been directly affected may be out of action for a long period of time, possibly several years. For the enterprises operating from the premises, this can prove disastrous. Enterprises much further from the blast area will also suffer loss of business and reduced staff morale. In some cases it may become difficult to encourage staff to work in the area. This latter situation is a particular risk in a city, such as London, where staff travel in from considerable distances to work. This also presents a low risk opportunity for terrorists. By giving warning of a bomb at a railway station, they can ensure maximum disruption of travel while the area is cleared of people and checked for the device. It is not necessary for the terrorist to actually place a bomb to achieve this result. The false alarm has the virtue that he does not expose himself to the risk of carrying a device and planting it.

Commuters may find that the benefits of working in London are outweighed by the perceived risk and that employment can be found closer to home. Because so few people routinely review their life plan, the original benefits of working in London may have vanished some time ago and the terrorist incident provides the trigger to review personal objectives.

Crime figures have increased both because the police are not providing an adequate counter to the risks, and also because improved information technology enables us to see incidents which may have gone unnoticed, or unreported, previously. The most concerning figure is the increase in unsolved crimes. This suggests that the police are becoming progressively less effective as a counter to the actual risks. Some areas present greater problems than others. Computer crime is probably rising around the world at an alarming rate. However, much of this crime is undetected by anyone. Much of what is detected goes unreported. Violent crimes also seem to have

42

increased dramatically. This appears to be deliberate crime against a person, rather than crime against property where violence resulted. There may be many reasons for the apparent change in risk, but most individuals and enterprises are not adequately addressing the changes in risks which now face them.

This failure takes several forms. Whenever the news media devote time to an emotional issue, a new industry springs up, or an old one rapidly grows. One consequence of publicity of a new *crime wave* is that organizations marketing various security products step forward and claim a total solution. Very often, individuals and companies spend considerable sums of money on technology which will not provide total risk reduction and may actually be largely unnecessary in a specific case. Individuals often respond by adopting a siege mentality and avoid walking alone at night, or visiting particular areas. In some cases people take a fatalistic approach and assume that the problem is too great to be solved, when they could take steps to reduce the risk to themselves.

Risk analysis is made unnecessarily difficult by the way in which we view different types of risk. The urban terrorist presents a trivial risk to the majority of individuals and organizations. The risk increases on the basis of geographical location and also according to the target profile. Urban terrorists have prime targets on which they concentrate. If a prime target is well protected, they may select another target in the same area at random, or move to a new area. They will also increase their impact if they vary their methods by shooting a politician in one area and bombing a bar in another, because this makes it more difficult for police to establish patterns to aid arrest, or to use their limited manpower effectively to protect the wide range of potential targets. Given that urban terrorism is a trivial threat to the population, it may be appropriate to ask why this risk has such a high profile.

Undoubtedly, the news media play a key role in generating an emotional response. Graphic pictures of damage and injury are presented to an audience. The story is talked up and linked with other events which can easily suggest a growing problem, when this may not be the case. Formal risk analysis avoids this situation in two ways.

Firstly, formal risk analysis will identify a large number of potential risks, some of them being related. Each potential risk is then analysed and a probability figure is allocated. The analysis process will also consider the impact of a risk. A risk with a low probability may prose a significant threat if it occurs. A risk with a high probability may offer a low impact. Therefore risk probability is not the only factor considered in ranking threats. At that stage it is possible to rank the risks to produce a priority listing. Many potential risks will produce a low probability of threat, or impact, and can either be ignored, or left until after counter measures have been implemented to address the more pressing threats. This is the point at which a policy under regular review is essential. The common failing of reactive risk reduction is that once the high visibility risks have been addressed, the lower level risks are then forgotten.

In most cases, it will be possible to reduce a risk to an acceptable level, but impossible to eliminate it. However, all risks identified at the time of the analysis will have received appropriate attention. Therefore, a risk management policy has been established which relates risks to the activities of the enterprise. Any new information which becomes available from any source can then be related to the risk management policy. If the risk management system has been adequately produced, it will have already catered to some extent for all situations which are likely to occur.

Secondly, this process also identifies risks which must be watched carefully. When an incident occurs, which relates to a risk in the analysis table, it may provide information which changes the probability of risks, or introduces a new risk. This may require modification, or replacement, of existing countermeasures. Response can be rapid, but controlled within the framework of the risk table. Emotive response is largely replaced by logical response. It may be neither desirable, nor practical, to completely remove emotion. Any system which is coldly calculating and logically formal will relate well to a machine, but not to a person. Every system has to relate to human beings and will only succeed if they can relate to it.

The efficiency of a risk management system depends on a number of factors. An individual will have a relatively small number of risks to respond to. Theft of property and personal injury are risks which potentially apply to everyone. The same is true of risks such as fire. Although the range of potential risks is reasonably uniform across a number of individuals, the probability of particular risks will vary considerably. A person living in an area where crime is at a very low level will have a lower probability of risk from burglary. A person who owns assets of a high value is potentially at much higher risk of burglary than a person who owns little of value. Risk increases as the property becomes more visible. Therefore, two people may potentially share risks such as fire and burglary, but one may be much more at risk from burglary than the other. This difference in risk may be the result of one person being away from home for extended periods, and therefore leaving his home and possessions unattended. The impact of an incident will also vary greatly. A person who loses all of his assets will be in a more difficult position than a person who loses only a part of his assets, even if the value of the latter is greater than the former. The same holds true for any enterprise.

A large enterprise may have a considerably larger number of potential risks and may be subject to more frequent change than a small enterprise. There may be several risks with similar low probabilities. Managing a risk policy on charts and written documents may not be very easy and is likely to be slow. A computer based system would enable risk management to achieve reliable and timely results. Such a system should be built for the enterprise, using standard modules for cost reduction and proven reliability, where ever possible. The building of an enterprise policy will identify the way in which the enterprise is structured and functions, producing the information to build a reliable risk management system. It will probably be a statistical analysis system which is linked to the enterprise model but there are benefits in using fault tree analysis, either instead, or in addition. This will enable risk measurement to function as a part of any future modelling of the enterprise and ensure that all circumstances are known before changes are implemented.

The statistical risk analysis system provides a good method of establishing probabilities but it may also be necessary to introduce fault tree analysis which relates the consequences of one operation to another. Statistical risk analysis places a numeric value on a threat which has been identified and is therefore effective as a system to rank threats in order of priority, based on their probability factor in the particular enterprise. Fault tree analysis is good at identifying what happens in the event of a failure.

As an example, a nuclear power plant is a complex system which could cause catastrophic damage over a large area if it suffered a major failure. It is therefore a very sensitive undertaking and has been treated with extreme caution. It is possible to forecast the probability of the failure of any particular component. This is initially achieved by extensive and costly testing of components and systems before the start of operation. As with aviation, it is common to test a sample component to destruction before any are installed, or to begin testing of an example ahead of live installation of similar components and continue testing to provide pre-warning of failure. Frequent tests and inspections of the nuclear plant take place to identify any unforecast defects before they become the cause of a serious failure.

Producing a forecast of probable failure in any one component does not necessarily provide adequate security. If it is estimated that a water pump has a working life of one thousand hours, it is possible to replace the pump under routine maintenance before that time has expired. There remains the possibility that the pump could fail ahead of the replacement time, making it important to predict the implications of premature failure and plan a containment and recovery procedure. One method of achieving this is to use fault tree analysis as part of the risk management system. This will identify the consequences which will follow a pump failure and the relationships of back up systems. Therefore, a failure of a water pump may reduce the flow of cooling water, leading to a build up of temperature. A back up pump will bring the temperature down to the normal working level, but could also be subject to unforecast failure. In this event, the temperature will again increase. If the nuclear plant continues to operate, the temperature could reach a point where a series of other failures could result from the original failure. It is therefore necessary to identify the stages at which a controlled shut down of the plant will have to be initiated. It will also be necessary to identify the consequences of the controlled shut down.

It can be seen that a fault tree analysis routine provides a number of benefits. It provides a sizing of the risks which can result from a failure, or attack, and identifies potential containment and recovery routines. It also provides information to cost measure protective actions. A failure of a component may have a probability factor which increases until it reaches a known failure point. Therefore, from the moment that the item begins operation, it presents an increasing risk. Replacement of the component has a known cost and fault tree analysis will identify the actions necessary to correct a failure during operation. These actions will also have known costs. It will therefore be possible to calculate the cost of correcting a failure, against the probability of failure, against the cost of replacing the component before failure. As a result, it will be possible to decide the balance between predicted working life of the component and the time at which it should be routinely replaced. As the risk management system should be dynamic, it is possible to revise replacement times in the light of additional information which becomes available from operational experience, continued testing and changes to the system in which the component works.

This form of analysis within the risk management system is applicable to a wide range of risks. It is not confined to the risk component of an engineering management system. Established practices in the aviation and nuclear industries provide extensive test data and modelling to prevent a failure occurring. Other activities may have less available data and this reduces the accuracy of information produced by fault tree analysis. Never the less fault tree analysis is still valid because it enables the best use to be made of available data. It will also improve through use because there will be a desire to obtain ever more accurate data. The same is true of statistical analysis, where changing conditions will result in changes to statistical values already in use.

Used against a threat such as fire, or theft, fault tree analysis can evaluate the optimum procedures and counter measurers. A small company which uses a single computer to maintain financial systems is very vulnerable in the event of failure. This vulnerability comes from the fact that the company depends on recovering money from customers to pay for labour and raw materials and maintain a positive cash flow. If the company loses its financial records, many customers will be unable to remember how much they owe, but suppliers will remember how much is owed to them. If the suppliers learn that the company has lost its financial records, they will fear that the company may fail before paying its debt to them. As a result, they may press for early payment and make the cash flow situation worse than it need be, so speeding the failure of the company. This explains why so many companies fail soon after suffering a major fire, or a major computer failure. The incident does not directly cause the company to fail because personnel survive, possibly together with some stock and production facilities. Insurance policies may provide capital for rebuilding. The consequential risks resulting from cash flow disruption become the direct cause of failure.

It is therefore very easy to see, without complex analysis, that any company which has a computerized finance system is very vulnerable to a wide range of external and internal threats to the computers. A simple, but possibly expensive, answer would be to buy a number of computers and locate them at a number of different sites, make very frequent copies of computer records for storage at remote sites and install an array of defensive systems to protect against power loss, intruders and fires, backed by an array of systems to give alarms if the defensive systems are breached. Statistical analysis and fault tree analysis would enable the company to scale the counter measures to the probable risk and provide a more efficient range of protection at a lower cost. It would also enable a company to introduce protective measures in phases as funding became available, addressing the highest priorities first.

Risk analysis identifies possible risks, highlights probability and identifies the consequences which would follow, so that every risk may be catalogued and costed. At least that is the ideal world theory. Putting the analysis programme into operation may be a very different matter.

The creation of an enterprise policy will identify a range of risks because it will identify tasks, processes and tools necessary to the achievement of the primary objective. This will not provide all of the information necessary to the analysis of risk and the establishment of a risk reduction programme. If an enterprise policy has not been created, there will probably be no available data in anything other than raw form. This is a strong argument in favour of producing the enterprise policy first but, in the real world, it is not as simple as that because the information collected to produce the enterprise policy will itself require protection.

This means that a risk policy should be produced to cover the work of building the enterprise policy and protect the collected data, ahead of the completion of an enterprise wide risk policy. What may seem to be a circular argument over which stages come first can be broken and this will set the outline for all later risk analysis and reduction. The first stage would then become the decision on the sensitivity of data and access authorization.

In an enterprise, which consists of a single person, the process may seem very simple. No other person may be involved in developing the enterprise policy and risk reduction could consist of locking the developing document in a fireproof safe when it was not being worked on. It might be considered that a duplicate document is necessary, to be stored at another location as an additional fire protection measure. However, it is highly unlikely that every aspect of the policy can be restricted to a single individual. Eventually, parts of the enterprise policy will have to be disclosed to other people, such as banks, accountants, lawyers and even customers and suppliers. This may make it desirable to use a computer as a word processor so that the document can be copied into a series of documents for distribution at a later date. This could simplify initial security, because the document could be stored on removable disks and the security back-up copy would be up dated frequently. It might be wise to add an encryption system to the computer so that the removable disks could not be easily read by an unauthorized person.

For most enterprises, even very small organizations, the task will be more complicated because a number of people will be involved at some stage in the production of the enterprise policy. This means that some risk analysis and reduction work must be undertaken at the beginning of the exercise. The first stage is to decide what risks would result from disclosure of information and then to decide how access would be restricted. Later chapters deal more completely with the mechanics of the process but, at this point, we must look at the broad principles.

During the analysis and development of the enterprise policy a number of people may require a level of access to information, premises and assets. It is therefore important to decide who should have what level of access and what steps should be taken to adequately identify those people. In a small enterprise this is not too difficult and may not require particularly formal procedures. A number of companies, such as accountants, and their employees will already be well known on sight. The simple way of ensuring reliable security is to insist that every visitor carries acceptable identification, and that new personnel are physically introduced by a colleague who is already well known to the enterprise and trusted.

Where a new person and company may have to be included, it is essential to carry out some checks. This will apply to consultants who will need free access to all parts of the enterprise to be able to complete their work. Their access will include unsupervised access and may involve the issue of keys. This highlights one risk which we tend to ignore, or deal with casually. A bank or trade reference is largely meaningless. Someone who is a potential risk is unlikely to provide anything other than a faultless reference. A consultant who specializes in security and risk analysis work has a particular difficulty in providing a trade reference anyway because of the confidentiality of his work. Many of his clients may decide that disclosing the identity of consultants is a risk for various very good reasons. However, he may be able to provide a better level of assurance than any other supplier because he should be known to his local police force, or perhaps to a national security agency. These people will probably not be able to comment on his ability directly, but they may be able to provide a security assurance. No system is faultless, but if a consultant works for government agencies, he will probably have to undergo specific formal vetting to obtain clearances to work in certain areas. Even the most basic checks are more thorough than those usually available to a commercial organization.

Enterprises and individuals who specialize in security services to commercial organizations will normally belong to one of the security trade organizations. However, membership of a trade organization may have very little meaning. To join may require nothing more than mailing the membership subscription. Some trade organizations have very few teeth and even less inclination to deal with a member who fails to provide reliable service, even after a serious breach. As with any trade reference, membership of some trade grouping can be acquired by a disreputable enterprise and is an essential tool of their trade.

Where a positive assurance cannot be obtained, the wise course is to avoid granting unrestricted and unsupervised access, until you have formed your own opinion of the new person. Another simple protective measure is to use different people for different stages of the work and to ensure that you retain executive control.

Some enterprises will decide that the only acceptable risk is to avoid using external consultants, even though this may substantially raise the cost of the work. A skilled specialist may charge more per day than the highest paid employee of the enterprise, but that charge includes years of experience and knowledge of study projects, vendors, techniques and technology. Using employees of the enterprise means that they will have to be trained and that probably means that they will have to teach themselves. The result will be that the actual cost becomes much higher, the quality of the work will be lower and the enterprise will be exposed to unmoderated risks for a much longer period.

A consultant also has to learn, to some extent, during each commission. This learning factor is considerably less than many enterprises assume. Every organization tends to believe that it faces a unique situation with unique problems. Although every enterprise differs in detail from any other enterprise, the differences are remarkably small. A risk consultant is firstly an information gatherer. Not knowing initially the fine detail of the way a particular enterprise works is a considerable advantage during the analysis phase and is one advantage of employing external help for risk analysis. Someone who already works inside an enterprise has the disadvantage that he is used to doing things in a particular way and this familiarity makes it much more difficult to draw out the key information, and then question why a specific process exists. It is sometimes said that consultants only collect information which was already known and then present it as a written report. The implication is that the study was unnecessary. It may mean that the consultant has been very effective in drawing out information and presenting a picture of the enterprise which its workers can relate to, making recommendations which are easily understood and completely acceptable to the enterprise personnel. The mark of the truly skilled practitioner is that he makes the whole process look very easy and painless. Just like a skilled trainer, he should bring out the essential facts in a way which makes sense to a client. There is little to be gained from producing a complex and alien policy because it is unlikely to be implemented and maintained. If something already works, it is pointless trying to fix it. At the same time, the enterprise's management should be in control of the situation, and the executive decision, and not the consultant.

In addition to being a skilled gatherer of information, a consultant should have extensive and current knowledge of his subject. This knowledge must include an understanding of the possible, in terms of techniques and technology, but is not a major part of the analysis phase, coming in later at the risk reduction phase. However, a key part of the experience is in understanding what phase of the programme is being addressed. This may sound like an obvious point not worth stating, but it is the area where most enthusiastic do it yourselfers make their most serious errors.

As we can see, the research and construction of an enterprise policy entails risks and these should be addressed at the beginning, but many enterprises start with a security problem in one area and attempt to find a solution. This frequently results in a reverse of the correct process. It is not uncommon to find that an enterprise starts with the implementation phase without first defining the problem as a solution requirement and then selecting the most appropriate technology which is available for implementation of the solution. In the real world there will always be occasions when a reactive process is essential, but it must still follow the path of problem identification, requirements/solution specification, implementation. Taking any other approach will prove unsuccessful and probably dangerous. Without identification of the problem, it is impossible to judge the relative success or failure of the solution. By adopting a popular generic solution, it may be that much greater risks have been introduced and money will have been wasted.

If an enterprise decides to follow a logical process of building an enterprise policy and developing a risk policy, it is highly unlikely that everything else can be stopped until the work is completed. The only time when policies can be developed in this way is when an enterprise is being planned and has yet to begin operations. It may be possible to produce policies for a very small enterprise in a matter of a few days and this could make it practical to stop operations for a very limited period, in much the same way as factories used to routinely close for two weeks every year to enable essential maintenance to be carried out which was only possible if the product line was shut down. For most enterprises, this is a luxury which cannot be justified. For many large enterprises, a complete suite of enterprise and risk policies will take many months to produce, and even longer to implement.

Bringing in external consultants may be inevitable, especially for the analysis phases. The Board of Management should be able to agree the primary objective very quickly. It may require the services of a moderator to chair the discussion and a large enterprise may have to hold a series of discussions to identify the group objective and to agree the primary objective for each autonomous operating division. Once the objective has been determined, the work of analysis can begin. In some cases the two operations could take place concurrently and one view is that analysis is more accurate if it is carried out without knowledge of enterprise objectives, because the purpose of the analysis is to identify what happens, why, and how it operates. If the objective is known to the analysts, they may reverse engineer actual processes to match a known objective, which is what frequently happens when the enterprise uses its own personnel to carry out analysis.

A consideration will be the objective of the enterprise and risk studies. This objective may seem obvious, but there are at least two ways of running a valid study. The ideal situation is to agree on the enterprise objective and then work to provide the structure to ensure achievement. As part of planning a new enterprise, this will not involve research into the enterprise because it does not yet exist. In this approach, the Board decides what the enterprise must achieve and then identifies the tasks, processes and tools necessary for achievement. For an existing organization, the structure is examined to decide which parts fit the new enterprise policy. It could be decided that the existing assets should be sold off and new facilities built or purchased. In its most extreme form, this approach could be called asset stripping and is designed to achieve optimum financial yield.

The opposite extreme would be to attempt to improve efficiency and reduce risk without substantial changes to existing structures. The best path for most enterprises normally lies somewhere between the two extremes. In this case, the existing methods and operation must be understood.

Once the risks have been identified, it is necessary to begin the reduction process. As with the creation of the policies, the ideal solution would be to undertake the work while the enterprise is inactive, but this is not usually practical. The reduction process itself introduces potential risks. If implementation proceeds at the optimum rate for risk reduction, it may greatly impede normal work and result in a loss of revenue. This may be an unacceptable risk and the risk reduction programme will have to be adjusted to reduce this problem. It is also highly probable that implementation will have to be phased; for budgetary reasons; because a particular identified risk is considered significant, requiring priority implementation, or; because some measures must be in place and fully operational before implementation of other measures.

There will also be the important question of training. Having decided what training is needed for each worker, it is necessary to decide how they will be released for training without disrupting normal operation. Inevitably, work groups will have to stage their personnel through training to maintain adequate staffing levels for normal operations. If people are trained too far ahead of implementing counter measures, they will have forgotten much of what they learned. If training follows implementation, serious problems may occur because the systems are incorrectly used. A reasonable compromise is to take a small number of key people from each work group and train them just before implementing the counter measures. They then become responsible for training their colleagues, or for operating the systems while their colleagues are given training by a separate training team.

Whatever measures have been implemented to reduce risk, they are unlikely to provide either a total solution, or a permanent solution. The degree and speed of change will vary greatly. There may be periods when nothing changes to the extent that risk reduction measures have to be modified or replaced, but in most enterprises change is a continuing and gradual process with occasional bursts of higher activity. This requires careful monitoring. It may be obvious that a new risk should be addressed at the earliest time, and that improvements may be needed to cater for an existing risk which has increased. What may be less obvious is the need to address reduced risks and situations where a risk is no longer present.

Every risk reduction measure represents an overhead, and a return on investment. The return on investment only exists as long as the measure is countering a real, or potential, risk which represents a financial cost. The overhead takes several forms. If the measure involves the purchase of a product, there will have been an initial investment, but there may also be a maintenance cost. If the risk is no longer present, there is no benefit in maintaining the risk reduction system because this represents a continuing outlay of funds and must also be administered. A redundant counter measure may also divert attention and effort away from a real risk which should be reduced.

The question which must be addressed is what to do about a redundant system. For example, an area may have been used for storing paper which was required in a particular process. The paper was covered by insurance and therefore the most cost effective fire prevention system was a water sprinkler system. In the event of a fire, the paper could have ignited and caused a major fire which would have resulted in severe structural damage to the immediate building and threatened surrounding structures and personnel. In the event of the sprinkler being activated, it would have dealt with the fire effectively, but at the expense of destroying the paper through water damage. This provided the best counter to the threat, operationally, and the damage to stock was inconvenient, but not serious, because the insurance policy would have covered much of the cost of replacement. Had the paper been finished goods, the sprinkler system could have caused a greater financial threat and other precautions would have been needed.

Since fitting the sprinkler system, the enterprise has changed its production requirements and the storage space is now to be used for another purpose. In the new situation, the sprinkler system would not be appropriate as a fire precaution. This leaves the problem of what to do with the sprinklers. The system consists of an extensive network of pipes supported from the roof. When it was installed, installation labour was a significant percentage of total implementation cost. The pipework and fittings have a residual value, but this will be a minor consideration against the labour costs for deinstallation and removal of the scrap material from site. In addition to the pipework, the system was also served by a reservoir and pumps. If the reservoir is left full of water, it could present a health and safety risk, unless money continues to be spent on cleaning it and maintaining fencing. If the water is drained, there is still a danger of someone being injured through falling into the pit.

There are several courses open. The pipework could be sold for scrap, or for re-use, and the cost of removal may be partly recovered. The reservoir could be filled in and the area used for another purpose, such as car parking. The use of the storage area could be reviewed with the possibility that a process, which would benefit from a sprinkler system, could be moved into the area and the water sensitive process located elsewhere. Another possibility would be to drain the system and leave it in place in case it is required in the future. If this action is taken, the pipes will still need painting and the system will still need to be checked, because otherwise it will be unusable at some future date. It will also be necessary to post notices clearly stating that the system is non operational so that dangerous mistakes are not made as a result of someone believing the system to be operational, or reactivating it with consequent safety risks. If the system is removed, or disabled, the insurance company should be informed so that the insurance does not become void. Even though the water sprinkler system could now represent increased risks, an insurance company may insist on increasing premiums if it ceases to be operational.

Many enterprises treat redundant systems of all types very lightly and this introduces new risks. A frequent example is power and communications cabling systems on sites. Over the years new computer and communication systems are installed to replace older systems. New power cables are installed to provide additional services and meet new demand. Often the old cables are left in place. This creates some major risks. There is a danger of someone connecting mains voltage to an old cable by accident. Older cables may present greater risk of fire and produce toxic gasses. Fires and injury can result because new cables are damaged when they are forced through ducts which are already over full. One of the main reasons for enterprises running these unnecessary risks is lack of thought. A new system is installed by a company which is not interested in devoting labour to removing the old cable and no one thinks of finding a company which can recover the obsolete material. As metals become less abundant, and more costly, the old cable may have an appreciable value. This can reduce the total cost of the new system. Planned removal of old cable also has the virtue of ensuring that a new installer does not make extra profit be re-using old cable in areas where it may go unnoticed.

One risk in retaining a system in case it may be needed at a later date is that it introduces the possibility that it may become expedient to reuse something which is inappropriate. There is always a danger that someone may not carry out a thorough analysis of risk at a later date because they assume that the redundant system will be adequate and it has the great attraction that it is there and avoids a new procurement. This can be very dangerous. It can also prove very costly because the costs of training personnel and testing, repairing and maintaining an old system can prove more expensive than buying a new system which is also able to reduce risk more effectively.

Any risk policy which is not audited and maintained becomes dangerously defective. Some changes in risks will be very easily appreciated. A major change in enterprise activities should result in careful planning and ideally be modelled within the enterprise policy before any implementation. The greatest dangers come from gentle progressive change and from people becoming over familiar with risk reduction measures. The best way of addressing these risks is to establish a group of people who have a sole, or primary, role of risk management. Even then, this may not provide a complete solution. The use of external consultants to audit the risk policy is a valuable additional safety measure. Most enterprises take for granted the need to employ accountants to audit the financial activities of the company, and this may be a legal requirement, dependent of the size of the organization. This can result in a distortion of the enterprise and risk policies if similar specialists are not engaged to examine other areas of risk to produce a balanced view of the enterprise and its risk reduction measures. If external consultants are engaged in this way, it may be desirable to change consultants periodically because, after a time, they will become familiar with the enterprise and begin to lose their impartial objectivity.

# 4 People and legislation

People represent the real risk. Human greed, malice, and error are the primary threats. It could be argued that almost every risk, perhaps even every risk, relates back to human error, or deliberate human actions. If a city is flooded during unusual storms, we may regard it as an act of God. The deluge is certainly outside human control, but the city was built by people, in a particular way, and at that specific location. Engineering work may also have contributed to the disaster by constricting the natural way flood water is handled by river systems. Much of the damage and loss suffered during the floods could have been reduced, or even avoided, if the flooding risk had been adequately addressed and managed.

An example of this is the severe flooding, and consequent damage, which occurred across the Mississippi basin in the United States. A period of heavy rain caused the river to burst through its banks and inundate extensive areas of population, causing considerable damage and loss of life. There may have been several contributory factors and some of these might not have been reasonably foreseen.

However, the damage would have been greatly reduced, if not avoided, had an adequate enterprise and risk policy been established and maintained. It is also possible that inadequate research played a significant role in creating the situation. Natural disasters in many parts of the world are the result of unusual weather conditions, or other natural events. What may be a very long period of time in human and enterprise terms is only a very brief period of time in natural cycles. Planners often fail to research these cycles over sufficiently long a period and also fail to notice early signs of change which may demand actions to avoid a disaster. The fact that a river has never risen above a certain level in living memory does not mean that careful research will not produce evidence that it has not done so with great regularity in a cycle which extends across several generations. In some cases, the length of cycle can only be accurately identified by geological and archaeological research.

Sometimes research is restricted by financial considerations. Cost may also be a factor in blinding planners to risks which should be appreciated. Building development in river flood plains is often the result of land prices which are much lower than for higher and safer ground. As development takes place, and no flooding occurs for several years, others are encouraged to build in the same area and, very soon, a high proportion of industry and population is sited in a potentially dangerous location.

There may be some minor flooding and this encourages engineers to build systems of flood walls and drainage ditches to restrain high water levels. In some cases, the course of a river may be restrained, or altered, in the interests of flood prevention, or to improve navigation. Considerable effort is expended with apparently excellent results. Unfortunately, particularly high water levels may result in these risk reduction measures becoming counter productive because they create increasing forces which eventually cause the structures to fail and result in significantly greater damage than if they had not been built.

There are many similar examples of man failing to take adequate account of natural risks. Building in areas subject to bush fires, or earthquakes, or seasonal storms, are all similar examples of planning failure. Although inadequate research contributes to these failures, the most frequent primary reason for the situations is human optimism, driven by desires to cost cut, and simple greed where developers are able to make greater profits in exchange for their customers taking greatly increased risks. In extreme cases, dishonest developers and corrupt officials have suppressed information about identified risks in the interests of making greater profits, or avoiding financial loss.

We tend to divide human error into two arbitrary categories, accident and negligence. The dividing line is not well drawn, or consistent. Two actions may be fundamentally similar, but one is regarded as an act of negligence. The distinction is primarily legal and has a range of implications. The inconsistencies of treatment raise risk, not least because most people wish to avoid the legal consequences of accepting negligence and try to avoid liability by concealing information, or by presenting inaccurate information. When confronted by an accusation of negligence, the natural reaction of most people is defensive.

Theft and vandalism are products of greed and malice. Throughout history, legislators have striven to protect the community from these basic characteristics of human nature. However, legislation alone provides no real protection. There must be enforcement, and even that cannot be effective unless the majority of the population supports the laws and takes responsibility for risk reduction. Often, poor legislation promotes the lawlessness which it seeks to prevent.

It is very easy to accept that large areas of human behaviour are outside the control of the risk management team. This is not so. Every team member is a citizen with a voice and a vote, being able to contribute to the functioning of a democracy. Every enterprise is a collection of individuals who each have the same rights and responsibilities in a democratic country. Each enterprise has a collective voice which becomes potentially stronger as the enterprise grows. Any enterprise which does not set itself high ethical standards will contribute to increasing risks.

Some risk managers will also be legislators. Legislators must seek to produce laws which are appropriate and necessary, ensuring that the mass of the population sees them as such. This places a responsibility on legislators to carryout an adequate and effective risk analysis before attempting to produce legislation. They also have a responsibility to sell the concept to the population. In a democracy the population, citizens and enterprises, has a responsibility to support the legislators, both in making its views known to the legislators and in assisting the enforcement process by compliance and cooperation.

Legislators frequently respond to public opinion without objective analysis of the issues. This is classic crisis management and can result in defective legislation which may be counter productive. In many societies, the legislators respond to public opinion as expressed by the news media and, in particular, by the would-be opinion formers of the television industry. This may not represent the views of the public. Claims to be presenting public opinion often depend on the results of opinion polls. Opinion polls during elections are notoriously inaccurate, but continue to be used extensively. On occasion, they can influence the election result. Inaccuracies come from defective questions which consciously, or unconsciously, reflect the preconceived views of the pollsters Pressure groups may produce a noisy view which gains considerable media space, but may be the direct opposite of the views held by the mass of the population on that particular subject. Resulting legislation may not have the support of the population and may even be actively disliked.

Legislation sometimes criminalizes activities which the population may not regard as criminal activities, leading to an assumption that most laws are unreasonable. In addition, most societies have great difficulty in deciding how to deal with law breakers. Judicial systems primarily interpret laws, rather than deliver justice, resulting in a system which is penal rather than corrective, habitually slow and costly, frequently eccentric, often tragic and sometimes comic.

Regard for the law is a social process and is influenced by many factors. The typical citizen is in favour of every law, until he finds himself on the wrong side of it. Law abiding citizens regard criminals collectively with fear and dislike. Criminals have their own grading systems for crime and regard other criminals accordingly. This may explain why legal systems have an illogical approach to dealing with the convicted criminal. However, the legal system plays a vital role in the establishment of risk. Enterprises play a similar part to that of the typical citizen, but the corporate influence may be disproportionately strong. Every enterprise therefore carries a special responsibility to support the rule of law.

A professional criminal will weigh up the risk and consequences of being caught, before deciding to commit a crime. In opportunist crime, this risk analysis may be fleeting and instinctive, even non-existant. Therefore, the legal system plays an integral role as the deterrent to crime, just as much as the burglar alarm and the door lock, at least in respect to the professional criminal. However, professional criminals account for a small percentage of total crime, in terms of the number of incidents rather than the total financial value, and operate in fairly well defined areas where potential returns are high. A high proportion of crime is carried out by people who do not set out to make crime a life's career. These people may not respond to deterrents in the same way as a professional and are also difficult to counter because their behaviour is much more difficult to predict. For example, bank robbery requires a number of skills which have to be learned and execution of the crime demands careful planning. It will also require financing like any other enterprise. Therefore it is not a crime for the casual, or the faint hearted, and this reduces the number of people which a police force has to watch. This further increases the deterrent effect, demanding greater skill and premeditation on the part of the professional criminal. Fraud may follow a very different path. Much fraud at least starts as accidental and opportunist crime. For a variety of reasons, a previously trusted and reliable employee commits a crime. The potential numbers of criminals in this category are so great that a police force stands little chance of anticipating the crime, making arrest equally opportunist. Only effective risk management offers any prospect for combating this type of crime.

This means that the penal response has a potential deterrent effect which may range from negligible to strong. For each criminal, the penal deterrent may become weaker at different stages of his career. Fear of jail carries greater power against a criminal who has not previously been jailed. This is partly fear of the unknown and reduces after the first jail experience because the criminal knows what it will be like next time, having survived the first experience. The prospect of a fine may deter, but it carries less weight with a wealthy perpetrator. Fines for traffic offences may have no deterrent effect on the business driver because there is a financial benefit, even after paying any likely fine, from deliberately breaking the law. Some enterprises encourage their staff to behave in this way by treating fines for minor traffic offences as justifiable business expenses. There are also environments where a wealthy individual can see that the prospect of being caught is small and, even then, an expensive lawyer and inadequate court systems mean that conviction is a remote risk.

Most criminals start in crime by accident, or because they start with socially accepted crimes. A child may take something, as much from curiosity, and find that no one notices. If his offence goes unnoticed, or no effective sanction is awarded, this first offence may lead to bolder activities. For some criminals, crime becomes a natural way of life, but for many it is a transitory stage. Some criminals suffer from a disability, physical or mental, which makes it difficult for them to exist within established behaviour patterns required by society. Each group requires different approaches. The mentally ill criminal will not be deterred and may not understand punishment, or respond to training. His illness may not respond to any know treatment. The habitual criminal has come to accept that police, courts and prisons are an integral part of his life. He becomes immune to deterrents and punishment and may be difficult to re educate.

Public support for law enforcement and the judiciary is reduced if the laws are illogical, the enforcement is variable and the courts cannot be seen to dispense justice. In this situation, lawlessness increases and the risks grow. Ultimately, this will lead to the destruction of a society but, long before that point is reached, the quality of life for most individuals will have been greatly reduced and enterprises may have extreme difficulty in functioning effectively. Increasingly, the population will have to take more steps to provide for its own protection and this can introduce its own risks.

A society able to enact laws which are seen to be fair and reasonable will reduce risks because the population will become more law abiding. Laws which are easy to understand are also much easier to enforce. Sentencing which matches the particular criminals and their offences will create an environment which reduces threats. A criminal who demonstrates that he regards violence and murder as a natural activity is very dangerous, probably incapable of re education, or cure, and therefore represents a permanent threat to society. That threat can only be reduced by removing that person from society. It is then a question of what form that removal will take.

All risks trace back ultimately to people, and people are infinitely variable. Legislation is inherently inflexible and therefore rarely meets the specific needs of a situation. In particular, legislation has difficulty in reaching a common basis for defining crime, negligence and accident. Most societies divide their laws into civil and criminal legislation. On examination, there will be two essentially similar situations, but one will be regarded as criminal, and the other as a civil matter, although the average citizen may have great difficulty in understanding, or accepting, that division.

An increasing trend in developed nations during the second half of the Twentieth Century is to over legislate. Laws penetrate ever deeper into the fabric of every day life. This has three counter productive effects. Firstly, this makes it much more difficult for the average citizen to decide what is a crime and what is a minor misdemeanour, or to keep up with the new laws which pour out of the legislative chambers. For an enterprise the problem is much greater because, increasingly, legislative output addresses commercial rather than social issues. Every new law must be studied so that the enterprise is able to fully comply with the new legal requirements. This places an increasing burden on every enterprise as progressively more management time must be devoted to this activity. Most enterprises do not regard new legislation as a central risk to be analysed and reduced. As a result, there is often no system in place to ensure that everyone who needs to know about the legislation does know and understands the risks. Equally, it is unlikely that many will attempt to map the new legislation against a risk policy, even though the legislation may be a key factor in the nature of the risk.

One example of this could be the use of guard dogs, often a common security measure at compounds and premises which are not staffed at night. The lowest cost method of deploying guard dogs is to allow them to run free inside the area, because handlers introduce substantial additional cost. Unfortunately, this practice can result in several laws being broken and expose the operator to civil damages claims, and even criminal prosecution. These risks are usually not considered fully, even though they may create a greater risk than the intrusion threats which they are intended to reduce.

Secondly, the deluge of legislation increases the number of people who will be offenders of one sort or another. Frequently, offenders are those who did not realize that their actions were contrary to new legislation. In some cases, badly drafted legislation makes it impossible for an enterprise to fully comply because new legislation contradicts existing legislation. Therefore, the enterprise can only fully comply with one set of laws at the expense of partial, or total, non-compliance with other regulations.

It is becoming increasingly common for new legislation to impose requirements which cannot be met economically by enterprises, especially smaller enterprises. There is also a worrying trend where large enterprises decide to break certain laws which they do not agree with and rely on their ability to hire expensive lawyers to provide protection. This places very unfair pressure on small enterprises who are at a commercial disadvantage if they do not follow the law breakers. If they do follow the bad example of the larger corporation, they run a much higher risk of being penalized for their actions.

Thirdly, the volume of legislation places an unbearable work load on the courts and therefore slows the trial process. This is most unfortunate because it encourages an environment where the fittest survive. Some unscrupulous enterprises have learned that they can use their financial strength to ignore those legal requirements which do not suit them. In some cases this may be a deliberate breach of trading laws which may be overdue for replacement but, once one individual, or enterprise, takes this type of action, it starts a process which becomes very difficult to halt. An even less reputable trend is for large enterprises to attempt to avoid their creditors, using the cost and slowness of the civil courts. This practice has become widespread in many countries and is morally little different from any other form of robbery or blackmail, even if this is not recognized by the legislative system.

The slow speed of the judiciary can create major risk. Increasing volumes of legislation result in increasing demand on court time in terms of the number of cases pending, but that is not the only problem. Much recent legislation is also increasingly technical and leads to very lengthy and expensive trials. It also leads to an increasing number of acquittals. It might be argued that this demonstrates the fairness of legislation, but the evidence suggests that increasing numbers of acquittals result from ineffective and incomplete preparation by prosecutors coupled with the inability of juries and judges to follow long and complex trials. Effective legislation must be simple, fair, and fast. It must also be affordable, without encouraging frivolous actions, a difficult balance to be struck.

The process of jury trial, common to many countries, assumes that the jurors are capable of understanding the evidence placed before them. When the process was originally developed, it was only required to deal with simple theft and violence, or to settle differences. The defendant was required to face the community, in the form of the jury. Many cases tried today involve very complex issues and concepts which are outside the direct experience of a jury. This can involve considerable and lengthy preparation by the prosecution and the trial can take many months to complete. A witness is required to remember events, which took place possibly years before, and the jury has to both understand and remember complex evidence which was presented several months before the end of the trial. Some evidence may be of such a technical complexity that only the Expert Witnesses can reasonably be expected to understand it. This places increasing responsibility on the trial judge to accurately sum up the evidence and give adequate direction to the jury. As a judge is primarily trained as a lawyer, it is unreasonable to expect him to fully understand complex technical evidence on a wide range of subjects. The whole process becomes so involved that it stretches human fallibility to the extreme.

Complex trials present a number of problems. The stress on an innocent defendant can be extreme and unfair. The outcome of the trial may be a lottery where the guilty are as likely to be discharged, as the innocent are to be unfairly convicted. The process will have caused considerable disruption for all concerned, not least the jurors who have been taken from their normal lives for many months, and the cost will have been considerable. In some cases, the cost of the trial may have exceeded the value of the alleged crime by a considerable margin. Worst of all, the judicial system will have been brought into disrepute and be seen as ineffective. If the population has no confidence in the laws, there will be increasing lawlessness.

There is little that an enterprise can do directly in the short term to influence legislation. In the longer term it can, alone, or with a group, lobby the legislators and ensure that its voice is heard. It can, and should, ensure that its work force is fully informed of the effects of legislation on their employment and well-being. Beyond that, the enterprise and risk policies must deal with the situation which exists now. Prevention usually costs considerably less than remedy.

The enterprise and risk policies should recognize the risks which arise from existing legislation and track changes introduced by new legislation. Risk reduction must aim at compliance with legal requirements and also ensure that all steps are taken to support the legal process. Nothing is more frustrating for policemen than to be forced to return stolen goods to thieves because the owner has not taken simple precautions to support proof of ownership. In civil damages actions, an employer may be unable to prove that reasonable steps had been taken to protect an employee, when steps had been taken but were not adequately documented. These are simple precautions which entail little cost to put in place to reduce risk. Some of these actions will not only reduce identified risks, but will also improve general efficiency and productivity. In this case, they will contribute a net profit, rather than increasing cost. It is also necessary for the policies to recognize human fallibility and take steps to reduce the risks which it produces.

A key element of enterprise and risk policies is the personnel policy. Enterprises can be remarkably casual about their recruitment, training and supervision of personnel. In addition to being the root of risk in the enterprise, personnel are also usually the most costly and valuable resource. Without people, the enterprise cannot function. The finest equipment will only function as well as the operators can use it.

Recruitment methods must therefore be reviewed with great care. Politically Correct recruitment poses a significant risk to an enterprise and several countries have passed legislation which increases this risk still further. The first and only objective of recruitment should be to find and hire the person who is most capable of performing the required duties. If any artificial positive prejudice is introduced into the process there is a potential for introducing high risks. Any negative prejudice may not only introduce similar high risks, but may also be a non-compliance with legislation. The only way an enterprise can reduce these risks is to accurately state the requirements for any particular job and that requires an understanding of both the enterprise and risk policies. For example, there may be some physical attributes which are unlikely to be met by a typical man or a typical woman. However, if a job advertisement mandates a single sex, the enterprise may be in breach of equal opportunities regulations and may also have missed the opportunity to hire the person most suitable to do the job because they do not match a pre-conceived notion of gender suitability but closely match the functional requirements.

Having accurately specified the real requirements of the job and stated the basis of reward, the enterprise will have to select from a number of applicants. The more accurately requirement and reward have been specified, the less work will be required to select the most suitable candidate. Many enterprises are remarkably inaccurate and incomplete in their specifications. This may be due to a lack of ability, but frequently the imprecision is deliberate. There are several reasons for this.

Some enterprises treat recruitment notices as general advertising and take the opportunity to paint an inaccurate picture of how well their business is doing, in the hope of influencing customers and competitors. This can waste the time of a number of serious applicants who would not apply if they knew the real situation. The problem is made worse when an unsuitable person is selected as the best of the applicants available. The most common omission from vacancy notices is an accurate indication of reward. Some enterprises seem to believe that this will enable them to fill the vacancy at a lower cost. In many cases, the reward will be negotiable at the final interview, but every applicant will know what minimum pay is acceptable to him. It is unlikely that a qualified applicant will accept pay below the competitive rate. The enterprise should also know how much the job is worth to the enterprise. Advertising a vacancy as; "Above average earnings for graduate, 25-28 yrs. old", when the real requirement could be filled by someone of any age who is healthy, educated to secondary school level and prepared to work for a relatively low wage, is not likely to be a successful recruitment.

Perhaps the real reason for behaving in this way is that some enterprises are simply not interested in the feelings of people and do not understand how important people are to the achievement of the enterprise objectives. If this is the situation, major risks are being run because employees will not perform well, or reliably. It will also produce a selfish culture which does not interact positively with any other enterprises and people, producing maximum risk and frequent contact with the legal system. A positive and fair attitude will cost very little and repay so much.

There is a limit to the amount of information which can be placed in a vacancy notice. It is a selling tool, in this case selling the benefits of working for the particular enterprise. Therefore it should be concise and attractive to be a successful advertisement. The information which is included should accurately reflect the company and its requirements. This will produce a higher probability that all responses are from potentially suitable applicants. Whatever information is contained in an advertisement, applicants will require more information to make a subsequent interview mutually productive. One method of reducing enterprise work load is to employ recruitment consultants, but this introduces a number of potential risks which apply to most sub-contracted services.

Recruitment consultants can reduce work load and bring specialist skills to improve the quality of recruitment. Success comes from selecting suitable consultants and managing the process. It is very easy to use recruitment consultants as part of the advertising process and then allow them to dictate how the process operates, leaving them to make important executive decisions. This can result in the consultants failing to understand the requirements of the enterprise and promoting the selection of applicants who are not the most suitable to fill particular vacancies. It is also very easy to leave much of the recruitment process to the consultant, in what is a critical operation, and this can lead to lost opportunity.

In any recruitment, there are usually a number of applicants for a single vacancy. That means that only one applicant can receive a job offer and the others will be disappointed. As some vacancies may require a number of stages to the process, a large number of initial applications will be reduced in number at each stage. Most rejections may even have to take place without an interview. When a large number of applications are received, this can represent a considerable work load, but accurate specification of requirements will reduce the number of totally unsuitable applications. Some enterprises act with gross discourtesy by only responding to applicants with whom they wish to proceed. When rejection letters are sent out, they may be terse, or even insulting. This can produce risk. Any unsuccessful applicant may one day be a potential customer, or be highly suitable for a later vacancy. A casual thoughtless action by an enterprise can therefore cost money at some point in the future. The action may not be confined to the insulted applicant. When people are unhappy they often tell their friends and, by offending one person, a number of people may now have a low regard the enterprise. This increases risk further because more people are included and also because the enterprise does not know who they are, or how their perception of the enterprise may affect it in the future. A prompt response to every applicant actually costs very little. Making that response polite and positive costs no more than being rude. Therefore a risk is reduced at virtually no cost and the enterprise may profit greatly in the future. It will also avoid the risk spreading to other areas of activity. The recruitment attitude can spread very easily through the company to relations with suppliers and customers.

As the recruitment process continues through its stages, many enterprises neglect to follow their own rules. Although every employer asks for proof of suitability, very few take the trouble to check that proof, but some rely unduly on references. If someone intends to defraud, they are not likely to offer a referee who will not enthusiastically support their claims. Equally, there may be little benefit in insisting on a reference from a current employer. The employer may be unhappy to find an employee seeking work elsewhere, or may be very pleased to solve a problem by speeding the employee's departure to another company. In either case, he may not provide a reliable reference.

Recruitment risks are usually a result of poor training. Every manager should be trained in interview techniques, and recruitment is just another interview in terms of information gathering and passing. To be effective, open questions should be asked, and the answers listened to. That may seem obvious, but remarkably few recruitment interviews follow that pattern. Closed questions are frequently put to interviewees. Asking the applicant if they are *familiar with an Ajax 10 Model 17 machine, or hold an operators certificate* is likely to result in *yes* being the answer. It may be that the applicant only knows what the machine looks like and does not have any idea how to operate it, or may hold a certificate issued some time ago and never have operated the machine at work. Equally the answer may be *yes*, but is then followed by further information which is not listened to because the first response was *yes* and the interviewer has already moved on mentally to the next question. This can result in an unsuitable person being hired and placed in a production area without sufficient training.

Few enterprises train anyone, other than personnel department staff, in recruitment. However, the new employee will usually be working in another department and that means that his new manager should play an important part in the recruitment because they will have to develop a working relationship. For this reason, it is highly desirable for the manager to meet each applicant at the earliest stage of the process because, however technically suitable any applicant is, if they are not comfortable with each other it is unlikely that a reliable working relationship will develop.

Having selected an applicant, it is essential that the letter of offer is accurate and complete. Any undertaking made, or required, must be observed. The greatest risks can develop because a commitment is not honoured. The most common failures arise because an employer has taken great effort to recruit a new employee and then made very little effort to receive him on his first day. It is not unusual for a new employee to arrive on the first day and find that no adequate arrangements have been made to receive him. It is also common for essential training to be unavailable at start of employment. This can create serious risk with a new employee being expected to function, possibly in a hazardous area, without any idea of the risks, consequently being a danger to himself and to others.

It is not only good manners, but also good sense, to ensure that a new employee receives induction training on the first day and that he is introduced to fellow workers by his new boss. It is highly likely that training must be phased over a period of time. This may be a result of pressure of time, but there may be other reasons why this is desirable and not simply expedient. If a new employ receives several weeks of training at the start of employment, he will be unable to make any direct contribution to the enterprise and much of what he learned at the start of training will have been forgotten by the time the course is completed.

There are two relatively inexpensive steps which can be taken to reduce early risk. The first step would be to issue the employee with a manual which details what is expected of him and what he can expect in return. This might be a relatively large volume in some cases and, if so, should also be issued with a brief fact sheet. The easier the manual is to read, the more likely it is to be read. It should also describe the objective of the enterprise and where this employee's duties play an important part in achieving this objective. Many personnel problems, particularly in large enterprises, start because the employee does not feel he is a valued employee and does not think that it makes much difference how well, or badly, he does his job.

The second step is to appoint a mentor, who may be a supervisor, but it is better to select a fellow worker of similar rank. The mentor fills a very important role. He holds experience of the enterprise and the job held by the new employee, so that he can provide immediate advice and instruction. That experience should be within the capability of a supervisor, but the most valuable service provided by a mentor may not be easy for a supervisor. This is to provide a sympathetic ear. Having someone nearby, with whom concerns can be frankly expressed , is very valuable for a new person in strange surroundings. However sympathetic and considerate a supervisor may be, a new worker may not be confident to share uncertainty with the boss.

Risk is increased through an inappropriate system of reward. An employee who is paid at a fixed rate has no financial inducement to do more than the minimum required of him. An employee who is paid on an hourly rate is encouraged to spread his work over the maximum number of hours. If an hourly rate is enhanced for working overtime outside normal working hours, there is strong encouragement to ensure that work is stretched out as far as possible to include the maximum number of hours at the higher rate. This may result in very little work being done during the primary operating hours of the enterprise and may force fellow workers to work overtime. By the same token, any employee who is paid on simple result, such as the number of pieces produced, or the value of sales booked, may ensure that he achieves the highest possible figure even if he knows that this will create other problems for the enterprise.

Many enterprises spend considerable effort looking for new payment systems as the single method of risk reduction. Management of personnel cannot be achieved by financial measures alone, any more than use of threats and sanctions can reduce personnel risks. The only method which has proved successful is staff motivation which requires a number of supporting measures. To achieve this, it is essential that every employee feels himself to be a valued member of a team, doing a worthwhile job for an enterprise which is making a valuable contribution to society. Pride is a more reliable motivator than greed or fear. This does not mean that rewards and sanctions are unimportant, rather that they have a supportive role instead of being a primary method of control.

Methods which work in one society may not be so successful in another. The achievement of Japanese enterprises in world trade has encouraged many enterprises in other countries to copy Japanese methods, often with very limited success and sometimes with negative results. When the effort to copy has failed, the enterprise usually assumes that this is a failure in implementation, and not a result of the concepts failing to travel well. The basic concepts of Japanese commerce are universal and apply irrespective of culture. They depend on dedication, hard work, careful planning, team effort and pride. However, different cultures present challenges in implementation because any enterprise has to recognize social attitudes, having to live with them and adapt methods to recognize their strengths and weaknesses. Many Japanese methods are very similar to the best methods employed in Britain during the Nineteenth Century when British society was very different from what it is in the late Twentieth Century. Methods which were successful then cannot be implemented with the same success a hundred years later, but that does not mean that the principles cannot be applied in a modified form which recognizes social change.

A Japanese worker identifies very closely with his company and has great pride in its achievements. He is also used to working as a valued member of a team in an orderly and dutiful way. As a result, he is motivated to give all of his effort to his job and operates in an orderly environment. The use of a company uniform by all workers is not so much a sign of democratic equality, as it is a common corporate identity where the individual is subordinated to the needs of the enterprise. Managers are still respected as leaders rather than as equals and the environment is basically paternalistic. It is however a two way street. A manager sets himself the same goals and standards as those he sets his staff. If the goals are not met, he will treat himself as harshly as he treats his subordinates, sometimes more so, accepting ultimate responsibility. This may not be ritual disembowelling, but it will probably result in resignation. This is alien to some other cultures where the individual's needs and desires are placed ahead of the corporate requirements. Some may see this as selfishness by the workers, but it runs right through the structure and probably emanates from the top. In some corporations, the only point of honour is to ensure that the consequences of all failures are visited on the most junior. When bad management results in reverses, the managers dismiss those subordinates who tried hard to reduce the consequences of their superiors failings.

However, there is no reason why any enterprise cannot ensure that its managers are trained to lead by example and be respected for their ability. What usually creates the barriers is poor definition of work groups and their relationship with other work groups. This is a result of poor enterprise planning, usually as a result of inefficient, or non existant, enterprise policies, originating from a lack of effective risk analysis. It is not unusual to find enterprises where the managers and their work groups neither fit the processes they are there to support, nor reflect the actual unofficial work groups which form by evolution. It is also common to find managers spending most of their time looking for problems and very little time looking for things which are successes. That leads to an environment where sanctions are given a predominant position, followed by financial reward and leaving no space for establishing pride in achievement. This creates serious risks which are made progressively greater as the work force becomes fearful and defensive.

Correcting this situation requires remarkably little effort and usually reduces the amount of effort required from managers. A worker who receives praise for a job well done is more likely to try harder to achieve even more. In contrast, a manager who is always looking for faults, and making free use of available sanctions, will encourage his staff to conceal errors and tell him what he wants to hear. Financial rewards will not compensate for ineffective management and bad training. However, giving workers a stake in the success of the enterprise and making sure that work groups are organized to support essential processes, under well trained and positive management, can turn an enterprise from failure to success in an amazingly short time.

A very important element in this process is the enterprise's ethics policy. This must include the standards which the enterprise expects of its staff and the standards which it sets itself. It should not be confined to internal issues alone, but include a code of behaviour in respect of dealings with people outside the enterprise.

The ethics policy starts with the recruitment process. If the enterprise has established its ethical code on the basis of fairness and equality, it is possible to project those standards to potential employees and identify how they relate to the code. Generally, an individual is looking for an employer who will give fair reward and treatment. Someone who is driven by greed and has low ethical standards is attracted more to an enterprise which has no obvious ethical standards, or has established a reputation for low standards. Once the new employee has started to work for the enterprise, it is essential to encourage observance of the ethics policy. This requires effective communication, good quality training and adequate monitoring. It also requires supporting measures.

It is very easy for an enterprise to encourage poor ethical behaviour by its staff, particularly in their dealings with customers and suppliers. This may be active encouragement, or it may be accidental. It is also very easy to establish an environment where general standards of poor behaviour inside the enterprise are regarded as normal. It may involve minor matters, but once a risk is encouraged it is likely to become progressively more serious. A common practice among workers is to take minor items for their own use. This may be the habit of copying personal documents on the office photocopier, using stationary for private purposes, or putting letters through the office franking machine. In some cases it may be common practice for employees to take stock for their private use. Although the value of the items may be small, it is still theft and the temptation will be there to take more valuable items in the future. Even low value items can result in measurable cumulative cost. One person using a single paper clip for private purposes does not cause a measurable loss but, if every employee takes one paper clip each week, the cumulative cost will soon become measurable. Even then the loss will not be significant but, having established the principle that this is acceptable behaviour, the loss soon grows into boxes of paper, pens, photocopies and a host of other items. Over the course of a year, even a small enterprise may find that the total cost of supplies diverted to private use is a remarkably large amount. If the practice goes unchecked, progressively larger and more costly items of equipment and goods will disappear. The real risk is the consequential risk which develops from petty theft. The challenge is how the enterprise can control the situation, and having an ethics policy will not in itself provide the solution.

Some enterprises, particularly food retailers, take a very firm stand on these issues because they know that unchecked petty theft can cause the enterprise to fail. A percentage of turnover is treated as 'permitted leakage'. If the percentage is exceeded, the shop manager is instantly dismissed. The cost of 'permitted leakage' is of course included in the price of products and so the customer is paying a percentage towards accepted theft. If an employee is found to be taking the smallest item out of the shop, or eating stock items, they are instantly dismissed and in some cases will be prosecuted for theft. This may seem harsh, but the enterprise will be at serious risk otherwise. Part of the risk is also generated by poor management, low wages, low regard for the staff, and management by fear is a natural component of this environment. What may appear as an ethical and firm approach to theft may actually be the result of a basically unethical company which condones theft, provided that only the customers suffer. It may also be the case that poor and inconsiderate treatment of staff contributes to the motivation to petty theft.

An alternative approach is to decriminalize petty theft. This may sound like the worst form of appeasement, but it can be the very best form of risk reduction. Some food manufacturing plants tell their employees that they can eat as much of the products as they want while they are working. This approach makes the eating of the enterprise's assets a permitted activity and not an act of theft, introducing a level of equally. Experience shows that new workers can enthusiastically consume a remarkable quantity of food during their first shifts. As the weeks go by the novelty wears off and the employees eat less and less of the products. Over a period of time, the cost of produce eaten by employees is insignificant and the cost of adequately enforcing a no eating policy would have been much more costly and not very effective. It is interesting to note that when losses are compared with those at a factory which prohibits employees from eating the produce, the losses of the latter are often much greater, productivity is lower, and money will have been spent in an attempt to prevent the problem. The factory which does permit eating of products also strictly prohibits any products being taken out from the factory and provides a shop where employees can purchase any of the products at low prices. The staff shop additionally provides a very convenient way of selling damaged products and products which are close to the end of their shelf life. When these measures are taken together, the enterprise has turned a potential loss into a profit and greatly reduced the risk of theft by employees. It has also produced a happier work environment.

It might be considered that this approach is only suitable for enterprises which manufacture food products, but the principle can be applied to any type of enterprise. When an office worker uses a paper clip, or puts personal mail through the office franking machine, it is often a matter of convenience rather than a deliberate attempt to steal. It may be that the location of the office and the working hours make it very difficult for the employee to go out and purchase a paper clip or post a letter. This will also apply to the use of the company's telephone for private calls. An enterprise which considers the needs of its staff may gain considerable benefits in terms of improved morale which leads to improved productivity. Therefore a system which identifies what is acceptable, or makes special provision, can enjoy returns which are greater than the cost of the provision. To achieve this there must be a method of accountability.

Some enterprises allow employees to post private mail and use low cost materials free of charge provided that the use is registered. However this is often tacit approval, an accepted *perk* rather than a defined permission. Other enterprises may provide the facilities at cost. Action is then taken against those employees who do not follow these rules. Where facilities are provided at no cost, those employees who are seen to be abusing the privileges are warned before the privileges are withdrawn. The cost of making these provisions is relatively modest and more than repaid by improved morale and effective theft prevention. Experience shows that employees police the system because they stand to loose the privileges if their colleagues consistently abuse them. This creates an environment where employees develop a regard for the company assets and assist in reporting any other thefts because they have a direct stake in the matter.

The principles can be extended to other areas of activity. Some companies have found that they benefit from allowing employees to use production facilities for private purposes. This is more difficult to organize because there may be a number of health and safety issues and it may be necessary to pay some employees to supervise the use of the facilities. One example might be a vehicle repair facility which permits employees to work on their own vehicles outside normal working hours, using company tools and materials. The privilege may not be free, but offered at cost price. It is an additional benefit to the employee and it removes the temptation to *borrow* equipment.

Removing an asset for personal use without permission may be theft, but another risk is created when equipment is *borrowed* from another department without asking. In some large organizations this can be a major problem and be responsible for creating other risks when the absence of equipment may result in injury or reduced product quality. For example, a very large hospital had been plagued by *theft*. One employee decided to buy security tags to mark every item of equipment in his laboratory. He marked hospital equipment and even personal items such as his kettle and mugs. He soon found that several marked items were missing and discovered one item in use in another lab. After this find he visited other parts of the hospital and recovered the remaining items. Nothing had been stolen and removed from the hospital, but *borrowed* by colleagues to replace broken or missing items in their own work area. Over a period of a few months, his idea was copied around the hospital and departments began to find items, which had been missing for some time, reappearing in their rightful places. In some cases, an employee had picked up something without thinking and walked off with it, but generally items had been taken as replacements because it was easier than raising paperwork to order replacements. In some cases new and unused equipment was discovered but no one would admit to ownership.

The lessons learned were that relatively inexpensive steps can be taken to keep equipment in its rightful place and overly bureaucratic ordering systems can create higher costs ultimately. Generally, unauthorized removal of equipment causes inconvenience and results in wasted effort, but in some cases it may mean that work is poorly, or even dangerously, carried out because the correct tools are not available. When the consequential costs are taken into consideration, significant expenses may have been incurred.

Although policy creation can produce substantial advantages, it can also introduce additional risk. This is a greater danger in a large enterprise where policies may become an excuse for new bureaucracy which will represent a financial overhead and produce limited benefits because the policies are unwieldy. To be effective, policies must be easy to understand and practical. They should fit the people rather than requiring the people to fit them. Unless the enterprise is a new venture in the planning stages, analysis and planning has to take place around an existing operation. Inevitably many employees will need to be retrained because process re-engineering is usually required to improve the enterprise's ability to meet its objective. Some employees will not be suitable for retraining and will no longer be able to fulfil a role in the enterprise. This will require sensitive handling and is an area where many enterprises fail miserably. If the employee was hired to do a particular job and has worked loyally to do that job to the best of his ability, it is not his fault that he no longer has a valid role to play because that job will cease to exist. The enterprise should make an adequate allowance for the cost of ensuring that each redundant employee is generously treated. This is not an altruistic action, but a very practical risk reduction measure.

When a company embarks on an analysis exercise, many employees fear for the security of their jobs. If this fear is allowed to develop, poor performance and even acts of sabotage may result. This can be avoided by keeping all staff informed of the progress of the study and involve them in building policies. They may well be able to make major contributions to the effectiveness of the programme. They should know that the enterprise will take every step to find a rewarding place for each of them in any revised structure and that every help and support will be offered to anyone who cannot be redeployed. However, the management should not make any promises which they are unprepared, or unable, to keep.

In small enterprises communication is easier, but redundancy can be a traumatic experience for everyone because they have been working together closely. The small enterprise also has less ability to cushion the blow. Even in a very large enterprise the work groups may be relatively small and redundancy may be just as traumatic. This factor is often overlooked and can produce a range of problems, especially if the notification is seen as heartless and uncaring, emanating from some faceless higher authority. When this happens, many of the anticipated gains of process reengineering are cancelled out by loss of performance resulting from demotivated staff.

Even a small enterprise will provide a considerable volume of information if it adequately builds a comprehensive suite of policies within the enterprise policy. One danger of analysis and policy production is that it can develop a life of its own and result of vast quantities of material which no one has the time to read fully and everyone has difficulty understanding. To make the exercise profitable, information has to be turned into valuable knowledge. Even if the data is stored on a computer based system, it still has to be accessible and that means that someone has to know that they need to search for the information. The only information which the computer will volunteer is that which is required during report generation. For enterprise modelling this can be very helpful because the entry of new variables can prompt a report which identifies any consequential changes and issues warnings of essential actions required if the changes being modelled are to be implemented. However, this does not cater adequately for the needs of employees in their day to day tasks.

The most reliable method of communicating essential information is to produce a digest which can be carried at all times, or stored in an accessible location close to the place of work. Any policy should be capable of summary on a single page, with an index to identify where additional information can be found, or who should be contacted for further instructions. In a typical enterprise, the best method may be to issue a small pocket book which contains key information and can be carried at all times. In some operations, such as a food processing plant, it may prove better to print key information on durable cards, which can be cleaned with the same chemicals used for cleaning the work surfaces and walls, and fix them on a wall in a prominent place. A more comprehensive document may be issued to each employee, tailored to their specific job. Each department may then need even more comprehensive documents, possibly in several volumes, and a number of manuals will be required to cover every aspect of enterprise policies. If this approach is followed, adequate information will be available to assist each employee in their work, but it does not guarantee that the policies will be observed, or even that they will be read.

The only way in which an enterprise can ensure that policies are implemented reliably and uniformly across the enterprise is to ensure that all training relates to appropriate rules and that careful monitoring constantly takes place. This monitoring will be most effective if the emphasis is upon reward for getting it right first time, rather than on penalties for making mistakes. It also requires managers at every level to fully understand what the policies are, how they should be implemented, and what to look for during monitoring. This must be linked with the system of rewards. Many enterprises only monitor output and major errors. There is no merit in encouraging a worker to produce a certain number of units per hour without tying production to quality of unit and observance of the other policy requirements. Quality of production is the most important issue but quality is much more than just the adherence to a product specification.

The achievement of high quality products is the natural consequence of implementing a suite of policies across the enterprise which ensure that the work force is motivated to achieve the enterprise objective through sustained effort over a period of time and at an acceptable level of risk. It is becoming increasingly common for enterprises to be forced to obtain independent quality control certificates. There are both advantages and disadvantages in this trend, but one common failing is that the issue of a certificate is taken as a reason to relax. The nature of Standards is that they require considerable documentation and impose a methodology which may be unnatural for any particular enterprise. That is an unfortunate situation because it means that only sustained effort and vigilance will ensure continued compliance.

It is usually uneconomic for the Standards body to carry out adequate auditing once a certificate has been issued. It is not uncommon for an enterprise to spend considerable effort and funds in preparation for the first assessment. For most enterprises it is a beneficial process which identifies a range of weaknesses and provides the means to improve quality and efficiency. Once the assessors have gone, the procedures are soon abandoned, until it is time for the next assessment. There is then a great deal of activity as people try to create documentation of events during the previous twelve months, which the quality manual requires should be recorded at the time to provide a method of testing that all quality assurance steps have been taken and to identify problems at the earliest time when their solution will present a smaller challenge. At the time, it was accepted that people were too busy to spend time writing notes and the records were not kept. A much greater amount of time will now be devoted to re-creating records from memory and by searching those basic records which have been kept at various locations. This is a travesty of the principles of quality management and serves no constructive purpose. It is also fraudulent because the quality assurance certificate has been obtained by a lie and maintained through deception in order to obtain trade. Very few enterprises accept that this is the consequence of what is a widespread and generally accepted behaviour.

The situation is an example of bureaucracy creating a new group of criminals. It is also an example of a basically sound and worthy principle being subverted. The principle is being applied ineffectively and in some cases the criteria of evaluation are seriously flawed. Because a *standard* exists, government procurement agencies seize upon it as a method of avoiding responsibility and blame. A strange belief exists that just because a vendor can tick a box to say that he has certificate for compliance with a standard, such as ISO 9000, his quality assurance is exactly equal to that of every other vendor who can tick the box, but a vendor who has not spent money on obtaining a certificate has an unacceptable level of quality management. Once this becomes a mandated requirement, a perfectly reliable vendor may lose a market overnight. This may put him out of business and therefore the pressure is on to obtain the magic certificate. Large commercial corporations jump onto the band wagon and follow the government lead in mandating certificates.

The pressures are now immense and the sudden demand for certification places great strain on the assessment teams and fuels a huge new growth industry of consultants who will write the necessary manuals and coach the enterprise through assessment. Hard pressed assessors then come to expect manuals set out in a particular manner. Provided that they are presented with manuals in this format, they may fail to look closely at some practical aspects of the enterprise. As the consultant has made the company fit a standard concept, he has taken it away from its natural and established methods and organization and the pressures of business demands will rapidly take it back to these methods again. Very soon after assessment, the enterprise is no longer following the procedures laid down in the quality manuals. This failure to follow the manuals, or to report the risks being created by adherence to the manuals, is usually not a company policy from the top, but omission much lower down the structures. The failure is

77

covered up at many levels and only considerable effort will recover the situation in time for the next assessment. On occasion, necessary items of equipment will be specifically hired in for the period of inspection and returned after it is over. This creates another new industry of suppliers whose primary profit is from helping other enterprises to fraudulently obtain and maintain certificates. This is nothing new, just being an extension of extraordinary lengths to which enterprises have gone to fake conditions for other inspections by fire officers, health & safety instructors and all the other people who have a right, or duty, to carry out inspections for compliance with mandatory standards.

Ironically, evasion is often more costly than correct compliance. If the enterprise had taken the opportunity to carry out a real analysis of the enterprise, all the policy manuals would have lined up behind the identified objective. Training requirements would have been correctly identified and the whole process would been monitored to ensure a smooth operation. Efficient management would have ensured all personnel were doing their best to avoid risk, but to identify errors speedily and correct them. This costs money and takes time, but it does not place the enterprise, or its employees, in risk of committing criminal offences. It costs much less to operate within the established method than it does to follow another method and then go back to fake documentation. It also produces savings because the enterprise is working efficiently and not faking it  All assessments and monitoring inspections can be performed without disruption, because they will only be observation of an established and reliable operation.

One difficulty which may have to be addressed during the development of compliance manuals is the interface with inspectors. The ideal situation for any enterprise is to produce a set of manuals which directly relate to the organization of the enterprise in a form which is recognized by the work force. This may not meet the expectations of the multitude of inspectors. The fire prevention inspector will have his own set of documentation, as will a health and safety inspector and a quality management inspector. Each set of documentation is likely to differ from the other sets and may not recognize the organization of a particular enterprise. Introducing a single risk management team within the enterprise may be relatively simple, but the enterprise will have no control over the many external agencies which set and police specific aspects of risk. These agencies also have different cultures and approaches. As with any organization, each will consider that their specialization is the most important and that the needs of others is of secondary importance. There is no simple solution to this challenge.

If an enterprise attempts to match each inspectorate's format and approach, the result is likely to be confusing to the work force, introducing risks as a consequence of the confusion. The most effective way of dealing with the issue is to develop an enterprise policy manual to match the objective of the enterprise, so that all tasks and processes follow logically and effectively to support objective achievement. As this manual builds, it will identify risks as they affect the objective achievement. Training manuals can be drafted to support this approach and will combine all the activity elements. Therefore, a worker being trained to operate a particular machine will be taught to manage and avoid risk during the operation. To operate within acceptable risk levels, the worker will also need to be taught how to interface with other activities and processes. This training should be arranged to combine seamlessly all of the aspects of work rather than consist of a series of individual sets of instruction. Therefore, the training programme will not identify risk management as a separate subject. The worker should then be able to learn all of the necessary aspects of his job function to develop good habits, automatically coping with the range of activities which make up his job.

Having produced a set of documentation and training programmes in support of objective achievement, the enterprise will need to have an inspectorate in place to ensure that all activities comply with the authorized procedures. In some enterprises, it may prove desirable to establish a risk management team with a number of specialists and those specialists may relate directly to external inspectorates. If that is a natural consequence of the enterprise plan, it is a useful bonus which may assist in dealing with external agencies. If it is not a natural consequence, there will probably be a need to produce a second set of documentation which is derived directly from the enterprise policy and its associated risk policies. This set of documentation will be organized into segments which relate directly to the external inspection agencies. In this approach, the risk is that the two sets of documentation are not always in step with each other. If the enterprise policy is maintained in electronic form, including a modelling facility, this should not present any difficulties, because any changes to any elements will be modelled and the system will identify any points of conflict. It must include all mandatory requirements imposed by external agencies and should be capable of identifying how these have been met, where they are exceeded and why the additional risk reduction is necessary to the objective achievement. Where the policy documents are only produced in hardcopy form, great care must be exercised to ensure that all documentation matches.

# 5 Risk management for sites

Risk management usually begins at site level. Virtually every enterprise operates from a base. In the case of the smallest enterprises, this base may be domestic premises which act as a mail address, even if the main business is carried out from a vehicle. The level of control over the base site may vary according to several factors, such as whether the site is owned, or rented, solely occupied by the enterprise, or shared with others. In addition, there will be other important factors, such as the level of access which must be provided for external agencies, individuals, or other enterprises.

The majority of risk studies begin with established facilities. This usually results in a policy which accepts that the existing sites are already fixed and fits risk management procedures around those sites. This approach may be a mistake. An established enterprise may occupy existing sites for a variety of reasons, some of which may have originally been justified but, several years later, no one can really remember what the justifications were. The enterprise will also have changed to some extent and any original valid justification may no longer apply. However, the selection of a site plays a very important role in risk management at the site. When an enterprise first acquires a site, remarkably little thought may have gone into its selection. The location chosen may have little more behind it than the fact the founders lived in the area, or it was close to a major customer. Financial resources may have driven the decision more than operational requirements. In some cases there may have been little time available and the selection criteria could have consisted of little more than a financial budget and a requirement that the site be available for immediate occupation. Since moving to the site, the enterprise may have failed to allocate time to reviewing the ability of the site to meet current requirements, or to consider what external factors may have influenced the continued suitability of the site.

One of the most common problems experienced by enterprises is that vehicle parking space is no longer adequate. There may be several reasons for this. The reduction in public transport facilities may have forced workers to use private vehicles to travel to and from site. In the case of small enterprises which have grown and prospered, it may be the workers who originally could not afford private vehicles are now more affluent and have spent some of that money on vehicles which provide a more comfortable and convenient method of commuting to work. Another common factor may be that changes in housing availability, road networks and increased personal wealth have resulted in workers moving out from the centres of cities and commercial areas and commuting longer distances. To these factors may be added the changes in commercial transportation where materials and goods are moved in and out of the site in different ways, including the use of large commercial vehicles which require what was car parking space to be reallocated to these goods vehicles.

Changes in social and economic conditions will result in changes to the environment in which the site exists. What was a site in a mixed commercial and housing area may now be in a depressed and largely derelict area, where crime has a much greater influence. This leaves two basic choices. Either a new site is sought, or risk reduction measures are applied to the existing site. If risk is treated in isolation, as is often the case, time, money, and effort will be expended improving risk reduction at the existing site. A more cost effective solution may be to relocate activities to new facilities. This can only be judged effectively if a complete enterprise policy is produced. It is an example of the importance of treating all issues on an enterprise wide basis. By locating to a larger site, it may be possible to simplify matters, such as vehicle parking. Crime prevention may become less costly because local conditions at the new site make some measures unnecessary. Operational requirements made be met more effectively and reduce pressure on quality management and in the provision of satisfactory health and safety facilities. Access to markets may be improved and provide additional profits to fund improved conditions which would previously have been difficult to fund. New markets may be opened and transportation requirements reduced. All of these factors will apply to all aspects of the enterprise's activities.

The major factor which discourages such an action is the size of the task. For most managers it seems simpler to adapt existing facilities and, sometimes, a modest incremental approach is seen as a way of avoiding the need to admit that some management decisions have been defective, or untimely. There may be many other additional factors. People generally resist revolutionary change, or any significant evolutionary change. There will also be considerations prompted by concern for existing workers. This applies particularly to the smaller enterprise where the work force may have been together for some time and have become an extended family. In moving to the most suitable new location it may mean that a number of existing workers will be unable, or unprepared, to move with the enterprise. These are all difficult issues which test the will and ability of the management to support the best interests of the enterprise. However, this is all part of the process of enterprise planning and the duty of management. There will be occasions when difficult decisions have to be made. What may seem to be a popular decision could well prove ultimately to be unpopular. Failure to respond to the demands of changing circumstances can result in a far less popular result eventually. There are many examples of enterprises failing all the workers and stock holders as a consequence of misguided attempts to assist them.

An enterprise which defies change will usually cease to exist and the period between key decisions and the eventual failure will have benefited those who depend on the enterprise far less than the eventual outcome. A company may have been located in a particular place for very sound reasons, such as proximity to markets, or essential materials. The fact that the company was once the main reason for the development of a community does not mean that the best interests of the community will be served by a slow decay because managers shirked the responsibility to face change. If market changes, or other factors, now make it necessary to move to a new location, some people will suffer. If a decision to move is taken promptly, the company will be able to support some relocation costs for employees which will eventually become impossible if the decision is delayed, and the company becomes financially weak. There may also be sufficient resources to assist the development of a new enterprise to take over part of the old site and provide employment for those who will not be able to move with the established enterprise. There will always be a number of positive options open, provided the enterprise is under control and opportunities are not avoided. Some courageous actions may be necessary, but they will only be effective if they are taken on the basis of sound research and planning.

One distortion may have been caused by government intervention. In several societies, changes in technology, markets, and economics, have made traditional industries unviable. If the situation is allowed to develop under market forces, enterprises will either fail, or change dramatically. During this period there will be a loss of jobs, possibly significant job loss. As a major enterprise feeds the community around it, the knock on effect may be dramatic. Governments have proved susceptible to pleas for financial support in the forms of subsidies and stock purchase. The motives behind government support may be well intentioned, but the final result is usually damaging to the people the policy was intended to help and also damaging to the tax payers generally. It is an example of crisis management where inadequate research has been done while a *quick fix* has been attempted. It is a crude form of inefficient risk management, applied to the symptoms of a deeper problem, carried out too late in the risk development. The enterprise site plays a major part in the process because it is visible. A steel works, or a shipyard, are major landmarks and provide the basis of emotional appeal. They also tend to be monolithic sites employing thousands of people. A government may not notice the failure of several small companies, but one large enterprise may represent voter power which could result in the government losing several parliamentary seats at an election.

Had enterprise and risk management been carried out correctly through the life of the enterprises, the dangers would have been identified at a time when they could be reduced to acceptable levels. A major enterprise, and more so a major industry, does not come to the point of catastrophic failure overnight. The situation develops progressively and the signs should be seen several years before. What clouds vision is that a major enterprise occupies one, or more, large sites and appears impregnable. When ship building has taken place on a stretch of river for several hundred years, generations have worked in the enterprise and come to expect that it will prosper for ever. Over the years the site has developed and massive machines tower over the landscape. However, the enterprise management should have been observing commercial risks and general developments in transport industry. They should have seen the impact on order books and the need to invest in new equipment and techniques to maintain their ability to achieve the enterprise goal. Their enterprise has reached the point of failure because they did not do this effectively.

Had the enterprise followed an effective enterprise policy, it would have been able to respond to the new opportunities and new threats. It might have been possible to move to a new location, develop the existing site more appropriately, adopt new technology, or even move into new markets. As this has not been done, there is panic, and a fearful government may be prompted to inject large sums to support a failing enterprise in the interests of keeping voters in work. This very rarely succeeds ultimately. Eventually a point will be reached where the government is no longer able, or prepared, to continue its support and the eventual failure is usually even more dramatic for a number of reasons.

Evidence suggests that the injection of panic funding eventually increases the size of the threat and that any relief is short lived. The workers of the enterprise come to expect continuing generous support and enjoy a false sense of security. To their original impression of permanence, which was generated by the substantial nature of the site, is added the comfort of a

84

bottomless purse of government money. Rather than encouraging fresh effort to succeed, subsidy most frequently encourages reduced effort because pressures have been removed and a dependency culture is established. This is not confined to the main enterprise. Most of the smaller enterprises in the area see this new mirage of permanence as an assurance that their life and business will continue for ever. Where they might have begun to look for new markets, and even re-locate geographically, they continue as before. When the government support is finally removed, they feel only betrayal and the sudden change leaves them with little ability to salvage their own situations. Where the failure, or major change, of a large employer would have been more progressive, and the results less dramatic, a whole community will be blighted, possibly for many generations. Eventually, government may have to inject further funding to support the community from total disaster. No nation is immune from these risks. Democratic governments may be more susceptible to individual pressures, but totalitarian regimes also follow similar paths and often end up with even greater problems because they acted in a uniform way, making an even greater intervention.

Government intervention will always be ultimately limited because even a government runs out of money if it spends freely. The eventual size of the problem is greater for two reasons. Firstly, governments are even slower to recognize that the point of limit has eventually been reached because no real attempt is made to apply true enterprise and risk policies and the flow of information is even slower. Secondly, no government is spending its own money. It may be raising the funds through taxation and the cost of collection raises the cost of support, in that to raise one unit of currency in taxation can cost up to 85% of the value of the money raised. Therefore the total funding requirement may be several times greater than the funding requirement at the enterprise. Alternatively, a government may borrow money to avoid becoming unpopular as a result of increased taxation. Sometimes, a government may be forced to borrow at very high interest rates because it is seen as a poor commercial risk. The total costs are further increased because of the knock on effects of the government intervention. Successful enterprises and individuals will be forced to pay the price of someone else's inefficiency. That means that they are less able to use their own profits to maintain the efficiency of their own enterprises and may become uncompetitive because the cost of taxation is all part of the cost of production. As the process continues, the government has to intervene in a growing number of industries. If a government borrows massively, interests rates will rise for all borrowers and a recession can be triggered, during which many otherwise successful enterprises will fail. The cost of saving a few thousand jobs in one area may result in the eventual loss of several million jobs throughout the economy. The recession may even become international with severe consequences around the world. That will not directly result from one government intervening to support one enterprise, but result from a chain of actions which naturally follow from the basic policy. Once a government has acted to subsidize one shipyard, it is very hard to resist demands from other shipyards for similar support. That support may become necessary because the system of subsidy has placed the first recipient at an unfair business advantage over neighbouring yards. Once the cycle has started, it is very difficult to break.

In the late Twentieth Century, this situation is made much more difficult because of technological revolution which applies strongly to the old concept of enterprise sites. The development of automation, and the new industrial processes employed in electronics and chemical production, does not require the huge sites which were essential to heavy industries. They also require lower air pollution levels and that often means that they have to be located away from the *dirty* industries. Once these new industries have established in other areas, and are producing the major revenues, communities expand in the new areas and accelerate the decline of facilities in the older industrial areas. A more productive use of funding in old industrial areas may be to make them more suitable for new industries and that may require government intervention, to tackle anti-pollution activities, and to provide management of shared areas of activity, where it is unreasonable to expect enterprises to take responsibility effectively.

Hopefully, the enterprise is carrying out enterprise and risk studies from its early days, but most probably it will be a formal exercise introduced at a later stage where an operation is already established, possibly for several years. The most dramatic situation is where an enterprise and risk study indicates the necessity to relocate the complete operation, possibly to a new site some distance away. Often it will prove possible to make less dramatic changes. It may be that the movement of one process to a new site will produce the necessary improvement. By study of the objective, and the means of achievement, a particular process may account for a substantial percentage of new costs in support of adequate risk management. The cost of relocating this process to another site may mean that no additional measures are required at the established site, and the cost of measures at the new site will be much lower. It could also prove attractive to sub contract the process to another enterprise. There are several examples of this situation. A common situation may be the need to introduce a new process which brings high levels of risk because either the process, or the materials, are hazardous, or have a very high value. If the process is introduced into the existing site, it may be necessary to apply risk reduction measures to the whole site and not just the small area where the process will be located.

That could add considerable cost to the enterprise when an alternative approach might avoid the problem. If the process is located on a new site, the finished product may not have the same high risk and could be transported to the main site. Alternatively, the low risk products could be transported to the new site and combined with the high risk element. When all issues are considered, it may prove more cost effective to employ a sub-contract service at a remote location, but that decision can only be made if the enterprise has a detailed knowledge of its objective, tasks, processes, and tools. The decision is made much easier if the enterprise has the ability to model the options before having to take a firm decision.

Maximum control is possible at a site which is owned and occupied exclusively by the enterprise and does not have to provide any access for external agencies. Such sites are rare, but do exist. In most cases though, a tightly controlled site is one of a number of sites operated by the enterprise and is most likely to be a government facility, where highly sensitive operations have deliberately been grouped together away from all other activities to provide a very high level of security. They are exceptional, because a minimum level of access is usually necessary for power and communications equipment and for the delivery and collection of mail. A closed site has to make special arrangements to avoid the need for this minimum level of access by external agencies. The cost of these provisions is likely to be considerable and requires the very special needs to be justifiable. It may be an essential requirement for the existence of the site to be kept secret.

These requirements introduce several special difficulties. It was once considered essential for high security prisons to be built away from population centres and in geographical locations which are difficult to navigate. Before the Nineteenth Century, it was common to export convicted criminals to new colonies across the oceans, to house some in ancient fortresses, or to employ them as slaves. By the Nineteenth Century many societies were beginning to consider these practices barbaric, demanding new systems of punishment. The use of the death penalty was reduced, deportation to colonies became unacceptable, not least because these colonies were developing national identities and their growing populations did not want other people's problems dumped on their doorstep. These factors combined to increase the prison population and in Great Britain a major prison building programme was started. This programme included the construction of special facilities for the most dangerous prisoners. Dartmoor Prison is an example of a Nineteenth Century High Security Prison, being built in the isolation of Dartmoor, where the terrain is a component of the protective measures. Difficult to reach from any population centre, particularly at the time of construction when the motor vehicle had yet to appear, it was also a wild expanse where strangers would be noticed and escapees would have to contend with a difficult terrain and unpleasant climate. The practice continued into the Twentieth Century and some prisons, such as Alcatraz in North America, were built on islands where fog and strong currents produced natural outer defences.

The construction of this type of prison appeared to offer a number of important risk reduction benefits. Being located away from public gaze, in areas which the population might regard as hostile, it was possible to create mystique and legend to make the prisons harsh and hostile, hell on earth. That greatly enhanced their potential for deterrence. They were also much more secure, with escape from the site being challenging, and recapture, in the difficult terrain beyond, reasonably assured. It might therefore be considered that prisons of this type would be highly successful and would continue to provide a necessary service.

A similar approach has been taken with particularly sensitive government activities. Military sites have also been built in a remarkably similar style, but in this case to keep hostiles out, rather than in. There has been the additional dimension of secrecy. In some case, there has also been a further consideration of safety to the population. An example of this would be nuclear weapons facilities, where the work is not only highly sensitive, but also potentially dangerous. For these reasons facilities have been built in hostile and unpopulated areas such as deserts.

Where both prisons and military installations in remote areas have a common weakness is isolation of the personnel. Although some might consider this appropriate for convicted criminals, prisons require guards and guards expect humane conditions for themselves and their families. Prison guards ended up serving almost the same sentence as the prisoners and it has become increasingly difficult to find suitable personnel who are prepared to work in such conditions. Similar personnel difficulties apply to sensitive government sites. To the difficulties of attracting personnel to serve in the location and maintaining morale for those on site, there is a further risk. When people are isolated from mainstream society for periods of time, they can unwind too quickly when they return to population centres for rest and recreation. This creates several security risks. All of these risks can be addressed, but some of the original benefits of security by isolation have been removed by advancing technologies. Greater mobility offered by motor vehicles and aircraft has reduced the effectiveness of hostile terrain as a reliable outer defence. Satellite surveillance and television journalists open remote sites to the public gaze, but perhaps the greatest risk to the remote site is that people are no longer prepared to tolerate working conditions which would have previously been accepted as part of the job.

Most sites have to provide a much wider range of access permissions to carry out their business. The most extreme cases are, typically, retail outlets, where economic trends have led to the progressive reduction of storage space with restricted access and the maximum use being made of point of sale floorspace. This means that virtually every part of the site is open to the public and suppliers, whilst the number of employees is deliberately reduced to the minimum necessary to support sales. The trend has further complicated risk management because suppliers' personnel now carry out duties formerly performed by employees of the retail outlet, such as for merchandising. This means that these visitors have to have access to all areas of the site, including any stock storage which is not open to customers. They may also take responsibility for the maintenance of stock records.

Assess control into, and within, a site as frequently viewed as a crime prevention exercise and placed under the control of a security officer, generating potential conflict between the security personnel and other work groups. This is a narrow and ineffective approach. It can generate a *them and us* situation where the security officer tries to tightly control access and other work groups are equally extreme in fighting any form of access control, leading to maximum cost and minimum performance. The principal function of access control is to provide the greatest practical and desirable level of access, rather than the provision of the minimum level of access. Crime prevention has to cater for external and internal threats, but is not the only reason for providing access control. Health and safety requirements often depend heavily on access control, and access auditing. Fire prevention has a number of access requirements. Quality control demands access control and auditing. In most cases, the methods which are most cost effective to meet one set of objectives will come into direct conflict with the most cost effective methods potentially suitable for the achievement of other objectives. The Risk Policy is therefore always a compromise and this can be most graphic in the case of site control.

Site control begins at the perimeter of the site. It should then become defence in depth. The classic, and perhaps most extreme, example of this approach is the mediaeval town. A town wall encircled the whole area, with a series of road and/or water gateways to allow adequate traffic flow under normal circumstances. All these gateways could be closed quickly to deal with an emergency and would be routinely closed during the hours of darkness. At night a restricted number of access points would be opened on demand, and every gateway was a defended area. To increase the effectiveness of the walls between gateways, defensive positions were established at regular intervals, serving as watch points. Even with this type of defence, a determined attacker could eventually force an entry. Also, it was not desirable to include all town facilities inside the walls. Plague houses where built outside the walls and some housing was constructed outside, this need increasing as the area inside the walls became fully used. Rather than extending the walls, it became common practice to encourage the less essential citizens to build outside the walls but, to retain the defence effectiveness of the walls, building was not allowed close to them, so that an open area was maintained and had to be crossed by an attacker before he could attempt to breach the wall defences.

Within the walls, every building provided the potential for further security measures and merchants houses, storerooms and other business and private premises would have been secured to the level which each owner desired. The castle provided maximum security for the local government and usually also provided the prison. The castle itself was rarely a single building. In fully developed form, the Moate and Baillie presented a series of defensive features designed to provide maximum resistance to attack and the highest levels of attrition to the most determined attacker. A series of defended walls and gateways protected the central fortified building which was sited on the highest ground, often artificially created, to provide maximum visibility and defensive advantage. Therefore an attacker was faced with progressively stronger defences as he advanced towards the most valuable assets and became progressively weaker in the process. The same defences also provided the means to stop people leaving and those, such as prisoners, most likely to attempt escape were held inside the strongest building, usually in dungeons beneath the castle keep at the very centre of the defensive systems.

It is often assumed that defensive systems of this type disappeared centuries ago but they have continued to be built to basically the same form, and are now showing a return to popularity. The materials used may be different, but the basic principles are the same. The main reason for the demise of the fortified town was that the threats changed and the fortification technology did not exist to counter those threats. Principally, the introduction of canon made the stone walled town and its castle vulnerable. The occupants became trapped inside the defences, which could not resist the relentless assault of artillery. The introduction of explosives also made effective mining of walls much easier and more destructive. However, this was not the only factor. Rapidly increasing populations made it prohibitively expensive to continue to enlarge the fortified area, and increased mobility made the fortified town seem restricting and less attractive. As a result, fortified towns became the exception rather than the standard and restricted their continued use to areas which suffered significant levels of civil unrest. The reason for their increasing popularity today is that urban crime has dramatically increased in many countries and the cost of effective domestic security measures has increased to the point where a fortified village offers effective security with the economies of scale.

Although the fortified village may be making a comeback, most individuals and enterprises have to take their own measures to reduce and manage risk and, even in a fortified village, there is still need and scope for individual counter measures. These measures should be designed to reduce specific risks, but also relate to other risk reduction measures and not introduce unacceptable restraints. Striking the right balance can be a challenge, and maintaining the effectiveness of risk management is no small task. It becomes viable only when frequent reviews are carried out, all personnel understand the need for the Risk Policy, being both willing and adequately trained to ensure that all systems are used as they should be. For that reason, many enterprises will decide to err on the side of weaker risk reduction measures to ensure that they are used, and used correctly, without unduly impeding the day to day working.

The simplest site to secure will be a site owned by the enterprise and used largely by employees of the enterprise. Even here, there are external constraints. There will be public access in the forms of paths and roads around at least part of the perimeter of the site. There will also be local planning restrictions to contend with. In modern society, an enterprise which decides to erect a thirty foot high wall with searchlights and machine gun posts around the site perimeter is likely to face considerable resistance from legislation, local planning authorities, and people working and living around the site. Therefore, funding and available technology are often not the first considerations which may restrict the freedom of action.

Many of the lowest cost techniques for building an outer barrier are also very unattractive. Chain link fencing and razor wire are relatively inexpensive and can be erected very quickly but, unfortunately, are not visually appealing, especially after they start to corrode and sag. This ageing also reduces their effectiveness. As both chain link and razor wire can be easily cut with pocket sized tools, they present little deterrent to a determined intruder unless they are augmented with sensor systems, such as 'shakers', which detect vibration caused by attempts to tamper with the barrier. If the site is industrial, and away from domestic housing, chain link fencing is often satisfactory because the area around the site is utilitarian and aesthetic qualities may not be as important. It has the virtue that it provides a simple barrier, which an intruder has to climb, and is animal proof in either direction. This potentially offers the option to release attack dogs inside the site during periods when it is only occupied by security personnel, but this may introduce new risks. In some countries, an intruder will be able to take civil action for damages if he is injured by a guard dog. If the animals have been released and left unattended, animal rights organizations may present a further risk, using the legislative processes to bring an action for cruelty to the animals. Irresponsible *rights* groups may take violent action against the enterprise, its employees, or even release the animals to create risks to others. The posting of warning notices may not adequately reduce legal liability and the employment of this form of intruder prevention may present risk to someone, such as a fire-fighter, who has a very valid need to enter the site in an emergency when it may not be possible to contact the dog handlers.

There are alternative approaches which combine aesthetic qualities with effective risk reduction. The first step is to decide where the outer defences must be sited and the number and location of entrances. Some countermeasures can add to the visual attraction of the site. A very effective barrier to people is the thorn hedge, which was also one of the earliest methods of perimeter control. Relatively inexpensive to install, it can be attractive, particularly if it has colourful flowers and berries, although some berries may be poisonous and therefore introduce a new threat. Natural hedging has the disadvantage that it requires regular manual maintenance and, once penetrated by an intruder, provides cover from observation. Most varieties of thorn hedging also take time to grow to a size which provides effective resistance to intruders, but still provides little resistance to vehicles.

Another ancient barrier to intruders which can be an attractive feature is water. To be effective, it must be deep and it will take up surface area from the site. It also introduces the risk of drowning and therefore needs some form of fencing to prevent people falling in accidentally. However, it is an effective barrier against both people and vehicles. Landscaped into a site, and provided with features such as fountains, it can be very attractive and it will provide a reservoir for fire fighting. In some areas, especially where water sprinkler systems are used for automatic fire extinguishing, a water reservoir may be essential because the water mains do not provide sufficient pressure for fire fighting. In this case, two risks can be reduced by a single measure, and the visual amenities will be improved as a secondary benefit. A similar ancient, but still effective, barrier is the dry moat which does not help in solving the problems of water supply for fire fighting, but does not offer the same accidental dangers as a water barrier. As with a wet moat, careful landscaping will turn this protective measure into an attractive feature.

The weak points in any perimeter control system are the gateways. The most effective perimeter system employs a number of concentric barriers, each with a single gateway, and no two gateways being directly in line. Although this architecture is effective in controlling access, it is also restrictive and takes up a considerable amount of land. It is acceptable on a large high security site, such as an airfield, or military installation, but for most situations it heavily constricts traffic to an unacceptable level and imposes excessive transit delays. Even on a large site it can present as many problems as it solves and a journey of half a mile in a straight line from the outer fencing can become a trip of several miles as the vehicle drives round to each successive gateway. It introduces a need for good surveillance of the access roads because, otherwise, a vehicle will be unsupervised for some time between check points and the barriers will slow the arrival of essential services, such as fire fighters.

Any gateway has to provide the means to control traffic without creating unacceptable delays, or congestion of the roads leading to the site. A common error in gateway design is to place a single gate close to the site boundary. This will inevitably introduce risk to vehicles queuing to gain entry and the other vehicles using the road in which they may be forced to queue. A probable consequence is that the gate will be left open to avoid this risk, and that will defeat the object of the gate. A more logical arrangement is to plan a checking area where the first gate is at least one vehicle length back from the access road outside the site. Sometimes, this is done at an industrial site, but the vehicle length is based on a car length. Unfortunately this can create greater risks when a large truck arrives and is too long for the allocated space. Any space allocated must be greater than the length of the largest vehicle which may want to gain access.

The first gate opens into a fenced area with parking and a turn round space and gives onto a second gate into the site. The area will provide sufficient space for vehicles and occupants to be checked before allowing them into the main site, and long term parking areas. The space must be large enough to cope with the highest traffic flow levels and the time that it will take to check visitors and their vehicles. It will remove the vehicles from the public road outside, preventing congestion and risk there, but it may require a large surface area. Checking times are likely to vary according to the type of vehicle and its reason for requiring access. It may therefore be highly desirable to segregate cars and goods vehicles into separate holding areas. It may also be necessary to introduce a one way traffic flow through the site and have one gate for entry and a second for exit.

The use of a holding area may simplify gate design. The outer control to the holding area may only have to cater for vehicles and therefore a line of steel or reinforced concrete posts could be sited on either side of a retractable steel ramp. This provides the gatehouse with an unobstructed view of the area in front and will be visually more attractive. This outer barrier should be resistant to the heaviest vehicle travelling at the highest speed towards the barrier to prevent an attacker ramming a way through.

Inside the holding area, space will be restricted so that the inner barrier does not have to be so heavily built, but it will have to be solid and higher to be effective against pedestrians. The height of the inner barrier may have to allow for the possibility that a person could climb across from the top of a vehicle, so that a seven foot high chain, or railing, fence might have to be extended to a height of fifteen feet or more. The alternative to building a high fence, or wall, would be to prevent vehicles from being parked close against this inner barrier.

Having provided a perimeter barrier with the minimum number of gates practical, a complete solution has not been provided. Even on a small site, security personnel in the gatehouses may not be able to observe the full extent of the perimeter. It is also necessary to plan manning levels at gateways. Gatehouses are often manned by a single person, who is exposed to risk when outside the building, with no immediate backup. A solution is to make the gatehouse, and holding area, the reception area also. Higher manning levels are economically possible, with visitors fully supervised until their escort arrives, unless they are known and cleared to enter unescorted.

Having constructed a security control room and reception building, it is then possible to plan all supervisory controls back to the building. If the risk policy indicates strong risks for the site, the security control room can be physically secured and the area divided into public areas, for reception purposes, and private secure areas accessible only to security personnel. It may also be desirable to introduce two separate facilities which would normally deal with traffic flowing in one direction, but could handle incoming and outgoing traffic in the event of the other facility being disabled. This would of course require all sensor and surveillance systems to be linked back to two separated facilities, preferably with the second set of cabling systems following a different path. Planning this type of facility makes possible protective measures which might be difficult to incorporate in the main site buildings. It allows the security building to be safety sited away from the risk of fire spreading from the main buildings, ensuring that the security personnel can function and monitor the site even when the main buildings have to be evacuated. Equally, it provides an area where mail can be screened, away from the main site population, so that a letter bomb would not cause damage in a main area.

The control room should be equipped with close circuit television surveillance of the site perimeter, all internal access roads and parking areas. This may require a number of television cameras and these may be remote controlled motorized camera systems with zoom lens, or fixed cameras with fixed lenses. Fixed cameras cost less per camera and guarantee to provide a set coverage, but remote control cameras will cover a much larger area and may provide lower cost coverage. The weakness of a moving camera is that it cannot be equipped for automatic detection of movement in the surveyed area and may be pointing away from an activity which should be watched. In either case, the number of cameras in use could require a large number of television screens in the control room, each dedicated to a single camera. This has several weaknesses. A large bank of screens is difficult to watch and takes up a considerable area in the control room. Security staff become bored watching a large number of static views and are slow to react to incidents. A large number of screens will also represent a higher cost, for equipment purchase, maintenance, and power consumption.

There are several methods which can be employed to reduce the number of screens in the control room. A common method is to have a single screen connected to a switching device which cycles through the cameras in an automatic sequence. The operator can stop this automatic switching and select a single camera. That then makes him blind to all the other cameras. During the automatic cycle, there are long periods when a particular view is unavailable and too rapid a cycling can induce the same concentration problems caused by a large number of static images. One solution is to use a split screen display where a number of images are displayed segments of the screen of a single monitor. This may be acceptable for a very small number of cameras, but the images are usually so small that they are ineffective in the security role. An alternative is to have an automatic switch cycling a number of fixed cameras which each have the ability to report movement in their field of view. A second monitor screen then displays either a view from a camera which has detected movement, or a view commanded by the operator. The system can be further enhanced by adding a number of remote control pan/tilt/zoom cameras which each have their own monitor screen and are used to sweep the site boundaries, overlapping the coverage of at least some of the fixed cameras. A better solution would be a comprehensive, fully integrated, multi risk, monitoring system which included cameras as just one element.

There is a choice of mono or full colour CCTV systems. Colour systems have a higher cost than mono, but provide more information and tend to be watched more effectively. At night there may be a particular problem with colour systems. Most modern CCTV systems are effective in low light levels and colour systems will operate well if floodlighting is employed at night. Floodlighting can prove a useful additional deterrent to intruders and will offer a safety benefit for authorized personnel moving around the site during the hours of darkness. However, there may be a number of reasons why floodlighting cannot be used. In this situation, infrared spot lights can be mounted on the camera housings, providing light which is not visible to an intruder, but will effectively illuminate the area viewed by each camera.

Some colour cameras may not perform well in infrared light and monochrome cameras may be more suitable. There are also cameras which will operate in very low light levels by using an image intensifying system similar to a starlight sight on a sniper's rifle. In most cases though, it is usually necessary to employ a mix of camera technologies, rather than take a single approach which is optimized in one area at the expense of overall surveillance effectiveness.

Many enterprises will need to record CCTV coverage for future use. This will require a number of video recorders and a large number of tapes will be produced in a short period of time, even when using long play techniques. The cost of tapes soon mounts up and they will take up valuable storage space. In consequence, many enterprises re-use the same tapes only shortly after a previous recording. This inevitably means that a recording is not available when needed and heavy re-use of video tape can result in a poor quality image from a worn out tape. The alternative of keeping tapes for several months, and having strict limits on the number of times each tape is reused, solves those problems, but means that an indexed storage system is essential if the recorded video is to have any real value.

One way of tackling video management and recording is to implement a digital multi media system. This approach can solve a range of problems effectively at reasonable cost. The same type of cameras are employed, and therefore the considerations of camera type and location will apply as for a traditional CCTV system. The difference comes in the integration of systems and the presentation in the control room. This is very similar in principle to the techniques employed in radar systems for a number of years. The sensor system, CCTV camera or radar scanner, captures information which passes to a computer processor, before being displayed on a screen. A traditional CCTV system operates like early radar sets, where the information from the scanner was amplified as an analogue signal and presented directly onto the cathode ray tube as an image. If a digital system is employed, the information can be presented in a form which is easier to understand, including additional information from other sensors and databases. It is a major advance in risk management.

Many existing CCTV users employ television surveillance as the primary method of detecting unusual or unauthorized activities and their security personnel do not venture out from their control room. In event of an incident, they call for help from the local police force. This causes great dependence on the CCTV system and the operators who view the screen. In the later part of the night shift, attention will have flagged and monitor screens will not be effectively watched. Failure of a camera may excite no real attention, being logged for maintenance action in the morning. Local police may have been called out on a number of occasions when their

96

presence has not been merited. Blind spots may exist in the camera coverage and an intruder can watch motorized cameras, although a dome mounting will hide the camera, and wait for them to point away from him before crossing the area. An integrated risk management system removes, or greatly reduces, these problems.

The integrated control room is equipped with computer terminals, or workstations, which present composite information from a range of sensors. This reduces workload for the control room personnel and increases the range of information available for effective decision making. A variety of sensors are employed to cover all parts of the site and will include sensor systems inside the building. If a sensor is triggered, the screens will display a graphic presentation of the site with the location of the alarm source. A window within the display will also provide live video from the camera which covers that area and all information is simultaneously recorded onto computer disk storage. The sensors could include vibration sensors, *shakers*, mounted on chain link fencing, infrared detection beams and area sensors, underground detection cables and other appropriate devices. Each sensor has the potential for false alerting and by using a series of matched sensors, each system will provide a check on the others and live video image enables the security personnel to observe the area and make a human judgement. As a result the complete process is event driven and no single system is totally relied on. When an alarm occurs, recording is limited to each event, greatly reducing the amount of recorded material but, for each event, a greater range of information is recorded and the record is date and time stamped. If the event requires action, the actions are also recorded by the system and retrieval of information at a later date is simple and rapid. At any time, security personnel are also able to carry out a routine manual video scan of any part of the site without becoming blind to an activity elsewhere within the site. Because the system is based on a computer controlled core, a number of terminals in different locations can simultaneously view the same, or different, information which is held within the system as database information, or data in real time.

Where a high level of site control is required, an integrated system offers a number of additional benefits. A live picture of a visitor, or his vehicle, can be compared with a previously stored picture. All necessary information is immediately available and the potential for error is significantly reduced. For example, a visitor can be identified against a visit authorization record. That record will also contain a range of additional information, such as the need to escort the visitor, or the areas where he is authorized to go during the visit. If site evacuation becomes necessary, the system can identify every person in each area of the site to ensure that all personnel are accounted for and any special circumstances identified, such as the fact that a visitor may be confined to a wheelchair and perhaps require special attention in the event of a fire.

When integrated risk management is available, a wider range of measures can be reliably implemented and much closer supervision becomes practical. In a typical traditional site security system, a visitor arrives at a gatehouse and is allowed onto site with a cursory check, being directed to a parking area and then having to report to an internal reception point. Once at reception, the visitor is already inside the site and that may be the first point at which any real form of identification is carried out. The visitor may be issued with a visitors badge and wait in reception for his host, or be directed to his host's location and allowed to make his own way there. This leaves many risks and is often the adopted system, not because of a low regard for risk management, but because integrating a series of controls manually is time consuming and conflicts with operational requirements.

The integrated risk management system can work more effectively at a greatly reduced workload. The visitor arrives at the checking area and is identified before being allowed into the site. The vehicle is checked and a magnetic identity device is attached. This device is a visual indicator, normally a plastic cube with a number on each face, and is colour coded if necessary. It also contains an electronic signature device which can be scanned as it passes electronic sign posts within the site. This means that constant direct supervision of the vehicle becomes unnecessary because its movement within the site is automatically monitored and compared with the expected route and position of the vehicle. If any variation occurs, an alarm is given and checks are then carried out, such as through CCTV surveillance. The visitor is also equipped with a badge which provides a visual indication of status and can be scanned electronically. This may remove the need for an escort because the visitor can only pass through authorized points and his progress is noted by the system, with any deviation being reported as an alarm. A great benefit of this approach is that employees can be issued with similar badges and vehicle tags, the only difference being that they may be issued with the equipment at the start of employment. Once every vehicle and person is equipped in this way, doors and gates within the site can all be controlled by the same system and no one need be aware that any barrier is normally locked because it will automatically open as they approach, provided that they are authorized to pass through the barrier. The risk management ideal has then been achieved in that very tight security can be implemented without in any way impeding an authorized person. Security enforcement becomes significantly more effective because an incident driven system of this type does not rely on a security officer successfully fighting off boredom, or concentrating on something insignificant at the expense of a significant event. It is also much easier to cater for otherwise conflicting requirements. For example, barriers can be controlled remotely during an incident, such as a fire, so that personnel are directed away from danger and all barriers along the route are opened, while the affected area can be sealed off. The ability to track everyone on site also ensures that no one is unaccounted for in an emergency and so placed at risk, or someone else, such as a fire fighter, is not unnecessarily placed at risk searching a burning building for someone who has escaped, or was never there in the first place.

Effective site control is not solely a method of protecting against malicious intruders. It can secure a site so that people cannot leave and therefore provides a method of containing internal malicious threats. It can also provide the evidence necessary to a successful prosecution. However, site security also addresses risks other than deliberate aggression. It provides a reliable method of locating authorized personnel and ensuring that vehicles are parked in the correct places. An incorrectly parked vehicle denies a space to an authorized vehicle and this can result in wasted time and money, in addition to causing frustration and potentially creating health and safety risks. In most cases, vehicles are incorrectly parked in error, but there are some cases where this is a result of selfish, or thoughtless, actions. It is important that any deliberate and persistent offenders are identified and dealt with before a serious risk develops. If a situation is allowed to continue, chaos will result. Personnel, who would normally take care to park correctly, will begin to ignore procedure out of frustration, or operational necessity. In the worst cases, essential access points will be blocked. Generally, personnel will have to waste time walking greater distances and risk injury by moving loads. In some cases, incorrect parking may be the result of poor planning of parking spaces and site control provides the means of identifying this problem so that it may be corrected.

Every site has a maximum capacity. The capacity for people may be more than adequate, but insufficient parking facilities may mean that all authorized personnel cannot bring their vehicles onto the site. Where there is a lack of site control, this usually leads to all space being taken up by employees at the expense of visitors. A visitor who has had no option but to drive to the site, and may have spent some hours travelling, does not receive a favourable impression of the enterprise if he has to waste time finding a parking space elsewhere and walking to the site.

It may not be possible to dedicate sufficient space for all possible vehicle requirements and this is a regular problem for older sites which were planned when parking demand was much less than it is today. As a result, existing space must be rationed to the most essential vehicles and to provide adequate reserved space for visitors. This will introduce some risks to the enterprise. If parking is difficult for employees, they may look for an employer who can make reasonable provision. Those who have to park away from the site may be placed at risk, especially when arriving and departing in darkness. The cost of organizing transport for employees may prove a sound investment and solve this problem. In many cases, employees only drive to work because there is no suitable alternative method of transport and will greatly appreciate an employer who provides an alternative method of getting to work.

# 6 Risk management for buildings

Site control provides an environment of reduced risk, but is not usually adequate on its own. It provides a first level of defence against a number of risks, but it will not address all risks within the site, or even adequately reduce all of the risks which it does address. Within the site there will be a building, or a number of buildings. General site security is designed to control the area within the total site which is not occupied by buildings. Each building may present a different range of risks from those faced in other buildings on the site, although there will be a number of common risks and some risks will be extensions of risks addressed by the site control measures.

The site control system will allow authorized entry and exit and it should control traffic within the site area. Many sites will have a simple two-way traffic flow between the public access road and the parking area. Larger, or more complex sites, may have a one-way traffic flow with separate entry and exit gateways, or even provide access to a number of sub divided areas, each with its own traffic flow system and parking areas. Even in the latter case, it is likely that access to, and within, the buildings must be further controlled. In most cases, the control of building access should be from the same control room which manages the site access control. Some sites may require a separate control room and security personnel for some, or all, buildings. This will depend on the level of sensitivity for each building. The majority of enterprises have a common level of sensitivity across most of the site and buildings and may be able to leave internal access control reliably with the particular work groups which occupy the buildings. Historically, policing of buildings and sites has been a labour intensive operation, therefore costly, and has led to either a single, or a double, level of security. Intelligent integrated systems are reducing the cost of multi level security and making it practical to apply this scaled approach to a wide range of enterprises.

Where a manual security system is in place, a simple level of access control to and from the site is augmented by simple locks on internal and external doors. In most cases, these locks are only engaged when the building is unoccupied, and at other times anyone already within the site is free to go to any part of any building. Even the more sensitive areas, such as cash offices, are not locked while an employee is manning the area. This may create many risks which could have been avoided and may have been identified. The main reason for this approach is that it is not considered cost effective to employ sufficient guards to lock and unlock doors during the day and it is believed that the time lost by employees in locking and unlocking doors will be considerable. In some buildings, it may not be practical for a worker to unlock, or even open, a door because of the nature of the processes, such as carrying bulky items, or wearing dirty protective clothing. The remote control of door locks, and the surveillance remotely by CCTV, has been available for a number of years and some enterprises use this technology to enable security control staff to control doors inside buildings. Where this technology is employed to provide access control in buildings, without greatly increasing the staff levels, it is often applied to only the most sensitive areas within the site and requires a person to attract attention by ringing a bell. Control room staff then use the CCTV image to verify that the door may be opened by them. This can still be time consuming and inconvenient and is used sparingly, often providing inadequate sub division of buildings and work areas. There is also a danger that the system will be subverted. If traffic levels through a doorway are high, control room staff may not take sufficient care in making sure that they are admitting only authorized personnel. Equally, it is not unusual for employees to become frustrated and jamb the lock open.

Manpower intensive risk management inevitably leads to a single level of security which is either set at a destructively high level, or an inadequately low level. Across the total site and its buildings, the same level of security will be too low in some areas, and too high in others. With considerable good luck, it may be that security is set correctly for a few isolated areas. A dual level security system provides a closer fit between assurance and availability, but even simple enterprises will not be adequately treated. The only way to provide a reliable and acceptable reduction of risk is to employ a multi level system of measures and provide the means to vary them to suit changing needs. Ideally, this suite of risk reduction measures should be largely transparent to the work force and to visitors.

Intelligent integrated solutions are now possible. The low cost of computer processors, and rapidly reducing cost of memory and storage, has

102

made it possible to automate and control complex processes which were previously manpower intensive. The computer is not very good at making intuitive judgements, but it is excellent at managing routine boring jobs. It is also extremely good at producing many analysis reports from a small number of data entry types. By selecting appropriate sensors, and arranging them to feed a computer, routine operations can be handled automatically. When something abnormal occurs, the system produces an alarm and leaves decision making to the human in the control room. The same system allows the human controller access to any of the sensors and sub systems at any time to make a manual check and assessment. It will additionally provide the means to rapidly change levels of control, in any selected areas, from the central control console.

This is a major step forward because it both reduces costs and improves service. Service improvement comes in two ways. When a human is tasked with dull repetitive jobs, such as watching a CCTV screen, attention levels drop progressively through a shift and adequate surveillance probably ceases early in the shift. By installing a range of sensors and feeding a computer, this repetitive operation is automated reliably. The other advantage comes through information management. When an incident arises, a human being concentrates on that situation at the expense of everything else. The most visible incident may not present the greatest risk, or demand the highest priority. A computerized system is able to present a composite picture, drawing on several information sources. While the controller is dealing with this situation, the computer continues to monitor all other aspects and provide alarms when another emergency occurs. The system may also be developed with a level of artificial intelligence. If a form of fault tree analysis is built into the system, it will be able to do much more than provide an initial alarm. It may present a number of options, from which the control room staff may select a course of action. As the incident proceeds, they will initiate actions which introduce consequential events. An intelligent integrated control system will be able to display new options and alert the personnel to new risks which may either be introduced by their chosen course of action, or by developments in the nature of the incident.

For example, a fire alert may have been triggered and the control room is informed of the location of the incident. The system may advise which areas should be evacuated, and in what order of priority. If the control staff then decide to seal an area, or operate an extinguishing system, the risk management system could provide a warning that not all personnel have safely evacuated the area. As the fire develops, the computers will continue to relate this to the fault tree, and advise further options for action. This might include further evacuation of personnel, or require processes on parts of the site to be shut down as a safety measure. This type of system has been used for a number of years in particularly sensitive operations, such as explosives manufacture and in nuclear power installations. Depending on the nature of the enterprise, the system may also provide warnings to be relayed to essential services which may require the evacuation of facilities outside the boundaries of the site. In the example of the fire, it could be that dangerous gases are potentially about to be created as a consequence of the fire and chemical interaction. This could result in a dangerous cloud being created which will drift across populated areas. If this is a potential risk, the management system would need to include sensors to report on wind speed and direction, together with an ability to predict the size and location of the area beyond the site which may be affected. Although this may fall into the area of responsibility of the essential services, only the enterprise will have detailed and current information on the volumes of materials present on site and their exact location relative to the seat of the fire.

Beyond the general level of service improvement, the computer may further reduce workload by offering these recommended options, using artificial intelligence, to aid in the reduction of risk on site during the event and to avoid risks in the neighbouring area. This can be an emotive subject, but should always be addressed as part of the risk analysis process. The weakness of a computer is that it is unable to think in the same flexible way as a human. It can only perform a task which it has been programmed to carry out. It is possible to build some level of artificial intelligence into a machine, but the creative learning capability of the human is absent. Therefore, the computer does not yet have the capability to make valued judgements and produce a best judgement in a new situation. Any recommended options will therefore be pre-recorded instructions which are triggered when a set of foreseen circumstances arise. This can be very helpful in risk management, provided that no one makes the mistake of slavishly following the first recommendation of a machine. The computer can list all manual checks which should be performed and remind the controller that there are several possible options for dealing with the incident, but the controller should always be free to make a human judgement and take responsibility which is something that a machine cannot do.

There will also be the issue of who is in command. Until essential services arrive on site, the responsibility clearly rests with the site operator. However, once police, fire service, and medical services are present they will have to take control. This may introduce new risks, not least because there may be no clear overall command structure and there may not be a common communications system. Each service tends to guard jealously its own individual position and in some societies this can result in dangerous confusion during an emergency. In some cases, total chaos is only avoided

104

because individuals on site work together and partly ignore their chains of command. That can create risks because the personnel on site may not have a sufficiently wide picture of the overall situation. The availability of advanced risk management systems on site should always assist in satisfactory action during an incident, but there is the issue of familiarity with the system and the site. In the ideal world, the essential services would exercise with the enterprise personnel so that they may best cope with a real emergency. Unfortunately, that is only rarely possible, and then usually only at high visibility and sensitivity enterprises such as nuclear power plants. The main reason why the ideal is not achieved is frequently a result of financial considerations, but there are also cases where the reasons are political. In this latter case, the enterprise may be highly resistant to disrupting normal activities to exercise with essential services and may be very uncooperative with these organizations. However, there will also be cases where the essential services consider the enterprise personnel a potential liability during an emergency and consider that any joint exercise is a complete waste of time. The only way for these situations to be avoided is for the enterprise to take every opportunity to inform those services of the risk policy and its operation in an emergency and to do everything possible to cooperate with them. Generally, most essential services respond well to an enterprise which can demonstrate a professional approach to risk management and fully appreciate that this will make their task easier and reduce risks to their personnel.

Once the core of a risk management system is computerized, there is considerable scope for providing flexible, tailored and transparent containment and reduction measures. Every worker and visitor can be issued with an identity card which responds to both site and building access control systems and this control can be extended down to processes, and even to individual machines. A common approach has been to issue an identity card which has a bar code, or a magnetic strip, and the trend is now towards a *smart* card with its own computer processor and data storage. This may be a very inappropriate path to follow. All cards of this type, currently available, have to be presented to a reader device and either touched against its surface, or inserted into a slot. Insertion may be a matter of *swiping* the card through a slot, or may require the complete card to be inserted fully, read, and then ejected. The process is therefore not unlike the process required to operate a simple mechanical lock. The first risk reduction benefit is that, unlike a mechanical key, a card of this type not only authorizes access, but is able to transmit the identity of the user and provide additional information. The other major benefit is that, in the event of a card being lost, a few key strokes at a computer terminal will remove it from the access permissions, where a lost mechanical key requires every lock which it fits to be changed, and every key holder issued with a new key. This is both costly and slow to achieve, against instant change for lost card, at virtually no cost.

The first disadvantage of the *swipe* and *touch* read cards is that the user has to stop, locate the card, and then place it in the reader. There is also a potential problem in wet, or dirty, work areas where the card becomes contaminated and difficult to read, or even introduces contamination into the reader, so preventing operation by clean cards. In addition, cards of these types are able to carry much more information than just an identity number. As *smart* cards become more popular and their storage capacity increases, there is a temptation to fill them with information about the card holder. This introduces a number of risks which are addressed in a later chapter, but it also slows the process of using the card. The more information held by the card, the wider the range of checks and read/write sequences, and the longer the card needs to be in contact with the reader. One general risk with information is that it can become addictive and the best risk management systems are those which are as simple as possible, at least in operation, if not in technical design.

A better solution may be to use proximity cards. Various types of proximity reader are now available and have high reliability levels. Some cards, or tokens, can even be carried in pockets and still be read from several feet away. However, most are designed to be worn as identity badges, and a few have to be held against a reader. Unlike *swipe* cards, there is no need to insert the card into a machine to be read. The cards read by proximity readers hold very limited information and this is an advantage. It is always much easier, generally cheaper, and certainly more reliable, to limit the transaction between card and reader. An identity number is all that the reader has to see. From that number, the computer system can check authorization records and operate a lock, or an alarm, as appropriate. The speed of checking is much faster than a person walking, or even driving a vehicle. The first check is that the number is a valid issue and has not been withdrawn. Further checking is only necessary if there is doubt about the validity. The result is that use of doors, anywhere within the site and buildings, appears completely open to users, unless one of them attempts to go through a door which he has not been authorized to use. The system can even extend to the point where not only is the lock disengaged, but the door is opened automatically. In this situation, two theoretically opposing requirements have been met with a single system. The electronic closing and locking of the door and the requirement for a token to unlock and open the door will achieve a level of assurance which will be relatively high and could be raised easily to a much higher level. At the same time, every authorized user has apparently free access to every area and does not even have to open a door. The automatic process can meet the different requirements for fire and safety because all doors will be closed and locked, providing fire barriers, but will be unlocked automatically if the system fails. The control room can remotely open all doors on a signed escape route and the system will provide an alarm in the event of default unlocking.

A further benefit of an integrated system of this nature is that all personnel can be located within the site, down to buildings and even individual areas and rooms. In the event of an emergency, a complete roll call is available by area and all personnel in buildings on site can be accounted for. Other records can be up dated automatically to reduce other risks. Poor attendance can create risks as it damages morale amongst previously reliable employees. In some cases, payment may relate to time worked and the access control system makes a very simple job of tracking the number of hours and the days when each employee was on site. Unlike a traditional *clocking in* machine, the system with its proximity badges does not caused queues at starting and finishing times and can provide much greater detail, possibly down to the machines used by each worker in particular buildings. Although ease of data collection for payroll purposes may be a great advantage, there is a quality management benefit which may be more significant. Knowing who used which machine, and for how long, can require extensive and costly analysis in many enterprises. Extension of the access control system to individual machines can provide this information at little cost. At the same time it will address health and safety issues because an unqualified worker can be denied access to dangerous machinery and the risk management system can report overcrowding in particular areas.

The scope of these systems for monitoring in fine detail does present a possible threat in that employees may be resistant to this level of constant supervision. The degree to which this becomes a real risk depends on the personnel policy, internal communication and the past reputation of the enterprise. Close monitoring in its own right is not the real issue, but what the information is used for, and how it is used, can raise emotions and introduce risks. A highly automated integrated supervisory system can reduce the level of personal scrutiny. After all, the system is basically there to watch in fine detail and report anomalies, whilst reducing visible barriers and reducing workload. The more detailed the information collected, the less likely it is that one individual will look closely at another employee. If the information is used sensitively and wisely, it will offer greater general freedom, improved morale, greater productivity, more effective risk reduction, and greater profitability, so that everyone benefits both financially, and in life style. If the information is used insensitively to grind down the work force and introduce rigorous policing, it will increase risks through reduced morale and increased acrimony, but that is a consequence of usage and not of technology. The main danger is that old attitudes which evolved in traditional management environments are heavily ingrained and the new opportunities are not seized.

A system which integrates various sensors with a computer based management system, and remote control of access points, offers the ability to build a more resilient system. Computer processors and cabling systems can be duplicated and any suitable authorized computer terminal, or workstation, can become a control point. The system will be capable of configuration from a single point, even on very large and complex sites with large numbers of buildings and processes. This means that changing risks can be accommodated more effectively, rapidly and at lower cost. Reconfiguration can be automatically carried out several times each day. If a building is vacant for several hours each night, a different level of supervision is required and this can be achieved by automatic configuration at the start of each period. As the system will be counting people into, and out of, buildings through the day, it will have a record of how many people are still in each area. If the building is due to be vacant at 18:00 hours each week day, from Monday to Friday, the system can anticipate this vacancy, counting out the last authorized user and then activating additional sensors. However, it can be much more flexible. If every building is sub-divided into areas, or individual rooms, the system can automatically toggle between two or more configurations. Every time an area becomes empty, the extra sensors are enabled, and then switched off when an authorized person enters the area. This may be extended to environmental control. There is no reason why the management system cannot also switch lights on and off to meet demand, or to prepare an area for the start of work. Those areas which do not require heating, or cooling, during those periods when they are not occupied, could be heated automatically in time to receive the next working shift. This level of automation may be a natural extension of the system, using sensors already installed, and may produce a considerable cost saving without introducing any additional risk. When an enterprise reviews the cost of services, such as heating and lighting, it is likely that a large part of the cost of implementing and maintaining the risk management system will be directly met by savings in these area.

Where a high level of access control is required, card readers can be augmented by other devices such as biometrics. A number of different systems are available to provide additional identification of authorized users. Any card system can be subverted through a card being stolen, or its deliberate unauthorized passing to another person. The simplest method of additional verification is to carry out random CCTV scans of access points to make a visual identification of anyone accessing an area and comparing the image with a recorded image of the authorized holder of the card. A typical two dimensional photograph does not always provide a very reliable comparison, but it would be possible to hold three dimensional images in the system database which would be rotated to match the angle of view through the CCTV system. In some cases, a CCTV scan may be routinely recorded every time someone uses a card to access an area and the records searched either as spot checks later, or after an incident has occurred. Biometric systems provide a more thorough and immediate check and can prevent irregular access to avoid an incident.

There is considerable debate over the most effective biometric system. Early attempts have used finger print scans and required signatures. A similar alternative method is to employ retina scans. In all cases, a scan is compared against a record. The reason that these systems have not gained widespread acceptance is that they are not entirely reliable and can be unduly restrictive. There is the risk of a, high false reject rate. The user cannot wear gloves which may present problems in high and low temperatures, but a more common problem is that users may have dirty hands as a result of their work. Oil and other contaminants can result in the system failing to recognize the authorized user. Records also need to be updated because scars will invalidate an authorized print, and wound dressings will create a temporary problem.

A finger print can be *spoofed* relatively easily. One method is to take a finger print covertly of an authorized user and then manufacture a facsimile in the form of a latex glove which is worn by the impostor. A more aggressive approach is to use the *bolt cropper* technique. This entails the abduction of an authorized user and the amputation of a finger, or a complete hand, which would be recognized by the scanner as an authorized identity. An intermediate, but risky alternative would be to abduct an authorized user and force him to effect an entry. Similar approaches can also be used in the case of palm prints.

Signatures can be forged. A variety of techniques can be employed, and have proved effective, in defeating early signature scanners. Improving technology makes this approach less reliable, but it is still a risk which may be unacceptable. As with palm and finger print scanning, an authorized user can be abducted and forced to provide entry. The retina scan is generally a more reliable biometric, still capable of defeat through abduction and duress of authorized users. The disadvantage of the retina scan is that it requires the user to place his eye very close to the scanner. Many users are uncomfortable with this and there is a possible health risk in that contact between the eye and the scanner has been claimed to provide an infection path for viruses, such as the AIDS virus, through the tear ducts and fluid. Generally, medical opinion is that this risk is very small, and some specialists even go so far as to totally reject the possibility, but it is a potential risk which cannot be ignored. An enterprise which decides to employ a device, where there is even a small potential health risk, could be laying itself open to significant financial risk at some undefined point in the future. What makes this type of risk particularly dangerous is that there may be no advanced notice which would allow the enterprise to replace the device with some other technology. There could well be several years of operation before a definitive ruling is made by a court in a test case, as has occurred in the past with various work related health injuries.

A more promising biometric scanner uses infrared light to reveal vein patterns on the back of a human hand, scanned by a suitable CCTV camera and checked against a stored record. Each person appears to have a vein map which is as unique as a finger or palm print, and does not change through ageing. No physical contact with the scanner is necessary and contaminants, such as oil, do not impede the scan, which is also immune to scar tissue. The system does not directly counter a hostage being forced to effect an entry, but amputation is not effective, because the system relies on blood being pumped through the veins at normal blood temperature.

The use of hostages can be countered relatively easily. This approach depends generally on more than one person requiring entry. Proximity readers would provide a second line of verification and it is then only necessary to install a sensor which counts people through the gateway. Several methods could be employed, but a simple and effective sensor could be a pressure mat which would indicate more than one person attempting to use the doorway with a single authorization identity.

Greater security would be provided by installing additional checks and sensors. Each additional line of defence requires an additional action and therefore slows entry. The more information entered into the computer control, the slower the processing time. However, these delays are individually very small, and even composite delay may be less than one second. If the security requirements are extremely stringent, a series of doors may be used to delay entry to a specific area. Each door opens into a containment area, and a further door. This protection can be simplified by requiring manual control of the entrance, and using armoured glass tubes which are only large enough for one person at a time. The inner glass door will only open after the outer door has closed. A controlled entry of this type has the advantage that the person entering the area is fully visible, either to the naked eye, or to a CCTV camera, during the whole of the entry process and the system requires very little floor space. The disadvantage of these entry systems is that they can severely constrict access and do not make provision for any bulky items to be carried through. In special cases this may be a requirement of the risk policy because it makes it much more difficult to bring prohibited items, such as weapons and explosives, into the restricted area. The risk policy must balance the need for protection with the need for adequate access, and also consider the implications in relationship between security risks and other risks, such as fire and health threats.

One difficulty in providing access control is the need for safety and comfort. The ideal security approach would eliminate windows and other structural weaknesses in a room and ensure that there is only one doorway, with a number of checks to control the operation of the door. The result would be a room which could be unsuitable for the activity intended and would certainly increase fire safety and ventilation risks. An integrated computer based risk management system does much to reduce these difficulties because it provides continuous monitoring without demanding a large security staff. It offers the option to leave large areas normally open because it provides the means to remotely close areas down very quickly and to monitor and record activity.

In the same way, an integrated system provides the means to progressively approach risk as it changes through the day. Fire risk tends to increase when an area is unoccupied, as does the risk of theft. Equally, as these risks increase, health and safety risks decrease because of the absence of people. It is therefore desirable to modify the configuration of the management system to deal with these changes as they occur and that demands a dynamic and responsive system which is able to see all elements of risk together. It then becomes practical to install automatic gas extinguishing systems and high sensitivity smoke detectors which would be potentially dangerous and prone to false alerting in an occupied area. As soon as the area is unoccupied the systems are activated. If an authorized user needs to enter the area, the systems will be deactivated and the door will only open when this has been completed. The system's ability to monitor continuously, and to adapt to operational needs, also allows more freedom in the design of a building and the rooms inside. Larger and more numerous windows and doorways can be designed in without seriously increasing risk from intruders.

However attractive generally, the integrated intelligent system is not always the best way to approach building security. Some processes will be very sensitive to risk, and some will be potentially dangerous. This does not mean that an integrated intelligent system cannot be used, but it may require additional measures to satisfy the risk policy requirements.

If a building, or room, contains something of special value, or sensitivity, there may be no option but to reinforce the structure and accept some potential health and safety risks. A classic example would be the bullion vault. Risk reduction is eased because people will spend very little time inside the vault and, when they are present, a number of special measures will be taken, such as leaving the vault door open and having guards immediately outside the area during this period. Fire risk may be minimized because the contents may not be easily flammable, although this would not be true if the vault contained documents and paper money. Health and safety risks are also reduced because of the close supervision during the periods when people are inside the vault. When the vault is closed it will not contain people and careful checks will have been made to ensure everyone has left the vault before closing the door.

Against this, the risks of external attacks will be high, both because the contents will potentially attract the attention of skilled and well equipped criminals, and because the vault will be unoccupied for extended periods. Typical vault design offers only one face of the structure visibly, leaving five faces which may be exposed to a hidden attack. Risk is further increased in many cases because the building containing the vault may also be unoccupied for extended periods. To protect against these risks, vaults have thick reinforced concrete walls, floor and ceiling, with the smallest practical doorway which is closed by a very strong metal door, secured by a number of substantial shoot bolts securing the door even in the event of the hinges being removed. The concrete shell may also be augmented with several layers of other materials, such as steel.

Within this very strong structure, there will be a place for electronic sensors which include smoke detectors and CCTV cameras. Even with all these protective systems, a determined attacker may still be able to force an entry, particularly during holiday periods when the vault may remain closed for several days. The high value of the contents may also encourage attackers to take extreme measures, such as disabling guards in a control room. To counter this risk, it may be necessary to install a second sensor system which is routed separately and directly to a police station. One method of achieving this is to bury sensors in the concrete shell and feed a simple alarm indication to the police station, using different telephone ducts from those used for any other purpose in any other part of the building. This installation may be carried out separately from other risk reduction work to reduce the possibility of any one person having knowledge of all systems.

A similar range of extreme requirements may also apply to high risk manufacturing processes. Although normal financial and operational considerations might be best met by having a complete process in one building, the risks which this introduces might dictate that the process is divided up into several separate buildings, or even over several geographically separated sites. Typical examples would include explosives manufacture and oil refining.

The manufacture of explosives, or chemical processes which involve potentially explosive materials during manufacturing, calls for special care

112

to reduce risks to an acceptable level. The first stage of risk reduction is to plan manufacture so that the minimum amount of explosive material will be in any one location. It will also be essential to consider potential reaction with otherwise stable materials, and ensure physical separation. Having reduced static location risk, the variables introduced by transport must be considered and routes planned so that risk is not increased because potentially dangerous material in transit passes close by other hazardous material.

With the fundamental risks reduced, it is necessary to consider the area in which processes will take place. The first step is to ensure that people are kept as far away from the processes as possible and that only personnel who have been adequately trained and equipped are authorized to be involved in the processing. Where explosive material is involved, building construction will normally involve a structure with very strong walls and a much thinner roof. If an explosion takes place, the force will then be directed upwards in relative safety. Where ever possible, the production machines will either be automated robot devices, or be controlled remotely by personnel located in a protected area. In most countries there will be legislation which covers this type of potentially dangerous activity, but this does not mean that compliance with the law will adequately reduce risks. Legislation takes time to enact, frequently it is triggered by a disaster which has already happened, and sometimes not until a series of disasters have raised public concern. Therefore any enterprise which waits for legislation will potentially be exposing itself, its employees, and people near the site, to risk.

If an enterprise is handling materials which clearly pose a high level of risk, or is engaged in manufacturing explosive materials, attention will focus directly onto these risks. However, risk of explosion may be remarkably widespread, but less obvious, across a wide range of enterprises which would not consider this area of risk. Materials which are used in many processes are normally safe, until they are combined with other materials, particularly in the presence of fire, or just sparks. Dust can create an explosion if it is dispersed in the atmosphere, at the appropriate levels of density, where it ignites from a spark caused by an ordinary electrical fitting, such as a light switch. This phenomena is understood at enterprises such as flour mills, but it can apply to many other types of enterprise. Items such as electrical cabling can produce gases during a fire and this can combine with otherwise inert substances in common industrial and commercial use with disastrous results.

Some industrial processes also pose a threat to the area which surrounds the site. This is particularly true where risks may be carried by wind. Theoretically, risks of this nature should be considered by planning authorities before they agree to usage at the site, but the enterprise should be best qualified to judge the risks before that time and some risks will not become obvious until after the site is in full operation. A process previously considered safe may prove to introduce risks. An example of this is a material, such as asbestos, which was in widespread use for many years before its dangers came to be understood. A responsible enterprise will take immediate measures to deal with these risks, including the safe disposal of material already on site. There are many cases where this does not happen. It may be that the risk policy is inadequate, inflexible, or incorrectly maintained, allowing a risk to develop unchecked, or even unnoticed. In a great many cases the reason for inaction is financially motivated. Enterprises can fear that the cost of reducing risk will place them at a disadvantage against competitors who will await legislative pressure before acting. Alternatively, it may be that an enterprise considers the admission of an error, even one which could not have reasonably been foreseen, will damage customer confidence and adversely affect the business. In either case, the enterprise is running several considerable risks.

If an incident results in damage, or loss, to an employee or to someone outside the enterprise it is likely that a claim for damages will be brought. Ignorance of the risk will not be considered by a court as a complete defence, although the enterprise may succeed in limiting damages if it can prove that it took all reasonable precautions and the incident could not have been foreseen. This may still result in heavy cost and the enterprise will suffer adverse publicity, even if competitors have also been running the same risks. However, an enterprise somewhere may have employed a better risk management system and foreseen the risk, taking action to counter it, thereby avoiding a damaging incident. If this comes to light during a trial, it may greatly weaken the defence because it demonstrates that the risk could have been foreseen and action could have been taken to reduce the risk.

If an enterprise identifies a risk and does not take action to reduce it, considerable consequential risks are run. Whatever action is taken to keep the knowledge secret, it will probably be exposed, usually by a disaffected employee, or an honest one. Therefore even cynical greed does not support a decision to withhold action in reducing identified risks. When a court case results, the enterprise will be dealt with severely if it emerges that the incident was either completely avoidable, or could have been less damaging. The cost of punitive damages may not be the only costs of deliberate inaction. The reputation of the enterprise may have been so badly damaged that it is unable to retain employees, recruit personnel, or find customers. In some cases, insurance companies may refuse to provide cover of any sort and suppliers may be reluctant to be seen to deal with the enterprise. Temporary financial gain may be followed by failure of the enterprise.

A strong code of ethics and a determination to limit risks can be turned to commercial advantage. At the very least, it will reduce the probability of financial loss resulting from avoidable failures. It is difficult to understand why enterprises run these risks. Usually it is not a natural product of a corrupt and greedy organization, but a result of inadequate planning and a short term financial view. Cost cutting is easy to achieve and measure and may be a consequence of inadequate management. In the short term, it can require real management skill and courage to plan for a secure future.

The irony is that enterprise planning and risk reduction can result in lower costs and greater profits. This is evidenced strongly in the design and use of sites and buildings. One difficulty in appreciating this is accountancy practice. Two key elements of an enterprise are very difficult to guarantee, but one appears relatively simple. Cutting known costs is only a matter of mandate. If an enterprise decides to cut costs, the first target will be the work force. Halving the number of employees may more than halve the cost of labour. Even in the short term, and after allowing for the cost of paying off workers, the reduction in cost will be significant. Those employees who are mainly engaged on risk management in some form may be the first to go because they are not seen to contribute to production. It is also easy to avoid replacing plant and equipment and to sell off buildings. In the process, risk will be increased and the medium to long term result may be either to raise costs, or to kill the enterprise.

The two areas which are difficult to guarantee are productivity and business growth. An integral factor in both subjects is quality control. A building which is inadequately staffed, or overcrowded, will result in reduced quality management. Risks will increase and even if they do not produce added cost through damages claims and related costs, they will usually affect cash flows. Customers who do not receive goods on time and to specification will slow, or withhold, payments. Production costs may also rise because understaffing will reduce productivity and increase wastage. This loss will only become obvious after reducing staffing, at which time it will be costly and difficult to increase staffing levels with trained personnel. As this process is usually driven by general economic conditions, many enterprises go through a continuing process of expansion and contraction which is only broken when contraction continues to the point at which the enterprise can no longer sustain itself. This is a very real risk because once contraction starts it can build up its own momentum and prove very difficult to halt. In view of the fact that this is a repetitive cycle, it can be modelled and planned for. Cyclic change can never be eliminated completely because several important factors are outside the control of the enterprise, but effective enterprise planning can even the effects of peaks and troughs, and reserves can be maintained to cushion more rapid change. If this longer view is taken, it is possible to avoid many of the risks which would otherwise apply to the enterprise.

Every time an enterprise contracts there will be additional cost. Severance payments to employees is one visible cost, but there will also be less obvious cost. Buildings still have to be maintained and heating and lighting will still be required. Therefore the support cost for each remaining employee rises. Worn machinery will become less productive and cost more to maintain. This can lead to assets being sold, often creating new risks. Risk reduction measures, which were effective under original manning levels, cease to be effective. Parts of buildings become unoccupied, leading to increased risk of fire and attack. Reduction, or removal, of risk management staff will result in considerably higher levels of risk. Workers become less motivated, leading to increased error.

If the enterprise survives the period of contraction, it will then move into a period of expansion. This can prove as uncontrolled as contraction, developing its own momentum. Recruitment processes are a key element and introduce special dangers because, in the drive to increase the work force, standards may be relaxed to provide the numbers of people required. The key building risks stem from the difficulties in smoothly reversing a trend. New recruitment will require funding which may be obtained at the expense of adequate infrastructure funding. New and untrained workers may be introduced to defective equipment in unsatisfactory accommodation. Areas may become overcrowded and space lost to construction and installation personnel who are trying to provide improved facilities. In this scramble to profit from an upturn in trade, risk management is frequently neglected because it is not seen to contribute to production and may be seen as restriction. By the time that the expansion phase has run its course and the enterprise is just moving back into a contraction phase, risk management may just be achieving reliable levels. It is not at all unusual to see an enterprise growing to the point where site and buildings are inadequate and for panic action to be taken to find a new site or construct new buildings, only for the work to be completed after the enterprise has started the next phase of contraction when it no longer needs the new facilities. This is an appalling waste. When all the costs are considered through one complete cycle, which may be a period of five years, it will be seen that cost cutting achieves a negative financial benefit. A key part of the net loss will relate directly to personnel costs, but most of the remaining loss will relate to site and building costs, and may well be the larger proportion of net loss. The reason that buildings play such a large role in loss creation is the time factor they represent. The actual construction time for a building, or the modification of an existing building, may be a period of several months, and can even exceed one year, but, before that timetable can commence, it will

116

be necessary to obtain planning consents and run a procurement. The total time, from start of project to completion, can therefore spread across several years and easily run into the next period of contraction. Adequate risk management and enterprise planning can play a part in reducing losses because they introduce the need for analysis and the reappraisal of traditional ideas.

Most building construction grossly over engineers the structures. If trading cycles run for a period of five to ten years, there may be little value in constructing a building which will stand for several hundred years. The primary purpose behind a building is risk reduction. It is designed to protect the occupants from external threats. These threats include attack and the effects of the environment. By tradition, it has come to be accepted that these risks are best addressed by building in low flammability durable materials such as steel, stone, brick and concrete. As these materials are relatively costly, and require time consuming and expensive techniques, this can lead naturally to a desire to build for a long structural life to avoid the need to repeat the process often. This, in turn, leads to a building becoming a durable asset on a balance sheet and ignores the fact that the enterprise will change greatly over the life of the building and, in all probability, the building will outlive the enterprise. During the period, the building will cease to provide the most appropriate environment for the enterprise and its inflexibility will result in the processes, needed to ensure achievement of enterprise objectives, being modified to fit the building, rather than the building being made to support the processes. Part of this tradition may result from ancient views. When society was based on agriculture, and farming was a labour intensive activity, housing and storage buildings could serve generation after generation with little difficulty, and designing a building for a long working life made reasonable sense.

However, industrialization, and more recently computer automation and communications, has considerably changed the situation. Parts of the early industrial areas are now littered with rotting buildings which have not been used for many years and were less than entirely suitable in the latter part of their working life. At present they represent a number of risks and serve no useful purpose. Eventually someone will either have to invest in refurbishing them, or demolishing them. Much more recent construction is also not fulfilling current needs and contains redundant equipment. Overall, these buildings represent a considerable volume of valuable material and wasted energy. A major city, such as London or New York, could supply the world requirement for copper without the need for mining because of the tonnage of copper in redundant cables and pipes which still remain in place, no longer serving any operation purpose.

Addressing these issues is a major challenge. Both architects and their clients can be very conservative in their tastes, and materials traditional to an area are normally the first choice. This limits the choice of construction techniques and again tradition triumphs over analysis and logic. Part of the process will be financial analysis and this will tend to favour traditional materials and methods, not least because traditional materials will usually be those materials most readily available in the area. Where materials, not common to the area, are used, this is more likely to be a statement of wealth than an attempt to build a more appropriate structure. Most construction still takes place on site, using raw materials and very little use is made of prefabricated sections. Site construction also takes place without weather protection in most cases. This means that work can be slowed, or even halted, by bad weather.

In view of the fact that many enterprises are faced with changing requirements, there is a case for construction techniques which enable the rapid site assembly of a building from standard modules, which are manufactured away from the site in controlled and protected conditions. The only form of construction in regular and widespread use which follows this approach is the temporary portable building. This takes modular construction to the logical conclusion. Minimum site work is involved and concentrates on installing water, power and drainage systems, building access roads and laying concrete to make bases on which the largely completed buildings are positioned, direct from the transport vehicles. The most common systems in use consist of a standard sized module, similar to a freight container in size, which can be stacked beside and on top of other modules. A relatively narrow selection of optional internal layouts are available and access from one module to another is usually external. This results in a utilitarian appearance and only loose integration between modules. As the appearance is not particularly attractive, portable buildings tend to be used as site accommodation for construction workers, while they build a traditional structure for a client, rather than to form a flexible building system for longer term use. To keep costs low, most portable buildings have a very short designed life. That life may be ten years, but in typical applications on construction sites, the prime working life will be much shorter because users treat the buildings as expendable, and abuse them in a way which they would not for other types of building.

Some enterprises will use portable buildings to temporarily house personnel during the expansion or refurbishment of permanent buildings. The design of most portable buildings makes them suitable for administrative personnel and for use as catering facilities, but not for production purposes. The buildings introduce new risk, the first of which may be that they take up site space which is needed for other purposes and may disrupt risk management systems installed for site protection. As they rely on external access between units, they will present some health and safety risks, particularly where they are stacked and are accessed via external steps which may become dangerous in wet and icy conditions. They will also not include risk reduction measures which are considered essential in the permanent buildings, and may suffer increased fire risk because portable gas heaters and electric fires are used to provide heating in colder climates.

Perhaps the major risks associated with temporary portable buildings are that they are not considered as important in the same way as a permanent structure. In fact, they will introduce most, or all, of the threats common to permanent buildings on site and then introduce additional risk. The need for fire protection will be at least as great and generally greater. Protection against external threats will be at least as important because the work groups will take all of their normal equipment and materials to the temporary buildings. Reducing these risks can follow the same pattern as for a permanent building, although intruder and fire detection sensors may need to be connected to the main system by a radio link. There will also be a need for additional training and supervision to counter the casual attitude which generally develops in temporarily housed work groups.

Much greater use could be made of prefabricated structures and there is no reason why they should be less visually attractive than traditional buildings, less secure, less functional, or cost more. In many areas they could be much better, and certainly much more flexible. A series of well designed modules can be combined in a very wide range of permutations and can be built with a considerable variety of materials. The only real constraints are size and weight of each module to take into consideration limitations imposed by transport and handling equipment. Some prefabrication techniques are already in widespread use, but they are normally employed to speed the construction of buildings which are still designed as permanent long life structures. This approach has also given prefabricated construction a bad reputation, because materials used have not given long term reliability. The most frequent form of failure has been corrosion of reinforcing metal and the employment of prefabricated cladding on very large structures, such as high rise apartment and office blocks, which employ a steel, or steel reinforced concrete, skeleton. This may be a natural conclusion because prefabrication has frequently been used as a method of cost cutting, and the cost reduction approach has extended to the use of the cheapest materials. Most failures have therefore not been the result of a flaw in the concept of prefabricated construction but, the result of over enthusiastic cost cutting which has paid too little attention to risk analysis.

There is no reason why quality should suffer in the design and construction of modular buildings. Equally, there is no reason why the designer should be constrained in his use of materials. If prefabrication is approached as a risk management subject, the primary objective is to provide flexibility without introducing additional risk. The major challenge to this approach is the commercial attitude to property as an asset. Because traditional views of what buildings should be like is so deeply ingrained, we have come to accept the process of site acquisition, design and construction of a building, and the subsequent maintenance of the building, within the confines of the site. If additional building space is required, we expect to expand the existing building, or find a new building on a new site and then sell the old building with its site. This then establishes an asset value which we expect to at least be maintained in real terms, and probably increase in real value. The real asset value is probably the site rather than the buildings on the site. The main value of the buildings is that they exist and can be occupied with little delay.

There are exceptions, mainly in domestic housing. In some countries it is not unusual for a home owner to move to a new location, taking his building to a new site, rather than selling it and buying a new house. It also applies to construction projects where temporary accommodation and offices are erected to provide facilities for building workers during the construction phase. In these cases, the predominant material used in their construction is wood. As a combustible material, wood has a high potential risk of fire and is unsuitable in a number of geographic areas because it may be subject to attack by insects and climatic agents. To be economic as a building material, it is necessary for supplies of timber to be relatively close to the production facility.

As greater use is made of modular construction and demountable buildings, a wider range of materials is used in their construction. Plastics are becoming more common and the assembly of larger, and more complex structures, is now practical. Glass reinforced plastic is strong and light and can be produced in fire resistant forms. This may prove to be the most suitable material for sectional building. By sandwiching an insulating material between two skins of GRP, it is possible to produce sections which have very high insulation values and will reduce the energy required to heat, or cool, the interior of the building. Smaller structures may require no additional support, but sections can be used to clad a steel skeleton which permits large buildings to be constructed very rapidly to withstand extreme conditions, such as high winds.

# 7 Risk management for shared and public sites

An enterprise which does not share a site or building with other enterprises, and does not have to freely admit the public, is in a fortunate position because it has maximum control of risks. Unfortunately, most enterprises are not in this position. This presents a special challenge in producing and maintaining a reliable risk management system.

The general principles of risk management apply in much the same way as for a private site. Most of the technology which supports risk management on a private site will also be effective on shared and public sites. What is much more difficult is the achievement of the same levels of assurance, although the nature of risk may demand even higher levels of assurance. It is possible to express risk management diagramatically as a triangle which has Assurance, Integrity, and Availability at the respective apexes. As each category has the same value in an equilateral triangle, to produce a constant value, it can be seen that any attempt to increase the value of Assurance can only be achieved at the expense of Integrity and/or Availability. Any requirement to raise the overall values will result, potentially, in a significant increase in cost.

The principle of site security, as we have seen earlier, is to keep the barbarians at the outer walls. If they penetrate the outer defences, they will visible and each layer of defence will weaken their attack. Therefore, only the strongest and most determined attacker will penetrate to the most sensitive areas and that penetration will be visible. By slowing the attack, time is provided to call in reinforcements. This form of protection can still be provided on a shared site, but the outer defences will be under someone else's control. Within the site, building security is as strong as the weakest link. If the site has to provide free public access to most areas, an attacker can easily merge with bonafide visitors and the opportunity for collusion between employees and attackers also increases.

A private site can establish an outer defence which identifies any attempt to force an entry at the perimeter, and controls access to gateways where security personnel can be based. With this level of control, it is relatively simple to ensure that all visitors are known and identified as visitors. This means that any risk control within the site is increased because personnel are aware of the status of other personnel and reinforce any access control and intruder identification systems. Shared and public sites cannot function with this level of control. There are several reasons for this. Cost may be a very important factor because one reason for an enterprise using shared facilities may be to cut costs. Although a shared security force may be very cost effective, it depends on every occupant being prepared to contribute to the cost, but not every occupant will have the same risk reduction needs. It is therefore likely that any shared security will be provided at the level of the lowest risk and this will provide inadequate protection for those enterprises which face a higher risk level. Alternatively, some enterprises on the site may be required to pay for a level of risk reduction which they do not need.

There is also the question of motivation and accountability of the central security staff. A private site is free to decide whether to sub contract site security to another enterprise, or to directly engage staff to provide this service. Even with sub contract staffing, there is a single accountability, through the service contract, to the employing enterprise. There is also an identifiable motivation factor and the ability to security screen the staff to a level acceptable to the enterprise which owns the site. Shared sites rarely offer this level of control. A shared site and/or building is almost certainly owned by a landlord who rents parts of the facilities to several enterprises. Any central security provided will be under the control of the landlord, who either employs his own staff to provide the service, or sub contracts the service to a security company. He may be motivated to provide a security service because it is essential to the process of securing tenants, because he wants to protect his own investment in the site and its buildings, or because it is a profitable addition to a range of services which he includes in the rental package to his tenants. In each case, his motivation is personal and may not coincide with the real needs of his tenants. This does not mean that he is greedy, or uncaring, but he is unlikely to fully appreciate the needs of each of his tenants. His position will not be much different from that of an insurance company which offers a profitable commercial service and is primarily concerned with managing those risks which directly affect it, rather than those of the policy holders.

The tenant has a limited number of choices. The standard security service may be accepted as it is, and specific risks addressed within the area rented by the tenant. There is the option to discuss specific requirements with the landlord, who may be prepared to modify facilities, or increase them, but at an additional cost to the tenant. The tenant may join with other tenants to form a user group which will raise security issues with the landlord and work together to maximize the benefit of individual risk reduction measures. The tenant may choose to find another site, possibly buying one which can be controlled by him. Each of these choices has advantage and disadvantage.

The best time to discuss specific enterprise requirements is during the negotiation prior to signing the tenanting agreement. The landlord is more likely to be flexible because he wants to sell space and facilities. It also establishes a framework for continuing dialogue and demonstrates to the landlord that risk management is an important factor in your facilities requirements. In some cases, it will expose unacceptable attitudes on the part of the landlord, before the enterprise has committed to hiring space and facilities. It should minimize the cost of additional facilities because a landlord will attempt to achieve an acceptable price for the total package. If the enterprise is the first to occupy the site, an initial negotiation, which includes risk management facilities, may result in the landlord extending that level of provision across the site and dividing the cost across the total area to be rented, with a consequential benefit to the first tenant. If the negotiation takes place after the signature of a tenancy agreement, the landlord may well ask a higher price because the motivation has changed. It is also possible that the landlord may have difficulty in providing the required level of service without renegotiation of rental agreements with other tenants.

However the provision of risk management has been negotiated, there is great benefit in forming a user group with other tenants. Even the most enlightened and cooperative landlord will be unable to guess what each tenant requires. By forming a group, and agreeing common requirements, there is a much better chance of getting agreement from the landlord and maximizing the benefits and effectiveness of any resulting systems. The landlord is faced with a single set of requirements, and a single negotiation, instead of a series of conflicting requirements which may be very difficult to meet adequately. If the landlord is not cooperative, an approach by a group representing all of his tenants carries much greater weight than individual approaches which are easier to deflect. Having achieved a common awareness of risk, the tenants can work together to achieve the maximum benefit from any measures which are implemented. This is similar to the need on private sites to ensure that all employees understand how risk management affects and benefits them and how they should work with the systems. Even the most advanced systems are only as good as the people who use them.

123

If it is not possible to negotiate adequate risk services, there may be no other choice than to look for alternative premises. This may be easier said than done. Usually, industrial premises provide greater freedom of choice. Even if it is essential to establish a facility in a particular town, there are usually several sites available and specific location is probably not that important, provided that adequate communications, such as road and rail access, are available. In an increasingly mobile society, it will not matter very much where the site is because the work force will have to travel from different locations to work. Therefore, some employees will have to travel further than others and there is no guarantee that an existing workforce will remain unchanged for very long, or that existing employees will not move house for a variety of reasons. This means that there is not usually an strong reason for choosing a site in a particular area of town.

An enterprise which deals directly with the public may not have this freedom of choice. Retail premises may have to be located in the centre of town, as may some types of office premises. Location in a shopping mall may provide a considerably higher level of turnover, for a given sales floor space, than a shop in a back street, or at an out of town location. This will greatly limit the choice of available sites and weaken the negotiating position of a prospective tenant. These needs must be carefully reviewed as part of the enterprise planning process. Usually there will be alternative ways of achieving the same objective. One option could be to implement a marketing programme to persuade customers to go to a different part of town to shop. The cost of marketing could be offset by the reduced risk and lower cost of risk management. It may additionally reduce site costs because space costs less. A further possibility could be to move from floor sales to home shopping. This offers several potential benefits and dramatically changes the risk table by removing the need to admit the public into the premises. It is also a subject which any retail outlet must consider carefully because it is a source of major potential competition in the future, and therefore is a potential commercial threat. The economics of operating a home shopping service, even with delivery direct to the customer's door, should be significantly lower than a conventional retail outlet in a city centre. This reduced cost provides the means to significantly undercut retail prices and possibly be considered a more convenient service by the customer.

Even after looking carefully at all the options, many enterprises will still seek accommodation in shared premises and have to accept that their freedom to manage risk is limited to some extent. Where the site is shared, but the buildings are not, the area of difference from private sites is primarily confined to the shared areas. There will be two types of shared site, those sites which have a perimeter fence and some form of security force, and those which have a completely open site.

A fenced site can operate in a similar manner to a private site. Security personal could check every pedestrian and vehicle before admitting them and issue authorization badges in exactly the same way as for a private site. They are also able to operate surveillance cameras and intruder detection sensors. This means that they would be able to control access and parking, manning the site twenty four hours a day. The question is how much control should they have and how much responsibility should be sub contracted to them. The level of control will in part depend on the quality of communication between the security officers and the individual tenants. This is not greatly different from the requirements of a private site where the security personnel are employed directly by the enterprise. However, the management of the services will probably be more difficult, not least because each tenant may wish to have a slightly different service and the security officers are unlikely to have any responsibility for, or control over, what happens inside each building.

The intelligent answer is to agree a framework of rules which applies to all visitors and people who are normally working within the site. This means that regular visitors and workers will be issued with identity cards and vehicle badges which will allow them to enter and leave the site fairly freely, but may limit them to use only some of the site roads and parking areas. This provides a reasonably flexible access but assists the security guards in identifying people who are in areas where they are not authorized to be. The process is greatly improved if there is colour CCTV coverage because it makes colour coded badges effective and reduces workload at the security office. If someone is in an area where they are unauthorized, they should expect to be challenged, but dealing with persistent offenders is more difficult. On a private site, an employee can be disciplined for failure to observe the rules. On shared sites, there may be provision for this, but there is not a single management structure so that greater tact is required and, if that fails to achieve a result, it is much more difficult to impose effective sanctions.

Provided that each tenant has an effective means of communications with the security officers at the gates, there is no reason why the badge system cannot extend to cover ad hoc visitors. If every tenant notifies the gatehouse of anticipated visitors and details of their vehicles, the process of identifying them is greatly improved and delays are reduced. In some cases, the tenant may expect a visitor and wish to escort him from the gate. Where an unexpected visitor arrives, he can only be admitted after checking with the tenant he claims to be visiting, and who may wish to escort him. In either case, the system depends heavily on reliable communication between gate and tenant to avoid excessive delays. Where the system can prove difficult to operate, it is likely to lapse. This can often occur on shared sites, such as docks, where there is a very real need for tight access control, but many tenants are small companies and personnel will be away from their building in some remote part of the port. At the same time, there will be heavy traffic flows and this could peak at times related to tidal states. What frequently happens in such conditions is that gate security breaks down because otherwise the gateways would be jammed with vehicles awaiting clearances to enter, or leave, the site. Although this may be an understandable dilemma, it is not excusable because ports often suffer very high crime rates and can be very dangerous places which offer the inexperienced visitor a high probability of getting lost, or injured.

There is a relatively simple answer which may also be a profitable opportunity for the site owners. A central messaging facility could be provided and available to every tenant. Any tenant who is unable to guarantee that there will be an employee always by a fixed telephone would be obliged to use the service, but it would be optional for those tenants who are able to guarantee a minimum manning level. The messaging service would be linked to a mobile site communication system and could be dial in accessible from any telephone on site. This service would offer a considerable range of operational and risk management benefits to the smallest enterprises on site, and significantly reduce the problems of maintaining adequate security. As with a large private site, the system could include facilities to issue every visitor with a portable two-way communicator which has to be returned on departure. This is much more convenient and effective than relying on public address systems, especially at very large complex sites, such as ports, where an unescorted visitor may be driving for several miles inside the site on roads which may all look very similar. In these conditions, two-way communications provide the means for security personnel to contact, instantly, any vehicle which is deviating from its authorized route, and enables the driver to call for assistance in the event of any difficulty.

A number of sites will be completely open. Most industrial sites have an extensive network of access roads and vehicles may be using them at any time of day or night. This presents particular difficulties for risk management. There may be no way of knowing if any driver has a valid reason to be using the roads and vehicles may be parked at any location for extended periods. This provides excellent cover for thieves and terrorists. Every enterprise on the site will be occupied with its own activities and may have no reason to challenge anyone loading at a neighbouring site. This places great pressure on the risk measures taken for each building, because there is no advanced notice of suspicious activities, and the first barrier will be the structure itself.

Where the building itself may be occupied by several enterprises, the problems will be even greater. This is especially true in the case of shared office buildings where many occupants will issue a number of keys to employees who may need to enter the building outside normal business hours. Along with occupants of apartment buildings, occupants of this type of building may take little notice of the comings and goings of others. Any attacker may therefore be able to gain entry to the building unnoticed, and then be free to force entry to any area inside. User/tenant Groups can play an important part in reducing this risk in two ways. By meeting, they will become more aware of their neighbours and understand better what may be normal behaviour. Of equal importance, meeting to discuss and consider risk will make everyone more aware of the threats which exist.

Having taken all practical steps to secure the perimeter of a shared site, or the shared area of a multiple occupancy building, the main risk measures must address the occupied area over which the enterprise has maximum control and responsibility. Again, the occupier will have a more difficult task than someone occupying an exclusive site. The primary difficulty is that there will be perimeters which can only be secured from one side. To this may be added restrictions imposed by a tenancy agreement. When the occupier owns that building, he is fairly free to take any measure which he considers necessary. For example, he can rebuild walls, replace doors, or carry out other major structural alterations. A tenant will not be free to do this and, at the very least, will need to obtain permission from the landlord. This may also apply to an exclusive site if it is not owned by the occupant but, with shared accommodation, it will be the normal situation. It may be that the tenancy agreement requires the landlord to agree to any reasonable request, but what the occupant regards as reasonable may not be the same as the landlord's view. The fact that structural remodelling may improve facilities and reduce risk for the current occupant does not mean that a successor will derive the same benefits and the landlord must consider the value of the property to him. Modifications may make the property more difficult to hire out in the future. The landlord should also consider the impact of change on other tenants and the probability that those tenants may be encouraged to demand similar rights. A modification by one tenant may not reduce the value of the property, but modifications, inevitably each case being different, by the other tenants may make it very difficult to rerent the building, or parts of it, in the future.

If we assume that the landlord is flexible on these issues and allows tenants a free hand, there are a number of steps which may be necessary. Most standard doors provide very little security against fire and attack.

Replacement of outer doors and frames may therefore be necessary and, as the history of the accommodation is probably unknown, the locks should be replaced, or additional locks fitted. If the landlord already provides an electronic locking system, operated by *smart* cards under the control of a computer, it may still be necessary to fit mechanical locks to secure the building during the period it is unoccupied. In this case, it may be necessary to provide the landlord with spare keys so that entry can be effected in emergencies, such as fire, or flooding. Similar actions may be required for windows and emergency exits, but fire protection requirements must be considered.

Within the occupied area, the tenant can fit fire and intruder sensors with relative freedom and select those sensors which are most suitable to his conditions. Providing appropriate alarming may be more difficult. It is highly desirable to give warning to immediate neighbours, but it will also be necessary to provide alarm to someone who can provide assistance. Fire and police services are becoming increasingly resistant to accepting connection of alarms to their control rooms. In part this is because automatic alarms do go wrong and false alarms must be responded to, because they are assumed to be valid until proven otherwise. The other difficulty is space and control. If every home, office and factory wanted to install alarm indicators in local police and fire control rooms, the essential services would be faced with a major problem just in accommodating the terminal equipment.

One solution is to use a commercial district control room, often available from local security companies. This may dictate the method of financing the sensors in the occupied area. Many commercial services will only provide control facilities if they are also providing the sensors and maintaining them and usually wish to provide the service as a rental charge. There is considerable benefit in reaching agreement with neighbouring tenants. If every tenant in a shared building agrees to use the same service, the number of communications links, which can prove costly, is reduced. It will also be practical to include video surveillance of shared areas and of occupied areas.

The service company can install a multi-media system to cover every area of the building so that many of the risks are reduced because of the elimination of blind areas in which a threat can develop. The addition of video surveillance significantly increases the effectiveness of a system because it allows control room staff at a remote location to make a visual check from a safe distance and assess the threat indicated by the alarm. As soon as the control room receives an alarm, they can verify that it is not a false alert and can both select the necessary essential service correctly, and provide much more accurate information to police, fire fighters and medical control rooms. This further reduces risk and avoids wasted effort because the essential services have a high assurance that they are attending a real emergency and can dispatch the most appropriate response units. For example, an intruder alarm does not indicate the nature of the attack and a police force would probably send no more than two officers who might not be armed. If the threat is from armed intruders, possibly holding hostages, the response is not only ineffective, but the attending policemen have been exposed to personal risks. Many enterprises may fear that sophisticated systems of this type infringe their privacy and introduce other risks. This does not have to be the case. A well designed system will include warning lamps on cameras to indicate that they are operational, and an automatic arming system which is activated when the detector systems are switched on. Where appropriate, this can be set up on a zoning system so that detectors and cameras can be activated in selected parts of the building, or for every room.

If it is not possible to gain agreement from neighbours, or there is no commercial control service available, the enterprise will have to take whatever precautions are practical. Any alarm must be audible to neighbours and preferably audible outside the building. Taking the alarm back to the control rooms of essential services may prove difficult. Generally, direct connection will only be permitted if the systems are installed and maintained by an approved contractor, who can be called at any time to repair, or reset, the systems. In a number of areas, this may mean that several contractors will be involved because the fire service may not necessarily approve the same contractors as the local police force. Where a contractor appears on all approval lists, this does not automatically mean that he provides the best level of service. In some cases it may be that companies which specialize in fire protection or intruder detection provide a much better service than a company which covers all categories of protection. An alternative approach is to install a system which contacts the appropriate essential service by means of an autodialler, but this does introduce some risks. The system will only function if the telephone line is free. If it is engaged, for example accepting a message to an answering machine, or if the emergency number is unavailable, the system will continue to try the line for a pre-set number of attempts and may also try other preset numbers in the event of failure, or after a successful emergency call. However, once the machine has run though its pre-set cycle, it will then give up, even if it has failed to pass its alarm message. The other danger is that the system will malfunction and give a false alarm. Essential services cannot prevent enterprises from installing autodiallers, but they can make a charge in the event of a false alarm. Usually this is not done until after a warning notice has been issued, as a result of a number of false alarms, but the charge may be deliberately penal and represent considerably more than the actual cost of dispatching response units on a fruitless mission. The only alternative, in addition to a local audible and/or visual alarm, is to install an autodialler which calls a number of employees in sequence and they then have to go to the building to make a personal assessment of the situation before taking appropriate action. It could also be practical to hire direct lines to employees' homes which may offer greater reliability. The disadvantage is that time will elapse before they arrive and then call in the essential services. During this period, a minor fire could have become firmly established, spreading to neighbouring buildings, and major damage may result which could have been avoided if professional fire fighters had been called earlier. In the event of a criminal attack, employees may be exposed to risks which they are not trained to deal with, but could be handled effectively by the police force. Their presence on site may also further complicate matters for the police when they arrive, such as turning a burglary into a hostage situation, or robbery into grievous bodily harm, or even murder.

Even where systems can be satisfactorily be connected to the essential services, there may be advantage in also installing automatic prevention systems. Automatic fire extinguishing is an obvious possibility and the easiest to implement. The most effective system is one which discharges inert gas into those rooms affected by fire. Some gas extinguishing systems are easy to install, and remove, which may have particular benefit when premises are rented. The disadvantages of automatic gas extinguishing systems is that they can be costly and, when they operate, they work by displacing oxygen so that people need breathing apparatus to survive in the area. Oxygen displacement does not present a danger to fire fighters, who will be equipped with breathing apparatus, and there is no reason why employees should remain in, or return to, the affected area until it has been declared safe by the fire authorities, but it does present a real threat to anyone who is unconscious or trapped at the time the system operates. One solution is to include emergency breathing apparatus, sited at strategic locations, but this will entail additional staff training to ensure safe use of the equipment. The alternative to gas extinguishing is a water-based system which may spray water to reduce temperature, or pump foam which smothers the fire. These systems are only really practical if they cover the entire building and that will require the landlord to carryout the work.

Shared premises become even more difficult to secure when sharing includes free access by the public. It becomes impractical to screen visitors adequately and it may be that most of the people present at any one time have received no training in risk procedures and are visiting the premises for the first time. There is a high probably that visitors will greatly outnumber authorized staff and this will add further to the level of risk. In some cases, such as retail premises, most of the building will be open to the public. In other cases, such as museums and educational establishments, only part of the building, or site and buildings, will be freely accessible to the public. Risk will also change with patterns of use. Retail stores may have a constant flow of visitors who have never been in the building before, but will not be on the premises for very long. Entertainment facilities will have visitors who are present for several hours in large numbers and could be under the influence of alcohol. There may be additional factors, such as deliberately low lighting levels and emotional mood changes caused by the type of entertainment. Educational establishments may be largely populated by visitors who may visit regularly every day for a period of weeks, and then be absent for several weeks, or by those who attend short evening courses. Hotels may have visitors who are present for longer periods than those visiting retail stores, but may occupy the building for several days and will spend time sleeping, when their vulnerability increases. Hospitals suffer from virtually all these risk factors, and have added risks from the dangerous processes and materials which are essential to the provision of medical services.

Providing reliable risk management in these types of premises is very challenging and, for that reason, it is often ignored to some extent, or completely. The significant factor is cost, but there is also the challenge of providing risk management which reduces risk acceptably, without restricting availability to the extent which prevents the enterprise functioning. The profit margins are typically low and this has resulted in a major effort to cut overheads. A primary target for cost cutting is manpower and this is most damaging to risk management. Any enterprise which relies on a transient customer population has to recognize that it is not possible to train customers in risk reduction, and any notices which issue warnings and prohibitions are unlikely to be read. Therefore, the employees of the enterprise carry the responsibility of supervising visitors and this becomes increasingly difficult to achieve when the ratio of visitors to staff rises. It also becomes more difficult as the number of employees is reduced, and are barely sufficient to carry out the basic tasks required to operate the enterprise. As this trend continues, personnel become progressively less effective in any role, and those roles which are rarely performed suffer most. One further constraint is that realistic training is virtually impossible. The last thing that a hospital, or a retail store, wants to do is to carry out an evacuation for training purposes. In the case of the hospital, a number of patients will be so frail that any movement may prove fatal and should only be considered in extreme emergency. Some patients will be infectious and moving them, while maintaining isolation, will prove difficult. A retail outlet has a different motive. If customers are ejected, as part of the fire drill, they will not be able to purchase goods and some may not wish to return to the store., This means that although staff training may be carried out, it usually fails to simulate the problems which must be dealt with in a real emergency.

However difficult it may be to implement effective risk reduction, it must be done. Preventative measures are of great importance in reducing the probability of primary risk, but it is also essential to cater for risk reduction in an emergency when the numbers of people involved will create considerable consequential risk and loss. Fire is a major risk. The presence of a large number of people who are not familiar with the building, and its services, increases the risk of fire starting. Once it has started, fear will generate panic and other consequential risks result. As visitors are unlikely to read warning notices and instructions carefully before an incident, and will not have time to read them during the emergency, it is essential that everything is very clearly labelled and signed. Escape routes and emergency equipment must be indicated in a way which does not require the study of documents, or pause for thought. Hand held fire extinguishers must carry symbolic instructions which do not require knowledge of a specific language, but the encouragement should be to evacuate the area. The escape routes themselves should be adequate to allow more than the number of people likely to be present to escape down a single route. In the event of fire, or some other emergency such as a bomb threat, it may be that only one route is suitable for evacuation, and there is always the risk that an emergency will occur when an unusually large number of people are present. There have been many instances where fire in a public building has created panic and people have been injured in the stampede to get away. Some of the more extreme cases, exits have become blocked with people who have been injured, or killed, in the stampede and this has stopped others from escaping, resulting in their death from smoke inhalation.

Planning escape routes can be difficult. Existing buildings may not have been designed for their current use and may not have been intended to cater for the numbers of people who may now be present. Major structural changes could be necessary to improve escape facilities. As a result of the number of serious fires in buildings, such as theatres, dance halls and sports stadia, legislation has been introduced in many countries which requires the installation of fire alarms and emergency lighting. This is a step forward in that it introduces minimum standards, but it is has the danger of becoming the maximum standard as well. An alarm system only indicates a potential severe danger, and typical emergency lighting systems only indicate the routes to several emergency exits. In the event of a fire, it may not be obvious where the danger is and which routes lead away from that danger. It may seem that the location of a fire will be obvious, but the first threat is usually smoke which circulates through air-conditioning systems and makes it very difficult to see the source of the threat. Emergency lighting systems are usually mounted in ceilings and above doorways and dense smoke may render them virtually useless when people are trying to keep below the level of the smoke, the ground being the last area to be affected. It is therefore possible that people will struggle through smoke towards any point of light in an attempt to escape, but actually be heading towards the source of the fire, only finding out when it is too late to try another route. The solution is to fit lighting systems in the floor, or low on walls, which clearly indicate direction and have a system of controlling the lights so that people are directed away from the risk. This is technically possible and the system has been used on passenger aircraft, but has only rarely been used in public buildings. However, there is no substitute for having trained people present to supervise evacuation. This may be very difficult to achieve because the staffing levels may be totally inadequate for emergencies, although they may be adequate for normal business.

Some enterprises, such as hotels and hospitals, have a large number of external and internal doorways. Crime prevention requires doors to be normally closed and under some form of locking control. Fire doors must be unlocked in an emergency to allow evacuation, but close automatically to restrict the spread of fire. It is not uncommon to find that external fire exit doors have been locked as a crime prevention measure, or that fire doors have been jammed open to ease normal access. The most common reasons for this are that departments take measures independently without understanding the consequences and that there is inadequate monitoring of facilities when they have been installed. Affordable technology exists which provides the means to accommodate these apparently conflicting requirements. A comprehensive enterprise and risk policy suite will identify the requirements and the relationship of countermeasures. However, once a solution has been implemented, it is necessary to constantly monitor its use to ensure that it is operated correctly and improved to meet changing requirements.

# 8 Risk management for travel and transport

Every enterprise employs transportation, directly, or indirectly. This divides into transportation to, and from, the enterprise sites. It further divides into transportation of people and goods. Each category introduces a number of potential risks, of which the majority relate to human error, rather than to aggressive action. A range of technology is available to assist in risk reduction, but most risks can be reduced by planning and an appreciation of the potential threats.

Risk management of sites and buildings includes procedures and systems which are designed to reduce transport risk within those locations. Some of this protection will also reduce transport risk outside the site, but its primary function is to reduce risk within the site. For example, site security will be responsible for the correct identification of vehicles arriving at the site, and ensuring that the drivers are identified. By preventing the entry of unauthorized vehicles, one group of transport related risk is virtually eliminated. Those vehicles which are granted entry can be directed to the appropriate locations and will have acceptable documentation to support loading and/or unloading. Procedures within the site will control the correct handling of materials, and the supervision of drivers and any passengers. This reduces the risk of dangerous materials being handled incorrectly and visitors being exposed to risks within the site. In the case of loading, all cargoes will be correctly identified and loaded, so that the vehicle is not allowed to move off in a dangerous condition. If the cargo consists of potentially dangerous materials, any appropriate signs will have been attached externally so that emergency services are aware of the risks should the vehicle be involved in an accident after it has left the site. By documenting all activities associated with a visiting vehicle, the site security personnel will be able to supply necessary information if requested. As the time of arrival and departure will have been recorded, it will be possible to

135

fix the last confirmed location if the vehicle fails to arrive at another destination.

The enterprise will also maintain records in relation to its own vehicles, and those of its employees, if the vehicles are based at, or operated from, the site. Records will typically include information, such as next of kin and, possibly, include medical details, such as blood groups and allergies. The reason for departure should also be recorded, so that it is known if the vehicle is due to return to the site, and where it is headed. In some cases, details of intended route will also be known and this may be a legal requirement if the cargo is subject to special controls, or required by the insurance company if the cargo has a high value. Therefore risk reduction measures employed at the site will provide a basis for risk reduction outside the site.

An enterprise can do much to reduce risk for its own transport and personnel when they are off site and travelling. Unfortunately this is frequently ignored. A police force recently carried out spot checks on goods vehicles using a particular motorway, and were horrified to find that 94% of all vehicles checked had faults which contravened construction and use regulations. They were even more horrified to find that 37% of the vehicles had very serious faults which were liable to cause serious, and probably lethal, accidents. Other police forces have carried out random checks on private vehicles with similar results. This means that most road users are failing to carryout adequate maintenance and many goods vehicles are dangerously loaded. However serious this may be, it is further compounded by driver health and behaviour. Random checks have revealed that an alarming number of drivers have health defects which impair their ability to drive safely, the most common being eye defects. On the basis of this evidence, it is not surprising that road traffic incidents are a major cause of death and injury, only surprising that the rates are not even higher than the present unacceptable levels.

Many health risks are partly excusable in that the affected person may not be aware of the defect, and health services are not equipped to handle the necessary routine testing required to screen out problems. This is perhaps an example of the failure of risk and enterprise management in health service provisioning, with the services primarily dealing with cure rather than prevention. Part of the solution lies with enterprises. Considering how valuable personnel are to the enterprise in achieving its objectives, there is a strong case for employers to arrange and pay for the cost of regular preventative health screening of employees, because the cost of this will reduce the value of loses which result from health related risks.

Inadequate vehicle maintenance is totally inexcusable. Like any well maintained machine, a vehicle performs much better when it is in full working order. Defects will eventually have to be corrected because the vehicle will become unusable but, long before that, operating costs will increase because fuel consumption is likely to increase. Eventual repair, or replacement parts, costs will be much higher than if the faults were corrected early, or never materialized because preventative maintenance had been performed correctly. If the defect results in an incident, substantial costs may be incurred. The obvious costs are those of repair work and increased insurance costs as a result of claims. There will be lost production costs, and injury, or death, will represent a significant cost which cannot be fully addressed financially. Beyond those effects, there will be the risk of fines, or even imprisonment. The driver will be the obvious target because legally he is responsible for the condition of the vehicle, but legal penalties may rightly penetrate much deeper into the enterprise.

Given the circumstances, it is difficult to understand why enterprises run these risks and allow, or sometimes encourage, their employees to run risks of this magnitude. In some cases it is simple greed, but most frequently it is the result of ignorance and totally inadequate planning. In either case, the subsequent cost is much greater than the cost of adequate planning and actions. If the full consequential costs are taken into consideration, most enterprises would receive a very welcome increase in profitability, as a result of allocating more funds and resources to ensuring the safe operation of transport. Unfortunately, deficiencies in transport management are usually symptomatic of overall bad management and can only be addressed as part of a major restructuring of the enterprise, probably requiring a complete replacement of the existing management. If this is not done actively, it may be the ultimate outcome, through the legal process, as a result of avoidable incidents, but considerable, perhaps mortal, damage will have been caused in the meantime.

One barrier to a solution is perceptions of privacy and liberty. Enterprises are often reluctant to insist on regular health checks for employees, and employees are often reluctant for their employer to have any form of access to their health records. This often has a justified basis which stems from the narrow short term view of many enterprises, manifesting itself in a view that employees are expendable resources. In the long term, every enterprise will benefit from having a stable and well motivated work force. To achieve this, it must be recognized that every employee may have some personal problem at some stage in his employment and that this may be health related. By driving employees through fear, risk is not reduced, but increased. Under pressure, most people will take risks which they should not take, and conceal important information. Fear of dismissal is one reason why an employee may report for work when he is not capable, or agree to drive a vehicle which he knows is not fit for use. Human error is covered up for the same reason. An excuse for this environment is that the enterprise cannot afford to carry passengers, but this is not an intelligent argument because there will be a number of significant hidden costs which will make a more enlightened approach to management more profitable, as well as more enjoyable.

Vehicle maintenance also suffers from poor repair and maintenance services. An enterprise which takes great care over the maintenance of its production machines may take a much more casual approach to the maintenance of its vehicles. It is much more likely to hand responsibility to the vehicle servicing company and not check that work has been carried out satisfactorily. Any servicing operation is capable of making mistakes and some faults are not visible when the vehicle is serviced. This has two consequences. The vehicle may retain uncorrected faults, and the enterprise may have been incorrectly charged. Some incorrect charging will be accidental, but some will be deliberate. Failure to check a vehicle at acceptance will either be a result of negligence, or ignorance. Ignorance can be corrected by training.

Very few enterprises make any effort to ensure that drivers of company vehicles are competent to drive the vehicle issued, or to check that servicing has been correctly carried out. Complete reliance is placed on a current driving license for the class of vehicle. As a driving license only demonstrates that the driver was once tested for basic capability, this is not adequate proof that he is now competent to take responsibility for a vehicle. Since taking a driving test, conditions will have changed and the driver will have had to adapt with nothing but experience as a guide. The driving test will also have covered only a narrow part of the spectrum of skills and, in many countries, this will not have included motorway driving, handling hazardous conditions, or driving at night. The vehicle used for the test may have been very different from the vehicle which has been issued by the enterprise for business use. Therefore the personnel policy should include an appropriate training program for every authorized driver. There may also be merit in making this programme available to those employees who use their own vehicle for work, or use it to commute. By taking simple and relatively low cost precautions of this type, the enterprise can greatly reduce the direct and indirect losses which can result from driving offenses and accidents. The number of working days lost by industry through driving incidents off site can be significant, and will lead to other loss as the remaining work force attempts to meet objectives with reduced manning levels.

Travel risk can be further reduced by ensuring that personnel are not expected to take avoidable risks. Goods vehicle drivers may have to limit the number of hours driven in any one day, and take a minimum number of rest periods, both during each day, and between days. In many enterprises goods vehicle drivers are in the minority, with sales staff and field engineers making up the majority of company miles travelled. These people will not be governed by mandatory restrictions and more vehicle related loss occurs as a result of tired drivers, than from any other causes. It is unreasonable to expect an employee to drive for more hours than a goods vehicle driver is permitted and also work many more hours doing other work, but enterprises often demand, or encourage, this. If long commute journeys are occasional requirements, the driver should be encouraged to stage his journey with overnight stops, or use an alternative method of transport. If long journeys are a regular requirement, it may be that the work is badly planned.

Although most regular business travel is self drive journeys, there is also a need to use public transport to some degree. Greater use of this can reduce driving risks, but there are some additional risks. A car will only carry four people, and most business use involves only one or two people travelling in a single vehicle. Public transport has the ability to transport much larger numbers of employees together. This has proved very dangerous for some enterprises. A complete senior management team, together with their entire sales and marketing staffs, could be carried in the same plane. If the plane crashes, the entire critical staff can be wiped out in one incident and the enterprise may never recover. It is therefore very important that this situation is avoided by ensuring that only small groups travel together. In an unfortunate incident, a complete team of senior counter terrorist officers was transported in a large helicopter which crashed, killing all onboard, and crippled the counter terrorist capability. There was the immediate tragic loss of life at the crash site, but the loss of capability may have been responsible for considerably greater consequential losses, some of which might not become visible for some time. In that case, the crash may have been a result of mechanical failure, but it could just as easily have been a deliberate attack by terrorists. Placing all personnel in a single aircraft may greatly reduce the travel cost, but the saving would be insignificant in the event of a major disaster.

Where personnel are expected to travel long distances, it is very important to make sure that they travel in comfort and can adequately rest before starting work. The speed and relative ease of long distance air travel holds many unseen dangers. An assumption, frequently made, is that a business traveller can sleep on a long flight and be ready for work as soon as he gets off the plane. Some people are able to do this, but most are not, and loading a diary from the point of arrival will be very counter productive, and unacceptably increase risk. The traveller also needs adequate briefing before departure and there should be contingency plans. The large numbers of travellers routinely taking long distance flights, without incident, creates a false sense of security. When air travel was in its infancy, every flight was an adventure and travellers expected to plan with care. Today, the use of passenger aircraft is so common that most travellers assume, and hope, that there will be no problem. Many attacks take place on travellers who arrive in a strange country after a long flight, and then attempt to drive to a hotel. Every town has areas which it is best to avoid, and these should be identified. Even if the traveller is adequately briefed, he may still drive off and become lost as a result of fatigue.

The best made travel plans can go wrong and contingency planning will reduce the risks in the event of an unscheduled change. Making sure that the business traveller is adequately equipped for these circumstances will keep risk and inconvenience at minimum levels. A long journey may involve passing areas where there are particular risks which only apply if the journey has to be broken. Therefore additional health measures may be advised, and possibly additional currency and travellers cheques may be needed. Standard travel insurance may not be adequate to cover conditions in countries where the journey could be broken and it is advisable to plan an alternate route to cover disruptive events, such as air traffic control disputes, or unusual weather conditions. Knowing that good alternatives exist will reduce stress on the traveller and help to reduce the time needed to adjust at the destination. Travel to some locations can also present particular difficulties which can be planned for in advance. Although a range of medication is generally available in most of the places a business traveller is likely to visit, it may not be easily available and product brands are likely to be different. Therefore, extended journeys will be made easier by taking a small medical kit, containing familiar products of known quality. A number of business trips are jeopardized because the traveller becomes unwell with a relatively minor ailment which is made worst by taking locally available medicines, primarily because they have to be taken in different doses to those required by familiar treatments at home, or have different levels of effectiveness. Labelling in a foreign language can also make it very easy to take the wrong dosage.

Simple things like clothing and luggage can produce additional risk. Someone travelling from a warm climate to a cold climate will make sure that he has suitable clothing, but smaller climatic changes are often unplanned for. Heavy luggage can cause injury, increase risk of theft and introduce additional delays in travelling. With widespread risk of terrorism and smuggling, it is important that the traveller packs his own luggage, locks it, and keeps it close to him. This reduces the risk of bombs being placed in it, or illegal materials such as drugs. A businessman who is found to have illegal drugs in his luggage will have considerable difficulty in convincing customs and police officials that he was unaware they were there and that he was not responsible for them. For this reason it is advisable to take the minimum luggage necessary for the trip, possibly with some extra items for contingencies. Ideally, luggage should be compact enough to hand carry onto the plane and keep close by as cabin luggage. In addition to reducing a variety of risks, it will save a great deal of time in leaving the airport, particularly if there is a baggage handlers strike, or it becomes unexpectedly necessary to change planes. Only someone who has experienced it can fully appreciate the chaos which ensues when a plane load of passengers have to scramble for another plane because theirs' has developed a fault. It is not too much of a problem for those who can walk off one plane and onto another carrying their hand luggage. For those who have to fight to retrieve luggage from the aircraft holds and then struggle across to another terminal to board an alternative aircraft, weighed down with masses of luggage, it becomes a nightmare and they probably end up missing the other plane anyway. When the traveller reaches the destination, he will take a lot longer to reach his normal performance levels. He may also find that he has arrived in Germany, and his luggage has just arrived in Brazil. This is no longer the regular problem that it once was, but it does still happen. If it is necessary to take luggage which has to travel in the aircraft hold, it is very wise to take essentials in a carry-on bag. At least if you become separated from the main luggage, you still have a change of clothes and personal items with you. There are probably few things more galling than to suffer a nightmare journey, become separated from all your clothes and toiletries, and arrive in a strange hotel, with nowhere to buy emergency replacements, and be greeted by a smug colleague who had the forethought to keep his essential luggage with him through the flight. Being able to wash and change after a difficult journey can be a great restorer.

On any journey via a seaport or airport, there are some special risks which can be missed. The extensive use of x-ray and magnetic equipment for detecting contraband can damage film and magnetic media. Most hold luggage automatically passes such equipment on the conveyor belt in baggage handling, and carry-on luggage is inspected in the same way. To avoid these potential risks, material of this type should be carried through the security check points for hand search. The process is also helped if the employee has been given a list of company equipment, which he is carrying, to prove ownership and authenticity. The list should include a description of the items, together with any serial numbers, and the traveller can save unnecessary delays by also carrying a list, and any proofs of purchase, for personal equipment such as cameras. Any items purchased during a trip should be listed and kept with receipts. When passing through customs, this can save a great deal of time and embarrassment. Further time can often be saved by going through the *red channel*, rather than the *green, nothing to declare, channel*, because most passengers make straight for the green channel and, if there is a spot check by customs, it can result in significant delays.

Although long distance travel may form a minor part of the total employee travel in any enterprise, it frequently generates the largest number of problems. Most of these can be avoided with little or no additional cost and sometimes at a profit, because problems cost money. Like much of risk management, risks can be reduced dramatically by forward planning and taking simple common sense precautions. Where it is necessary to buy equipment to reduce risk, this usually has a fairly long working life and can be reused many times. Some items can be reissued to a number of different employees over a number of trips. As with any equipment, it must be kept in good working order and replaced before it is worn out.

One thing which is a major risk reducer in any business travel is good communications. Changing technology is making it much easier to obtain reliable mobile communications. The advent of digital mobile/portable telephones has begun to open cross border use of this form of communication and to make data transmission a reliable complement to voice communications. During the last fifty years, equipment has moved from bulky units, with a range of a few miles, which had to be mounted in a vehicle, to pocket sized radio telephones which can access via public switched telephone networks, and operate across large geographic areas. General confidentiality has greatly improved, but any radio based system can be covertly monitored so that there is a potential security risk. As systems become more sophisticated, monitoring requires greater skills, and more sophisticated listening equipment, which reduces risk for all but the most sensitive high profile targets.

Against reducing risks, the value of mobile communication increases as systems become more flexible. For most users, modern systems provide the freedom to change work patterns and reduce risks associated with travellers. Being able to communicate on the move extends facilities which have previously required people to go to, or stay at, fixed locations. In the event of a travel problem, schedules can be reorganized and help summoned. This is particularly valuable to the lone traveller. A vehicle failure on a motorway can be reported without the driver having to expose himself to additional risk because it is no longer necessary to walk to the nearest telephone. There are conflicting views as to whether the driver should remain in the vehicle, or vacate it. Certainly, a broken down vehicle at the side of a motorway, particularly in poor conditions such as fog, is potentially vulnerable to being struck by another vehicle. However, a lone driver may be safer from attack by remaining inside a locked vehicle until help arrives.

Vehicle security has always been a particular problem. Standard locking and alarm systems have proved vulnerable to the determined attacker and most vehicles spend more time parked and unattended than being occupied and driven. It is wise to assume that no security system will be invulnerable and some simple precautions can be taken to reduce the risk of attack. Parking in an area which is supervised by CCTV cameras or security officers greatly reduces risk, as does parking in a well lit location. All attackers prefer to target vehicles which are not easily observed so that they can work on the security systems undisturbed. Risks to personnel also increase when a vehicle is left in a badly lit location because vulnerability increases as the driver approaches the vehicle and unlocks it. A large number of attacks on vehicles succeed because the driver has failed to lock his vehicle. Thieves can strike quickly, even when the vehicle is briefly unattended at a filling station while the driver is paying his bill only a short distance from the vehicle. Easily removable items of value are left on open display in unattended vehicles and all a thief has to do is to break a window, grab the items and run. Attacks of this nature can be over and done in moments. As with most risks, first level risk reduction starts with an understanding of the threats and the development of good habits through adequate training. Very few enterprises make the effort to brief their drivers and personnel on threat avoidance.

Vehicle related crime rates are increasing, and in consequence insurance rates have increased, putting pressure on vehicle manufacturers to make greater efforts to design and produce better security protection. However, this increased effort has still to result in significant improvements for all vehicles and does little to assist in the protection of existing vehicles. There are some fundamental design challenges. The requirements for visibility and safety produce a number of weak points, creating attack risks. Large areas of glass must be included in the vehicle design and the size and location of openings for doors is determined in part by safety requirements. These weak points provide an attacker with several opportunities to access the vehicle interior. Door locks are improving, but a determined attacker can usually find a way of defeating them, given enough time. This means that an intruder alarm is often the main means of protection, but passers by usually ignore a vehicle alarm and the incidence of false alarms has resulted in legislation to limit the duration of an alarm sounder. Higher value vehicles are now being fitted with systems which make the vehicle undrivable in the event of a thief breaking in. Of course these systems do little to protect the contents of the vehicle, but make it more difficult for the vehicle to be stolen.

Drivers can greatly reduce risk by taking simple precautions. In general terms, items should not be left in a vehicle where a thief could see them easily. By locking items in a closed luggage compartment, they will not only be more secure because it is usually harder to break into the compartment,

143

but also will be invisible to the passing thief and therefore not entice an attack. Particularly valuable, or sensitive items should not be left unattended. An incident occurred, during the 1990/91 Gulf War, when an officer left a portable computer unattended in his vehicle. In this incident, it appears that a common thief took what he thought would be a valuable computer, but it could just as easily have been taken by an enemy agent. During the period that the machine was missing, it had to be assumed that this was the action of an enemy. Unfortunately, the machine contained very sensitive information and this resulted in considerable cost because equipment and personnel had to be moved in the war zone, just in case the information was in enemy hands. A similar situation could arise if the computer had contained sensitive commercial information, such as chemical formulae, or details of a forthcoming bid.

One of the more promising developments has been the availability of tracking systems which send a signal to a radio network, many using satellite radio communications. Systems of this type can be fitted to existing vehicles and may provide no indication that they are fitted, or that they have been triggered to send an alarm call. Reliance is placed on providing an alarm to a control room, and then providing indication of the vehicle's location and heading, so that police can intercept. One major advantage of this type of system is that it can be triggered automatically by a detector system, or activated manually by a driver. As the vehicle can be located and tracked by the control room, the police do not have to engage in dangerous high speed chases, but can set up road blocks, or wait for the vehicle to stop, before moving in. The ability to trigger the alarm manually means that a driver can call for help if attacked, or threatened, providing personnel protection and reducing the risk of high value loads being highjacked.

As mobile communications continue to develop, it will become practical to reduce several vehicle related risks. Onboard radio navigation systems can reduce delays and costs by assisting the driver to take the best route available at the time and to avoid areas with serious hold ups. By linking navigation and tracking systems, it will become possible to monitor the progress and status of every company vehicle. There will be resistance from drivers to this perceived reduction in privacy, but the benefits will be substantial provided that enterprises make reasonable use of the facilities to improve efficiency. The systems will be most effective for enterprises which avoid adversarial management techniques and harsh control of their personnel. There is also the prospect of improved safety because the systems could be extended, through additional sensors, to ensure that vehicles travel automatically at set distances from objects and other road vehicles. Inevitably it will restrict freedoms which drivers have become used to. It will not remove the need for adequate driver training, because the driver will have to take manual control in the event of system breakdown, and not every stretch of road will be covered by these systems, first deployment being to heavily used motorways. Whilst drivers may be initially resistant, a similar path has already been followed for aircraft. Many flights now take place on a largely automated basis, with the pilot primarily being required to monitor the systems for correct operation and to take over manual control in the event of system failure.

New technologies will introduce many changes, offer benefits, and introduce new risks. For most of the Twentieth Century, populations have become increasingly mobile. The great freedom of the motorcar has led to extensive road building systems and put great pressure on public transport. Much current planning is based on the assumption that this pattern will continue, but the assumption may prove false. The motorcar and the heavy goods vehicle have revolutionized business transportation, but encouraged enterprise to relocate to the best points along the road infrastructure and led to a significant increase in commuting. Working hours have been largely based on daylight hours, and single shift working is the most popular system of operation. As a result, populations have shifted into prime areas and placed ever greater pressure on transport systems, but are a very inefficient use of resources because heavy use is concentrated into short periods of each day, leaving resources at some point in the chain unused for most of each day. High speed long distance transportation has not fundamentally changed this pattern, but has extended travel risks to a larger proportion of workers and introduced new risks, such as the rapid introduction of sickness to populations which have not built up a natural resistance. It has also increased the percentage of unproductive time. The cycle cannot continue unchanged and has been waiting for new technologies to address the problems it creates.

New communications technologies are making travel time more productive by enabling communication for travellers. Increasing system functionality is also reducing the need for some travel and providing greater flexibility in working hours. As effective international communications become widely available, business across time zones will continue to increase and reliance on planning working hours to coincide with local daylight hours will reduce. This has the potential to spread the load of travellers across the full day, and therefore relieve peak pressure on transport systems. It will also free many workers from the need to travel to a working place. This may result in populations being spread out more evenly. Improving transport systems have already achieved this to a degree. The critical time period for commuting is generally 90 minutes. In heavily populated major cities like London, this once meant that workers would try to find accommodation, at least during the working week, within 15 miles of their place of work. The introduction of faster electric trains and motorways has increased the proportion of workers who now routinely travel more than 100 miles to work each day. Where workers used accommodation close to their place of work during the week, and then established a home in more attractive and comfortable surroundings within 50 miles of their work place, this distance may now be several hundred miles and family homes may even be in different countries. Already, people working in London, who used to have a family, or holiday, home within 50 miles of the centre of the city, may now have that accommodation in France, or even further afield. As telecommunications systems continue to develop, many of those people will work largely from home and travel occasionally to other locations to conduct business which cannot be carried on without a direct personal meeting.

Many enterprises have been slow to grasp the opportunities now opening up and to address the changing risks. People who would previously have had difficulty in working can now benefit from the new communications technologies. People with disabilities, which make it very difficult for them to leave their home, are now able to work remotely. Women are increasingly able to find work which allows them to be at home with their children for much of the time. This opens up new sources of labour with many implications, both social and financial.

Some countries will see greater change than others. Developing countries may be able to avoid the risks which developed countries have had to experience. Some countries, such as the United Kingdom, may see many changes, not least the habit of enterprises providing company vehicles. If the average business mileage drops, as it already shows signs of doing, the need for company vehicles will also drop. Business drivers may also show a greater desire to select a vehicle which suites their needs, rather than the needs of employers. There may also be a greater tendency for workers to provide their services on limited contracts and this will introduce a number of changes. As long as workers saw life as continued employment with one enterprise, they were captive to that enterprise, and many freedoms were restricted in return for security of employment. There are several signs that this is changing and the number of people who have several different jobs, or only work for part of each week, is increasing. This may in turn make some new technologies inappropriate, or reduce their benefits. If a worker provides his own vehicle, and does more than one job, it will not be possible for any one employer to benefit from vehicle tracking systems in the way in which they would benefit were they monitoring company vehicles. The variety of vehicles could also increase, or dominant types change. This has already begun to occur in countries, such as the United States, where privately owned vehicles predominate and many drivers choose multi

146

purpose vehicles rather than the standard business/family saloon car. Buying patterns may also change, particularly the rate at which vehicles are replaced, and this may introduce major change in manufacturing techniques. It would also create a number of changes economically, and to predominant risk groups.

As long as vehicles are replaced at short intervals, the major labour component will be occupied in manufacture. This has accelerated because new vehicle technology results in maintenance free components which are replaced as complete units. As this technology has become progressively more sophisticated, it has put pressure on vehicle servicing enterprises which have had to invest larger sums in personnel training and in automated test equipment. This favours the larger enterprise and reduces the number of small service enterprises. It also has a considerable impact on second users of vehicles who previously further reduced their motoring costs by servicing their vehicle themselves. Where police services have found high fault rates in vehicles which they have inspected, an important contributory factor has been poor, or non existent, servicing. A factor in this has been the rising cost of repairs and the need to use specially equipped facilities. This has a number of risk implications which will increase if buying patterns lead to predominantly private purchase, at least of light vehicles, and the working life with a first user extends. Social and economic factors have started this process which may be further complicated by the use of new long life materials.

When motor vehicles came to be constructed largely of steel, the life of the vehicle was limited primarily by the rate of corrosion. This factor set the pattern for designed life of mechanical components. At the end of the vehicle's life, it was practical to crush and melt down the vehicle for its metal value. Some risks were generated because the recovery process encouraged scrap merchants to strip off mechanical components and sell them for reuse. As the less affluent end of the market was the main customer base, this could easily lead to dangerously worn components being used by people who did not have the skill to judge quality and suitability. If vehicle manufacture moves to long life components, such as reinforced plastics for body construction, the whole market will begin to change. Longer prime service life will lead to reduced production rates. Long term pollution risks may be generated because recovery of materials may be much more difficult at the end of the vehicle's life. The second user market may collapse, and there are signs that this has already happened in some countries. What may happen is that vehicles are exported to poorer nations at the end of their prime life period. It could also lead to an increase in the use of suspect components to replace worn units. This already happens in the highly controlled aviation industry, where poor quality cloned

147

components and items recovered from crashed aircraft are sold through dishonest dealers.

Historically, vehicles have been divided into two broad groups, commercial vehicles and private vehicles. Commercial vehicles have been utilitarian, sometimes in the extreme. Most private vehicles are used to some extent for business purposes, including commuting, and some are largely used for business purposes, but they are designed with greater levels of comfort to make them attractive both to company buyers and private individuals. Although private vehicles may be less likely to carry high value items, they are often better protected than commercial vehicles which may carry very high value loads. The focus of vehicle design on family and business use resulted in the classic saloon car predominating and being designed to carry four to five people on surfaced roads. Company buyers prove reluctant to accept alternative configurations, and social attitudes to status make private individuals reluctant to use a vehicle which looked even slightly like a light commercial vehicle. That has begun to change and many multi purpose vehicles are designed on the lines of the light commercial van, some being commercial vehicles with redesigned interiors. Clubs and schools have also purchased personnel carriers, designed in a similar manner, to reduce the need to hire coaches. The consequence of these changes in buying patterns is that drivers, who have always been used to saloon cars with low centres of gravity and modest carrying capacity, are now driving larger, heavier vehicles, with high centres of gravity, and capable of carrying much larger loads and numbers of people. This introduces new risks. Handling characteristics are different and there is often no luggage compartment in which to place valuable items out of sight of thieves. Locks and other security devices may not be as effective as those on private cars, and passenger safety may be at a lower level. There is a potential for overloading which combines with these other factors to create a higher risk, increasing further if the vehicle has an all-terrain capability with higher centre of gravity, and general purpose tyres to cater for off road driving.

Where an enterprise is allowing, or depending on, employees providing their own vehicles, there is an increasing likelihood that the chosen vehicle will be a multi purpose vehicle. Where an enterprise provides company cars, they will be under increasing pressure from drivers to include multi purpose vehicles in the range of choice. This means that risk and personnel policies must be adapted to ensure adequate training and risk reduction. Where the business community is status conscious, it may be that multi purpose vehicles do not project the appropriate image to suppliers and customers and the consequential risks of this must be addressed.

As transport patterns change, the use of short term hire vehicles has increased and can introduce unpredicted risk. Hiring a vehicle at an airport, or rail station, is attractive for many business travellers because it retains the flexibility of self drive transport at the destination area, but offers the benefits of public transport for the bulk of the travel distance. Unfortunately it does also introduce limitations and risks.

The first risk is that the vehicle has not been adequately serviced or repaired. Selecting a known hire company does not necessarily reduce this risk adequately. Even a major international company is only as good as their local people and very often the turnover of hirers at busy airports can mean that someone forgets to do something. It is also possible that a previous hirer has damaged the vehicle, in a way which is not obvious during routine refuelling and cleaning work, and neglected to inform the owners. The second risk, which has a higher probability, is that the hirer will be driving an unfamiliar vehicle, on unfamiliar roads, in a country which has different regulations and sign posting. A surprising number of hirers carry out the most rudimentary checks before passing the keys over to the hirer. Provided he can produce a credit card and a driving license, no real checks are carried out. No one ensures that he is familiar with the controls, local driving regulations, or geography. The driver may receive the keys and a card which identifies the pick up point. If he is very lucky, he may even receive a small scale road map. At airports, the driver would then use the shuttle bus to get to the car park where he would have to search for the vehicle he has hired, possibly having to walk some distance, during which time he is very vulnerable to attack by thieves who can lurk in anonymous areas like airport car parks, and where passers by will not be keen to help a fellow traveller under attack. In some countries, rental cars carry distinctive license plates, and most carry advertising marks for the hire company. This can mark the vehicle for attack because thieves know that the driver is probably a stranger, tired, in unfamiliar surroundings, and vulnerable.

Having found the car, the driver only wants to drive off as quickly as possible to his hotel, or to a meeting. It may be his first visit to a country which drives on the opposite side of the road to his home country. Therefore, even the driving position will be different and the controls may be very different. A traveller, tired after a long flight and still adjusting to an alien time zone, is likely to get into the vehicle and drive off, hoping to work out the controls as he goes. Attention divided across a number of activities, and an inadequate road map, means that there is a considerable risk of getting lost, or breaking local driving laws, through ignorance. It is surprising that some vehicle hire companies take such poor care of their customers and increase their own risks as a result.

# 9 Information risks

Information Technology has come to mean systems which are computer-based, but this is only part of the range of Information Technology systems employed by every enterprise. Although computer based systems are a relatively recent innovation, every enterprise employs other systems based on technology which dates back thousands of years. Written correspondence still accounts for a major percentage of business communication and, whilst an increasing percentage is prepared on electronic machines, many small enterprises still depend largely on hand written documents, and letters written on typewriters, rather than on word processors. Where documents are produced electronically, and then printed out, important information is frequently added by hand in the form of margin comments and footnotes.

Telephone communication is also heavily used but, unlike the written note, is rarely recorded for future use. As a result, the typical pattern of business communication is to speak by telephone, and then confirm the details of the conversation by letter. For many years, the alternative was telegraph and telex communication but these forms of communications failed to achieve the dominant position of telephone and letter communication. A major reason for this was that they were less convenient systems, requiring trained operators, and combined several of the disadvantages of the alternative communications systems without combining many of the advantages. Like a letter, telegraphic and telex messages produced a visible record which could be stored, but it carried no firm proof of authorship and was limited in style and presentation. Although transmission from machine to machine was much faster than a letter, the overall transmission time could even be longer if timed from the sender arriving at a telegraph office, writing out a telegraph/telex form, the operator indexing the information and sending it, to the message then appearing on the desk of the addressee. Against this, most telephone calls are direct and immediate.

The telefax machine has come to largely replace both the telegraph and the telex machine, but does not necessarily compete with the letter, or the telephone call. Often, it complements both, because it requires a hard copy document. Typical business practice is to make a telephone call, write a letter, transmit a copy by telefax, and also post the letter. This can result in some verbal communication which is not recorded in any way, an electronic computer file of the letter on a word processor, a copy of the printout of the letter with a telefax transmission printout, and a letter, received by the addressee, which may also appear as a printed copy in the sender's correspondence files. In some cases, the word processor will have a telefax card and therefore transmit electronically from the word processor file, but a hard copy will probably still be printed for record purposes. The demand for filing space actually increases, although action in response to the communication may be speeded.

An increasing trend is to communicate by electronic mail. The technology has been available for many years and its initial adoption has been much slower than expected, partly because few people understood the operation of computers and the equipment was costly. As computer technology has reduced in cost, and become more freely available, the popularity of electronic mail has increased. The ability to include sound and images has also extended the value of electronic mail and the main barrier became the low availability, and high cost, of communications carriers. As these issues have been addressed, the use of electronic mail has greatly increased. In the process, it has replaced some voice and letter correspondence and will eventually replace the telefax machine as the use of document scanners becomes more widespread. It may be that electronic mail will eventually replace letter post and most conventional telephone communications. Most probably, the next few years will see the convergence of systems into a common local machine through which all communication will flow. That requires higher levels of equipment reliability as a single system becomes the sole method of communications.

A typical enterprise will therefore use a variety of communications technologies to send and receive information which is processed in various ways and stored in various forms. In the future, technology will become available to support two way multi media communication for every user, whether they are at a fixed location, such as an office, or are mobile. Current trends indicate that this is entirely possible, but it will produce so many new options that further unforeseen change may take place and create a very different environment. What will not change is the fundamental reason for communication and, with it, fundamental risk.

As computer-based systems have proliferated, it has come to be accepted that information has value. This is not entirely true. Information, as such, has no value unless it can become knowledge and be applied to some profitable purpose. As electronic communication becomes richer, and volumes increase, the information carried may actually become less valuable because it becomes harder to identify useful information, especially in the enterprise. The situation is very similar to a crowded room where a large number of people are all talking on different subjects. The room is filled with information, but each person is trying to concentrate on conversation with those people in their immediate group. The background noise makes it difficult sometimes to hear what is being said and concentration falters when a familiar name is heard from some other more distant conversation. The result is that very little information, from the vast amount potentially available, is of use and even this has a reduced value because it has been corrupted by the noise around. Therefore the primary risk in information transfer and availability is that it fails to convey knowledge which can be reliably applied to a necessary process.

In a simple society, communication is more limited and focused. For thousands of years, humans were able to rely on their natural communications abilities in sight, sound, scent and touch. Information was stored in the mind to be readily available and immediate. The disadvantage was that information tended to die with the person and misunderstandings could occur. Writing developed as a method of storing information beyond the life of any individual, and to provide a record which could be agreed at the time to reduce the potential for dispute. In addition, the written word provided a means of long range communication for complex information. The nature of writing, together with the normal method of use, identified the writer with reasonable reliability and the skill was confined to a relatively small group of people. As human knowledge was built in recorded written form, it helped to accelerate the growth and distribution of knowledge, but the records were fragile. Periodically, large sections of knowledge were wiped out by war, or by natural disaster. The accumulated wisdom of generations was lost for all time when the Great Library of Alexandria was destroyed by fire. Much of the knowledge built up by ancient civilizations died with them, at least until such time as it was unlocked through archaeological study. Even in this fragile environment, information was turned into knowledge and developed a value. It might have been a positive value, or a negative value. Some information was deliberately suppressed, or tightly controlled, and this need to control increased as literacy became more widespread.

By the Nineteenth Century, with the industrial revolution well underway, the volume of information was growing rapidly and control of the information, and therefore knowledge, developed a financial value. The situation had become very different from that in earlier societies. When iron was first produced, it gave advantage in war and peace to those people who knew the secret of its manufacture, and the knowledge of smithing might be handed down from generation to generation, but what maintained the secrecy was that there were no written records. As demand exceeded supply, the knowledge was passed to more and more people until it became common knowledge, but the fact that it was part of a craft culture meant that the techniques and technology were used differently in different ways by each family of smiths. This changed in two ways with the industrial revolution.

The first significant difference was that complex processes and technologies were recorded as drawings and written documents. Someone who had basic skills could remove a competitor's technical advantage by obtaining copies of the records. The second significant change was that the industrial revolution brought scientific principles to play and introduced the concept of repeatability. Where the craftsman had employed skill and creativity to produce each item in a slightly different form, industrialization introduced the ability to produce vast qualities of identical items at great speed. The knowledge of the manufacturing techniques, and the method of assembling assorted components into complex machines, became very valuable.

The sheer explosion of volume also introduced change. Where, only a few generations before, a craftsman would produce during his lifetime only a few thousand items, each item a little better than the one before, or certainly different, the industrialist produced tens of thousands per day, each to the same specification. This created a need for administrators to manage the documentation and the finances, and salesmen to find new markets. The complexity of products increased and this created a security dilemma, introducing quality control risks. The craftsman would generally manage a complete process to produce a final product, but the growing industrial corporations also had to produce items which others integrated into a final product. Many items of equipment, such as steam boilers, were potentially dangerous and these potential dangers increased as industrialists learned what we might now call value engineering. This technique aimed to reduce materials and processes to the lowest values practical. In craft manufacture, many products were over engineered because the craftsman had no basic formula to work to, but industrial processes depended heavily on an ability to work to a tight specification in the interests of cost cutting which became ever more necessary as the volume increased and the materials assumed a higher proportion of total production cost, creating the need for three broad classes of information.

Every manufacturer had developed proprietary knowledge which became a closely guarded secret. At the same time, the enterprise had a need to transfer information to others. A factory producing boilers for locomotives might consider that the full design and specification included information which had to remain a secret, but needed to purchase many components from other enterprises. Each boiler might require thousands of nuts and bolts. Every sub-contractor needed a detailed specification to ensure that the nuts and bolts would fit correctly and so that they could provide additional matching items at any time in the future. The manufacturer of the boilers therefore had to pass this information to his suppliers, but might require them to treat the information in confidence and protect it as though it was their own secret. There would also be the need to publish information in the form of sales literature, which might be freely available to anyone. In the early Nineteenth Century this was relatively simple because documents and drawings were produced first by hand. Making a copy was a potentially lengthy exercise and printed material was produced from carefully selected, or specially produced, documents.

Risks increased with the availability of cameras and has increased as copying technology has both improved and become more widespread. Today, copies can be made rapidly and easily in the form of film, plain paper copying, and electronic form. Sound can be recorded on tape and on computer storage media. Electronic transmission means that any copied information can be instantly transmitted around the world and legislation has failed to keep pace with the rapid development of new storage, copying and transmission technologies. Risk has increased rapidly as a result, but many modern technologies have failed to take this into consideration.

Any information is potentially subject to risk of attack, and at risk from human error and machine failures. Attack is still a low potential risk for most enterprises, but human errors and machine faults potentially affect every enterprise. To adequately reduce these risks, it is necessary to know where the information came from; who has been able to handle it; if the information has become corrupted; if the machines which have processed, stored, copied and transmitted it were working correctly at all times, and; where it has been circulated. To have real value, this audit information has to relate to the sensitivity of the information. Every person who has a valid need to enter, access, or modify information must not suffer any unnecessary restriction, or delay. The integrity of the information must be understood, and there must be an adequate assurance which relates to the nature of the information sensitivity.

The first task in risk reduction is to produce a system for classifying information. Governments have long employed a formal approach to data classification. Most data is rated as *Unclassified*, but this does not mean that

155

it is freely available to anyone. Most classified data is rated as *Restricted* or *Confidential* and these are the lowest levels of classification. A series of classification levels extend above and usually include progressively lower percentages of the total information held and used by government departments. A review system is employed to reclassify, or declassify, information so that information is not unnecessarily restricted, but is adequately protected. However, the system does not solely depend on classification levels. Each person is cleared to access specific information on a *need to know* basis. Therefore, a government employee, or contractor, may be cleared to access information up to and including *Secret*, but is not authorized to access any government information within these classifications, only specific information which relates to his essential activities. The system of classification and authorization has worked very well for hundreds of years, but is potentially placed at risk by new electronic technologies.

When government classification systems were introduced, they only had to deal with documents, drawings, charts and verbal communication. The cellular nature of government departments made it relatively simple to operate classification systems under the control of the senior officer involved in the activity. Therefore the person at the top of a particular tree structure was able to know everything within his operational area and decide what information was passed to subordinates. Each subordinate might be free to decide how much information to pass to those below him. Any information passing back up the tree was available to the person who contributed the information and those in the reporting line directly above him. At each layer, information from several sources was aggregated and passed upwards. As this was a manual process, it was easy to control and the source was personally known. Therefore the integrity of the data could be judged with reasonable reliability. The tree structure, and the discretionary powers granted, provided control of availability. Assurance was provided by personal knowledge of the people involved, and any techniques employed to restrict access.

From early in the history of writing, techniques have been employed to protect written information. Seals were used both to authenticate documents, and to make it more difficult for an unauthorized person to open the document without leaving an indication of the attack. Codes, ciphers and invisible inks were used to add further protection when the contents of the document were highly sensitive. All of these techniques could be subverted by a determined attacker, but they reduced risk. Merchants, priests and government officials all used the techniques to some extent and the commercial use of data protection was often more common than government use, where armed messengers and escorts were considered the most effective protection.

The data volumes created by the industrial revolution made it much more difficult to employ the ancient techniques. It was no longer possible to rely on the intimacy of a small group of people and correspondence had to be exchanged with a growing number of people, both inside and outside the enterprise. A partial solution was the introduction of government mail systems, where the government undertook to ensure speedy and assured delivery and collection of letters and packages. Careful selection and supervision of employees and the enactment of legislation provided reasonable risk assurance for the majority of postal needs. Reliability increased as customers became confident and made ever greater use of government controlled postal services. Speed of transmission was considered important, together with the security of documents in post. As new forms of transport have come into use, the speed of posting has continued to improve and the vast majority of all packets arrive within the time promised by the postal services, with a seamless transmission for international mail through a number of different national postal services and at an agreed scale of charges. This process may start to reverse as electronic mail systems begin to take business from the traditional postal services and it becomes progressively more difficult to economically operate postal systems.

In spite of the changes taking place, hard copy documents will continue to be an important part of private, commercial and government communications for some years. Some locations will not be served reliably by electronic mail for some time to come and it is possible that we may return to a system, not unlike the Nineteenth Century telegraph system, where a correspondent in a remote area will either have to travel to a centre which provides an electronic mail service, or uses some form of local postal service to send a letter to the centre. At the centre, the letter will be scanned into the electronic system and either sent direct to the addressee, or to the nearest electronic mail centre where the message will be printed out and delivered by local postal service.

Whatever form communication of data takes, the first task in risk reduction is to ensure that there is a system in operation which recognizes sensitivity levels and manages the authorizations for access. Every enterprise generates and handles information which covers a range of sensitivity. The degree of classification will vary and an enterprise will only have control over the activities within its organization. The way in which access authorization is organized will differ from one organization to another. If we look first at hard copy documents, the possible processes are easier to understand and control.

When a letter is produced, the writer is able to decide how and where the information is transmitted. To produce the letter, he may need to refer to files. In a commercial organization, the writer may have direct control over, and responsibility for, his own files. In this case, he can store them in a locked facility and may also be able to lock the room in which the files are stored. If he is the only key holder, he will be able to lock both the filing cabinets and the room when he leaves. While he is in the room, he may unlock the filing cabinet which holds particular documents and relock after removing a specific file. Therefore, he is physically in possession of any document which is out of the cabinet. To reduce the risk of forgetting to lock a filing cabinet, he can have a label which has *Locked* printed on one side and *Unlocked* printed on the other. Every time he unlocks a cabinet, he then turns the label to display the status, turning it back again when he has relocked the cabinet. If he writes the letter himself, and produces any necessary copies, he has full production control. He can also determine the circulation list and may be able to deliver the letter personally to the addressee. In this case he has full control over all documentation up to the point where he hands it over to the addressee. Provided that he has agreed with the addressee how the information may be treated, he also has reasonable control indirectly over the information once it has left his hand. Very few enterprises, outside certain government agencies, take this formal approach to handling documentation. The reason most frequently given is that it is too time consuming. This is not entirely accurate because once the system is put in place, and rapidly becomes an automatic habit, it adds very little time overhead to the process of communication.

The security overhead may be reduced by classification. The writer may decide that only a small part of his personal filing system contains information which needs protection and, therefore, the bulk of information at his disposal does not require protection, so that there is no risk management overhead. He will continually be adding material to the protected files, but some material may cease to be sensitive and could be refiled in open storage. Provided that he manages his storage system correctly, a given level of assurance can be maintained. The integrity level of the data is known, and maximum availability is possible at each level. If every person he corresponds with maintains the same system, the protection level for every item of data is known.

Certain government departments use a system of this type rigorously, to the point where communication is only permitted between people who agree to operate the same system of classification. This requires a policing authority to set default levels for all information and to audit the operation to ensure that there are no security breaches. Some level of discretion has to be allowed at a local level, but usually the consequence is that data will generally be protected at a higher level than is strictly required to provide a safety margin. This can result in operational restrictions, such as requiring an authorized person to carry out functions which might otherwise be delegated to a subordinate, and authorizations are generally assigned to a job function rather than an individual. Each job holder is then subject to a set of security rules as long as he holds the job and when he moves on he passes all files and keys to his successor. He may also be required to agree not to divulge any information gained in the job without limit of time. Although it is possible to enforce this type of system in a government environment, it is much more difficult to enforce in the commercial world because there is less control over employees and legal protection is much weaker. A government department can arrange for imprisonment of individuals in the event of a suspected security breach, but a commercial enterprise may have to rely on civil action which is slow, and any damage will probably have been done before the court acts. It is also likely that a commercial enterprise will not define personnel roles as clearly and strictly as some government departments.

In the example of the letter writer, most commercial organizations will accept some remarkably informal practices. The writer may not have physical control over his files and may routinely delegate tasks to colleagues. Information may therefore be freely available within a department. This may not present any particular problems, provided that every document is signed by the person who created it, or signed by a supervisor. If everyone, who handles the file containing the letter, signs the file in and out of the filing cabinet, it is possible to prove integrity levels. It is also possible to measure the progress of the information, if every copy made of the letter is registered, together with the circulation addresses. Very few enterprises take and enforce this system, and therefore have no real knowledge of availability, or integrity, and cannot rely on the assurance level. The larger the number of people who have access to any document, the greater the risks.

A major risk is created by the availability of photocopy machines which are usually available to anybody in the building and require little skill to operate. This can result in a large number of unauthorized copies being made very quickly and distributed to unauthorized, or even unidentified, recipients. It is not unusual for lax procedures to result in originals being left in the machine, to found by someone who should not have access to the information contained. This does not have to happen because control procedures can be introduced which do not significantly impede authorized use. When checks are introduced, it is common to find that a large number of unauthorized copies have been made of private documents and enterprise documents, which represents a financial loss to the enterprise resulting from the cost of each copy, and may also result in other losses consequential from the unauthorized distribution of enterprise data. Similar risks relate to the use of telefax machines and can only be dealt with by auditing systems and controlled availability.

Most written communication which leaves a department is carried by an internal post system, and then a public post system, before entering an internal postal system at the addressee's site, creating the risks of interception and loss. The potential for these risks generates a further risk, because an addressee may claim not to have received a letter although it has been successfully delivered. Where the safe receipt of a document is considered important, public postal services and private commercial couriers offer a system for recording and insuring any packet entrusted to them for safe delivery. The weakness of this service is that very few enterprises employ a matching service before and after the packet has passed through the courier. Maintenance of a postal record book is very easy to introduce and removes this risk because the movement of the document can be recorded from production, at least to the point where it arrives at the addressee's site. Even where a document does not have particular confidentiality implications, the introduction of such a system is still very worthwhile because the loss and delay of mail costs enterprises a significant amount of money through wasted manpower and loss of revenue.

Telephone communication generates a number of risks. The major risk is that there is usually no record of any conversation. Technology is available to record every telephone conversation. If the system is engaged manually, it is probable that essential information is not recorded, because the system has not been engaged at the right time. Where the system is automatic, it records large volumes of information which has no record value and locating valuable records can be very difficult and time consuming. As with video records from site surveillance systems, telephone tapes are often reused regularly and this both reduces record quality, and can result in essential records being over written before their value is appreciated.

There is no easy answer, but there are techniques which reduce the risk. It is certainly better to automatically record every conversation because that removes the risk of essential information going unrecorded. This will inevitably produce a large number of tapes which must be indexed and stored to maintain the value of the information contained. The cost of recording equipment and tapes is not high. Simple low cost equipment is available for the smallest enterprises and may be part of a telephone answering system. In the simplest environment, it may be necessary to keep a manual log of telephones calls in, and out. This makes it much easier to locate a particular tape at a later date and then find the specific conversation. As telephone systems become more intelligent, the need for a manual log reduces. Many telephone bills are now itemized by the phone company and this means that a small enterprise could identify the dates and times when calls were made to particular numbers. Larger enterprises are likely to have a telephone system on their site which logs every call made by every extension, even for internal calls. Equally, more sophisticated recording equipment will date and time stamp every record and, if the system is computer based, it will have retrieval tools to improve later searches, allowing records to be searched for conversations between specified telephone numbers, or to find all records made during a given period.

For most enterprises, the greatest risks are abuse of the telephone system by employees. When all telephone connections were made manually through operators, a level of control could be introduced, and users were much more careful about the way they used the telephone. When automatic electro mechanical phone systems and direct private lines became common, use of the telephone changed. Many enterprises found that the cost of metered calls rose alarmingly, but had little control over the situation. The only effective system of control was to deny particular extensions access to external lines, but this frequently placed undesirable restrictions on the specific phones and did nothing to control internal use. As telephone systems have become more intelligent, these problems can be solved. It is now possible to maintain an audit file which records how every extension is used, and it is becoming possible to identify the source of incoming calls. At the same time, the use of any particular extension can be finely controlled so that each user can be issued with an identity code. This grants every authorized user access from any extension and enables the audit system to record the person making the call, and not just the extension being used. When this system is linked to automatic voice recording equipment, it becomes possible to define which types of conversation, by which individuals, the recording system should record and potentially reduces the amount of recorded information to the minimum level required. Availability of the system for valid use can actually be increased and risks more accurately reduced.

The automation of telephone dialling will produce some financial risks which are much more difficult to quantify. The fact that a particular facility is technically possible does not necessarily mean that it is desirable. Manual telephone exchanges did have a number of benefits. The operators were skilled and had the ability to make connections efficiently. They were also relatively low cost labour. The improvement in speed of dialling for the caller is not great when moving to an automated exchange. Regular and frequent users will develop similar skills to those of switchboard operators, but most users will be slower and there is likely to be a need to significantly increase the number of telephone directories held by the enterprise. High speed dialling does not necessarily improve the speed of connection because the person being called may be unavailable, or slow to answer. This delay costs time, and therefore money. A switchboard operator can make the call and then call the initiator back when the connection has been successfully made to the required person. The amount of time this saves the caller is considerable and if the caller is paid substantially more than an operator, the savings will become significant. It is still possible to use similar techniques with an automatic exchange, but there will be inadequate resources available for more than a very small number of people to do this. The reason is that an enterprise will reduce the number of operators employed when they move to an automated exchange. Resource will probably be further reduced by giving the smaller number of operators additional duties, even to the point where they are no longer able to provide an efficient service to incoming callers. The lack of resource has been addressed generally by further automation. Most automatic exchanges now accept direct dialling for incoming calls. This then creates a new problem because, once a caller is given a direct dial identity to use, the incoming call will often be routing to a number which is not manned. Technology has been employed to deal with this situation. Automatic rerouting of a call may be employed so that the call is diverted to an alternate number. It is not unusual in some enterprises for the call to be rerouted to several successive numbers without anyone answering it. To avoid that inconvenience, electronic exchanges may employ voice mail and recorded voice assistance. In theory, these techniques make for an efficient use of the telephone system, but they may in fact be introducing some major risks. The service to callers is very poor and can generate considerable frustration. It will also greatly increase the cost of communication for the caller who is being charged while the automated system runs through its list of options, often very slowly. For the caller, a delay of one minute can seem more like an hour and high levels of frustration are created. This can result in a caller doing business with another organization which handles calls in a fast and friendly manner, or for someone with a complaint to feel even more aggrieved. In both cases, this may lead to a significant financial loss for the enterprise providing such poor communications service.

In producing a risk management policy, it will be necessary to establish a system for the classification of data and the method for granting access rights to authorized users. Although government departments may have a formal system of classification, it will not necessarily extend to cover all necessary levels of confidentiality, and most commercial enterprises will have no existing system. In the case of government departments, at least 80% of all data will be *Unclassified*, although particular departments may have their own system of dividing *Unclassified* data into a number of sensitivity levels. The main difficulty is that any methods which do exist may not extend outside the particular enterprise. The only description which does have some common international acceptance is *Commercial in Confidence*. Beyond that, data sensitivity may be addressed through specific *Confidentiality Agreements*. The great weakness of this approach is that confidentiality is required to the level which the participants would normally treat their own sensitive data. As the signatories may have no formal approach internally to data sensitivity and protection, the agreement is open to interpretation and debate. By the time it moves to debate, the damage may already have been done. As business is increasingly international in nature, there is the added complication that each country has different legislation, and terms in use in different countries may mean different things. Before any enterprise can hope to agree on data protection with business partners, it is necessary to implement an internal system which can be described, where necessary, to other enterprises to form a common understanding of how data risks are reduced and managed. In time, these issues will have to be addressed by national and international legislation and agreement, but at present inadequate legislation exists and, what does exist, addresses hard copy documents better than electronic systems.

In deciding how to authorize access rights to personnel, the enterprise must understand what each person actually does. That may seem obvious, but most enterprises do not actually understand the real structures within their organization. Many government departments do have a very formal definition of duties which is rigid and rigorously enforced. That may be both practical and necessary. Government departments do move personnel through a series of tours of duty and there may be a specific period, such as two years, after which each person is moved to a new job, probably at a different location. For this system to work reliably, it is essential to define duties accurately and ensure that each employee remains within the confines of the job definition. This level of rigid control is possible because governments generally are resistant to change and have not been subject to the influence of market forces. Commercial enterprises however must respond to many changes and tend to under employ so that each worker has to accept extra duties, which may not be formally defined anywhere, because there is no one else to perform them. The result of this is that patterns are constantly under uncharted change.

Most commercial enterprises draw up organization charts which look very similar to those produced by government departments. The resulting tree chart shows one person at the top of the tree with a number of departmental heads reporting to him. Each departmental head is then responsible for layers of employees below. In a government enterprise, the reporting structure will normally follow the tree chart so that an employee at the bottom of one tree will communicate with people in neighbouring trees only by observing the chain of command. This can mean that a message has to pass upwards to the top of the tree, before then passing back down through the neighbouring branches. The nature of public accountability in government encourages strict adherence to this system, even if it may introduce unacceptable delays in communication and introduce the risk that communication may be blocked at some point on its way up, or down, a tree. Unlike commercial enterprises, where personnel names are used, government tree charts usually list job functions rather than people's names. The intention is good because it allows job functions to be recorded, rather than personalities which will change, and caters for the fact that personnel are being rotated to new jobs all the time. Where it introduces risk, an individual sends and receives letters, and not a job function. Two job holders can start a line of correspondence just before they move to their new posts. Their successors do not fully understand the original motivation but do not wish to admit this. As a result, an unnecessary line of correspondence can be continued over successions of post holders to no beneficial purpose. As this unnecessary correspondence continues, the circulation list continues to increase and the generation of unnecessary documentation is fearsome. Most commercial enterprises would be unable to survive in their markets if they were restrained in this manner. This is a natural result of governments being driven by mandates and commercial enterprises being driven by markets. Further risks are introduced because commercial enterprises publish tree charts, but do not adhere to them.

The main risk of producing a structural chart, which does not match the reality, is that no one can be sure what the situation is and a number of false assumptions will be made. This does not mean that an enterprise cannot produce accurate charts, or that it has to follow a rigid structure which will not support the achievement of the primary objective. The enterprise and risk policies will produce charts which could be expressed as tree charts working down from the primary objective at the top. If that is the only way of expressing the policies, they will not work because each branch and twig has to work interactively with its neighbours. The company organizational chart has to recognize this need. For example, the receptionist/telephonist has to have some knowledge of most of the aspects of the enterprise to be able to function reliably. No caller is going to happily speak with a series of people sequentially and work slowly up or down a tree chart to the person who can answer the question. Unfortunately, very many enterprises expect a caller to do just that and the worst offenders are usually government departments, where a caller may waste valuable time, while his call is transferred to yet another voice, which will only pass him on yet again. The enterprise which starts out ahead of its competitors is the one which employs a happy knowledgeable telephonist who deals efficiently with every incoming call. It is surprising how few enterprises there are which have this advantage. Most frequently, a harassed telephonist attempts to work with insufficient information and callers are given the impression, probably accurate, that the enterprise does not know what it is there to achieve.

What may happen is that employees try their best to deal with the mess in the interests of getting the job done. This well intentioned action can be counter productive. Frustration will build up and maintaining a constant work force will become difficult, so exerting more pressure on the remaining workers and raising frustration levels, or encouraging total apathy. Further risk can also be introduced. If the published lines of communication are not followed, problems can arise which cannot be traced back and corrected. Many of these problems may be the direct result of a well intentioned employee doing something he is not qualified to do, or someone not realizing what work has already been done. The solution is to identify the real work groups and ensure that they have access to the information they need.

In a commercial enterprise, there may be a series of departments which have primary responsibility for accounts, sales, engineering etc. Although these departments are formal structures with someone responsible for their operation, works groups will be formed which cut across the structures. Usually, these work groups are informal. A customer who is chasing the delivery of a product is likely to contact the salesman, who then has to chase delivery which may involve contact with accounts, production, or dispatch. The customer will not wish to wait while memos gracefully flow up and down the tree structures, or want to spend his valuable time speaking with a succession of people. By the same token, there is great potential for risk. The salesman could obtain inaccurate information from someone, who is unauthorized to provide it, and pass that information to the customer in good faith, resulting in confusion and broken promises which turn an urgent matter into total dissatisfaction. Alternatively, the unofficial workgroups may function remarkably well normally and conceal an organizational problem which has serious consequences later.

Taking a commercial situation, a salesman is tasked with achieving a set of targets and searches for business. If a potential customer is currently in financial dispute, there may be little benefit in attempting to obtain further business until the problems have been resolved. In many enterprises, an accounts department might not think to appraise the salesman of the situation. If production delays are extending delivery times, the salesman may be unaware of this and make promises on delivery which cannot be met. Failure to notify production of a pending large order may result in insufficient stocks to meet it. If the salesman neglects to inform the research department of changing market needs, there may not be suitable products available when they are needed. Any system which allows this information to flow informally can face major risks. It is therefore necessary to provide a management system which can identify what is happening, and impose some structure on information flows, but is sufficiently flexible that it can allow for unusual and urgent situations. That system will need to adapt to changing circumstances and may require reorganization of departments, or the relocation of personnel.

In a small enterprise, with simple manual systems, the internal flow of information is straight forward and the enterprise adapts almost instinctively to change. As the enterprise grows, more sophisticated systems are installed so that the management of communication and change becomes more challenging. The great potential of computer based systems for improved efficiency and reduced risk is often turned into reduced efficiency and increased risk through misapplication. The two most common reasons for this are that either the enterprise attempts to fit the system, or the system is designed to meet theoretical requirements which do not recognize the reality of the enterprise and its requirements. If an error exists in a small manual system, it is more likely to be noticed, and be much easier to correct. If an error is built into a computer-based system, it can go unnoticed and unchecked, creating further risk until such time as the system fails spectacularly.

In recent years there has been a move towards the adoption of uniform quality management standards by mandating an independent assessment and registration agency. As a result national, and international, standards have been adopted, such as the ISO 9000 system. The motives behind this process have been well intentioned, but the result has not always been satisfactory. These standards have received considerable contributions from academia, governments and very large organizations, all of whom are used to bureaucratic management systems and large scale operations. Unfortunately, these standards are now being forced on smaller enterprises, introducing increased costs, without necessarily introducing any positive benefits. The main reason for this is that the people who drafted the systems did not understand how small enterprises operate, particularly in their organization and level of communication of information internally.

When electronic computers first became available in the 1940s, they were large complex machines, which were still in an experimental state. The hardware was available in early production form, but there was no suite of programmes ready for use. Each computer was specially built for each customer and programmes were developed to meet specific requirements to the extent permitted by the technology. In reality, technical limitations required the user to adapt to fit the machine The main application of the new machines was the automated processing of numerical information and this was handled in batches, a far cry from typical computer based systems today. As the technology was new, there were no established principles for design, construction, installation or operation. There was also no readily available work force. All data had to be gathered from existing hard copy records, and indexed onto punched cards, so that the contribution made by the early computer was to process large volumes of numeric data very quickly, and to print report documents, such as payroll slips and financial analysis reports. The first natural customers were banks, research centres, major corporations and the military, anyone one who wanted to automatically process numeric data. The high cost of early computers also confined the market to large organizations.

The first computers essentially performed relatively simple routine tasks and were set up to run one task at a time. This was not a problem for accounting systems because invoices and payrolls are traditionally paid in set cycles of, usually, thirty days. As the data preparation took place away from the computer, punch cards could be produced as source documents became available, and any cards which were not completed by the deadline missed that processing run and had to be included in the next. This batch processing of punch cards, which were produced off-line from the computer and unchecked, allowed people to blame the computer for any error. The old business excuse that *the cheque is in the mail* was joined by *the computer's gone wrong again,* or *sorry but it missed the computer run.*

During the early years, computers reduced the man power needed to perform routine tasks and produced analysis reports which had previously been difficult, or impossible, to produce. Against this, the computer was inflexible and unintelligent. It processed any data fed to it very rapidly. It did not mind what the data was because it was meaningless to the machine. Therefore, the first risk of computing has been that a computer could produce vast amounts of total garbage if the input data was rubbish. The second risk was that the people had to serve the machine and a late payment became a thirty day bad debt, just because the payment was a day late, or someone failed to make up the punch card, recording receipt of money, and get it to the computer on time. The huge volume of data was too much to check and commerce moved from an environment where the person sending out an invoice made every effort to check documents before they were mailed, to an environment where error checking was not possible and the addressee was relied upon to spot any error. This attitude developed because the enterprise producing the invoices was mailing millions, but each addressee was receiving only one. That sounds logical, but of course the recipient is actually receiving millions of invoices from millions of creditors

167

and therefore has an even greater quality management problem. The other fatal weakness of the position was that the system was handling, in effect, money. If the workforce failed to receive a bonus or an overtime payment, because the computer had not processed the data, there were a lot of unhappy workers. Customers would also become unhappy if they received threatening letters demanding a payment which had already been made. The only people who were very happy, apart from the computer vendors, were those enterprises which had received invoices, or who had not received an invoice on time.

The most unfortunate aspect of early computing was that it was introduced into enterprises which were most vulnerable to the dehumanizing elements of automation. Every large enterprise is inevitably more remote and unfriendly than a very small enterprise where workers are close together and close to their customers. The large enterprise also tends to attract more than its fair share of mean minded people who delight in hiding their inadequacies behind the power of the corporation. It may well be that people like this will not survive in a small enterprise where supervision may be less obvious, but actually be more detailed and constant. More probably, a worker in a small enterprise is more exposed to public gaze and may not have the opportunity to display the behaviour which has made *bureaucracy* a term of abuse. Machines provide depth to excuses because they cannot be questioned, and the mystery surrounding early computing added to this.

Computer operations teams compounded many of these problems by developing as a new empire with its own language. The technical nature of early machines demanded special conditions, where temperature, humidity and dust had to be carefully controlled. They had a high rate of power consumption, and the use of punched paper tape and cards produced a considerable amount of paper dust. Early mainframe computers had to be housed in large buildings, often constructed specifically to house the machine. Physical security kept the uninitiated away from the machine and some facilities required computer workers to wear white overalls and hats, giving more the appearance of a hospital operating theatre. The building was typically divided into three areas; a data preparation area, where paper tape and cards were punch encoded; an input/output area, which housed the punch tape and card readers/writers and the line printers, and; the holy of holies, the machine hall, housing the cabinets of equipment which made up the computer itself. In some major corporations, the mainframe computer took on almost the aura of a shrine tended by a priesthood. Senior officers of the corporations took visitors to see the machine hall and stand in awe of the computer and the wealth of the corporation which paid for it. That exposed another early computer risk, failing to regard the machine as a common production tool to support a process.

Early computers enjoyed a level of security by obscurity and rarity. The very small available work force was eagerly sought by employers and paid well. Not only were there very few computers, but each manufacturer produced a very different design, so that skilled operators needed retraining if they moved to a site with a machine from a different manufacturer. There was often great reluctance to employ someone who had been trained on a different machine. The result was that the computer industry fragmented in groups around each manufacturer. The potential for attack was therefore reduced because few skilled people were available, machines were costly and large, and the method of operation made it almost impossible to find any profitable way of attacking a machine. The only computers which might be at serious risk were those employed on military and intelligence duties, where the potential enemy would be able to justify expending significant resources to penetrate the system. Even here, the nature of early machines meant that they could be reliably protected with concentric defences in depth within the military site.

Computer risks have grown as the technology has become cheaper, faster, smaller, portable and communicating. The first main risk development occurred with the introduction of Remote Job Entry, RJE, machines which could be connected to a Front End Processor and, through that, into the central processing system of a mainframe computer. Once the computer suite was connected to a telephone circuit, the physical security at the site was potentially subverted. This was not quite the major risk it may seem, because communications protocols were constantly changing and largely confined to specific manufacturers equipment, so that risk probability was reduced somewhat. For most sites, risk was very low and the simple solution for the higher risk sites was to deny RJE connections. The next escalation of risk came with the development of departmental and business computers.

A typical mainframe computer would be under the management of an Electronic Data Processing Manager. He would have his own team of systems analysts and operators, whose first loyalty was to the EDP department. Operators were generally drawn from the traditional administrative functions of typing and filing. Systems analysts were mainly drawn from the Organization & Methods department and the Accounts department. Whenever another department wanted the computer to produce information, they had to go to the EDP Manager and plead for his agreement. The EDP Manager was in a very strong position because he had full control over the computer and could therefore demand whatever budget he wanted, and take as long as was convenient to him, to produce the necessary code to obtain the required information. Over a period of time, EDP departments became well staffed and a law unto themselves. They drew most of the most experienced and able people from the O&M department and began to dictate changes in the structure of the enterprise to suit their department and its machine. This began to cause considerable resentment inside some large corporations. Smaller corporations had been acquiring computer facilities by renting a service from a computer bureau, which owned a mainframe computer. In some cases, large corporations had offered bureau services to smaller companies to use spare mainframe capacity. A whole range of supporting specialist services had also grown up, including the Data Preparation Bureau, to feed this new industry. Unfortunately, friction caused by arrogant EDP managers and high computing costs began to force some rethinking about the whole basis of the computing industry. Another factor which was causing concern amongst users was the lack of control they had over the whole process. The use of various levels of people to handle data transport, preparation, processing and printout introduced time delays, deadlines and increased the risk of unnoticed human error at each manual stage. There were also work groups which required real time and virtual computers and could not use batch processing mainframe computers.

The answer to these concerns and needs was the development of the business computer and the departmental computer. Business computers could be relatively small, low cost, and suitable for use in normal office conditions, frequently being developments of earlier accounting machines. Departmental computers could be powerful medium priced machines, which were closer to mainframes in design and requirement.

Business computers were usually purchased by sales, technical and finance departments, not by EDP departments. This introduced many differences, the chief being that the machine was regarded as just another tool. It was expected to work reliably with minimum attention and not require highly skilled personnel to operate it. Most machines of this type looked like typewriters, or accounting machines, and they pioneered many of the niches which were later exploited by Micro Computers and Personal Computers. In particular, they pioneered applications packages because the new customers did not want to wait two years for programmes to be written and tested before the machine could be used. This meant that computer programmes were written for an average customer and might be slightly modified to appear to have been designed for a specific customer. The business computer also introduced word processing and began the revolution of document production.

Departmental computers were generally much more powerful machines and were bought typically by EDP departments, research and scientific users. Unlike mainframes, they had the ability to run interactively as virtual, and even real time, machines for their terminal population. They also made very much more use of data communications, both dedicated rented circuits, and dial access through public switched telephone networks. Progressively, they began to replace business computers and even to compete directly with mainframe computers. They were more vulnerable to risk than mainframes, because users were connected directly to the processor and could call up any service provided by the system. These services were largely provided through the use of applications packages which contained little specialist code. The result of these changes was that the system could be attacked by users, people attacking through the communications links, and attacks through the software applications packages. Although attacks did take place, the main threat came from human error and system failures.

Early mainframe computers were closely tailored, as far as technology permitted, to the customers requirements. Software development was often lengthy and, if a problem was discovered, it was usually more cost effective to change procedures to work around the fault. Very careful monitoring of conditions, and high levels of preventive maintenance, did much to produce high reliability levels, and many sites were equipped with standby power systems which would enable the computer to function for days without mains power. If the machine suffered a major failure, the worst situation would normally be that the punched paper data input had to be reloaded when the computer was working again. Departmental computers were a very different proposition, being expected to work in normal office conditions off a standard mains power supply. They were also subject to very different economic calculations. A mainframe computer would cost many millions to purchase but a departmental computer would cost tens of thousands. To provide the same level of preventive maintenance, as that expected for a mainframe computer, could come close to equalling the total purchase price for one year's cover. Customers were used to much lower proportional costs and therefore maintenance was reduced to produce a profitable cost at about 20% of the computer value each year. That figure has steadily reduced, and with it the level of service provided. The risk of hardware failure therefore increased because maintenance cover was reduced and lower quality accommodation was provided. Further risk was introduced by many users who tried to avoid using the highly paid computer professionals employed by EDS departments. In many cases, bitter rivalry developed between departmental users and EDS departments. There was often bitter rivalry between EDS Departments and Communications Managers. Communications already existed as a specialist duty in most major companies, long before computers arrived, and covered telephone, paging and telex facilities, sometimes extending to cover alarm systems. Data Communications developed after computers were introduced, and most corporations placed responsibility for data communications with the telecommunications manager, rather than with the EDP manager.

The next point of major change was the development of personal computers and widespread use of local and wide area communications networks. Computing had moved down to the cost of items purchased by most departments and were designed to be used with little training. Relatively low cost and simple operation made computing available directly to individuals who would previously have had to depend on EDP departments to procure equipment, or provide services. The explosion of computerization led to EDP departments loosing control of computing in many enterprises as PCs came to be regarded as tools in much the same way as pocket calculators and typewriters. Much of the early growth was in word processing, but users soon realized that their machines were capable of a much wider range of services. Enterprises which had previously been unable to justify the cost of buying their own computers found that this was no longer the case. Computer bureau suffered because smaller enterprises found that they could enjoy reduced costs, better and more flexible service, and direct control through buying their own equipment. In less than ten years, the early Personal Computer has developed with progressively smaller, more powerful, lower cost, easier to use machines being purchased for home, educational and business use. Where early PCs either operated as stand-alone machines performing a limited range of roles, the modern machine is multi functional and capable of international communications. Performance levels exceed those of the earlier departmental computers and, in some respects, are greater even than hugely expensive mainframe computers.

As PCs have developed in capability and been purchased in huge quantities, they have dramatically changed the risk structures of enterprises. In particular, they have made possible global computing communities which extend across millions of enterprises and individuals. They have provided an environment which accelerates the rate of change, reducing development cycles to the point where every enterprise has to struggle to keep pace with change, and which greatly exceeds the ability of legislatures to recognize the implications of new technologies. This creates levels of risk and opportunity which have never before been experienced by man, a true revolution more significant than the industrial revolution and probably equal to the revolution which resulted from the development of speech communication. The suddenness of the revolution has meant that many accepted values and structures are now deficient and unable to control conditions. Where it probably took several millions of years for man to evolve noises into speech, and several thousand years to evolve manufacture from craft to industry, the computer has developed over a few decades.

The first risk in computing remains *garbage in, garbage out*, but is now closely followed by the risk of unsupported dependence. Automation is adopted more to reduce costs, and labour costs in particular, than to increase production, or to improve quality. Early computers operated alongside older technologies and most data was duplicated in hard copy form. It was often true that manpower levels remained unchanged, or even increased. As a result, a massive computer failure was inconvenient rather than fatal. That is no longer true, with most enterprises becoming heavily dependent on their computer systems. This dependence is increasing and it is virtually impossible for some activities to continue in the event of a computer failure. The general reliability of computer systems has encouraged a belief that they will not fail and it is always an unpleasant surprise when a computer fails to do what is expected. What is even more unexpected is that the computer will make a mistake because we have been conditioned to believe that any error is human error. Even more dangerously, most failures go undetected.

The risk most often associated with information technology is *hacking*. This is certainly a threat and many attacks by hackers may go unnoticed, so that whatever figure is claimed for the number of attacks, it may only represent a small percentage of the total number of incidents. The hacker makes a good news story because it is so very difficult to put an accurate figure on the number of hackers, the number of attacks perpetrated, or the reason for hacking. The best horror story is the one which cannot be cross checked. Hackers also have a folk cult image which some people identify strongly with, particularly, *the individual against the giant corporations and the establishment*. This has led to the development of a new snobbery. While *hacking* has come to mean someone who is doing something illegal, or irresponsible, to electronic information, *hackers* have developed their own family of names for different forms of anti-social informational behaviour. This is somewhat like the distinction between misdemeanour and crime. The reality of hacking is somewhat different.

The majority of suspected hacking attempts turn out to be accidents rather than deliberate actions. There are at least four categories of hacker and that influences the likely targets. A large number of hackers, probably the majority, are computer enthusiasts who are exploring the cyberworld. They are curious rather than malicious, but that does not mean that they will not cause damage unintentionally. However, their general threat level is relatively low and they will be deterred by low level security measures. Rather like most ramblers out for a day in the country, they will go anywhere that they can easily get to and may climb a fence, or open a gate, but will respond to a notice which indicates a private area, barbed wire fences and locked gates, and not enter the area.

The next category, numerically small, includes people who want to feel important and superior and are often very inadequate as human beings. Their numbers are much smaller than the casual explorers, but they are much more determined. What they seek is a famous target. Being able to claim that they have hacked into the email box of an important person gives them status amongst their fellow hackers. A claim to have broken into a military computer wins maximum points because many assume that the hacker is a heart beat from launching a nuclear strike. The fact that he has broken into an unprotected system, carrying unimportant information which is already public knowledge, does not detract from his reputation. This hacker is most likely to target information systems owned by very visible enterprises and is therefore unlikely to waste time hacking into a small computer owned by a small obscure enterprise. It is also likely that this type of hacker will not deliberately cause damage and may have developed sufficient skill to avoid causing accidental damage. However, he does need to leave his mark in some way to prove that he was able to penetrate the system, and this may be destructive.

The third group of hackers are the cybervandals. They are a much smaller group. Essentially, a disruptive social element which probably corresponds with other vandalistic elements, such as graffiti artists, as a percentage of population. That means that although they are very visible, there are very few of them. They are more likely to attack establishment figures, but can be entirely random in target selection. When they do strike, they can be very destructive. Their close cousins are the virus authors who have plagued the personal computer population and caused considerable financial damage. The main difference between malicious hackers and people who write and circulate computer viruses is that the virus writer is dependent largely on the illegal acts of others. Although some viruses are maliciously inserted by disaffected employees, the majority circulate on illegal pirated copies of computer software and any user who only uses software from a known legitimate source is unlikely to suffer virus attacks. Several early viruses began life as a copyright protection system. Computer software was available for trial and contained aggressive code which was automatically enabled after a particular date. The software author provided an antidote to anyone who had decided to keep and use the software, and had paid a license fee. Early virus writers could therefore claim some justification for their activities, but cybervandals cannot produce any valid justification for their actions.

The forth group are the professional hackers. These may be security consultants hired to identify points of weakness in a system for the owner. Their service may be very valuable, although not without risk. The selection of this type of consultant should be undertaken with great care, because the

174

enterprise has to trust that the consultant will only test a system and not exploit weaknesses which he finds. Professional hackers are still a very small group and so far they have grown slowly. The hostile professional can create significant damage. He will only devote his efforts to those targets which will bring him profit. That may include government agencies, highly competitive market leaders, or political groups. In many cases, the professional will be employed by a government security service, but the number of professionals who concentrate on industrial espionage and sabotage is now growing rapidly.

In addition to these risks, there is the risk of equipment theft. Computers may have reduced in price, but they still contain high value components, some having a greater value by weight than diamonds. Theft of components is a growing problem. Memory chips are particularly vulnerable and some large organizations have discovered on a Monday morning that their systems will not function because thieves have removed all the memory chips during the weekend.

The great challenge presented by these hostile groups is that their attacks are difficult to predict and, whatever their motives and objectives, they can cause substantial damage to those systems which they penetrate. The fact that attacks are a low statistical probability means that many legitimate computer users are reluctant to take adequate measures to protect themselves, and there is a high cost attached to providing effective protection against the range of attacks which are possible. When an attack does occur, it is often unnoticed at the time and discovery is more likely to be accidental. When an attack is detected, the victim is likely to wish to conceal the incident for a number of reasons. This may be true of a range of risks, but the percentage of victims reporting an attack is lower than the percentage of victims reporting attacks such as rape and robbery.

In general terms, less than 60% of common crimes are reported to the police and through the news media. Of those crimes reported, less than 50% result in successful prosecution. The figures are worst for some types of crime than others. A crime, such as rape, can be difficult to prosecute because only one victim and one attacker are involved and it can therefore be difficult to obtain corroborating evidence. The nature of the crime also discourages many victims from reporting the incident. Other crimes such as burglary may have a higher reporting rate and a lower conviction rate because one person may commit a number of burglaries in a random pattern, victims may compound the crimes through fraudulent insurance claims, and overstretched police forces may concentrate resources on what they consider more serious crimes with a higher probability of successful conviction.

Computer crime most closely equates with rape. A victim may suffer more if the incident becomes public because his reputation suffers. There is a similar assumption that the victim in some way was responsible for encouraging the crime, and there may be no prominent visible injury after the attack. Damage to the victim's reputation may cost more in financial terms than the attack itself. Achieving a successful prosecution can be even more difficult than in the case of a rape. Corroborating evidence can be equally elusive and this is made more difficult because legislation lags far behind technological development, so that it will be difficult to find a law which can effectively cover the nature of the crime.

What makes information technology especially difficult to protect is the nature of the technology and the history of its development. Any industry which grows rapidly from humble beginnings is bound to contain a number of risks which have been ignored in the race to develop products and market them. No industry has grown as rapidly as electronic information technology and it is perhaps understandable that it contains the high risks which exist. That does not of course make those risks any less painful for victims, but it can make it much more difficult to reduce the risks. This frequently becomes the user's excuse for not attempting the solution. The belief in many cases is that risk reduction is unacceptably costly, ineffective, and rapidly made obsolete. There is evidence that vendors have encouraged this belief because they fear that a drive towards risk reduction will reduce their profit margins, weaken their market position, because new companies could build new low risk systems more easily than mature products could be modified, unsettle markets which have been susceptible to vendor influence to keep buying more, and restrict creative design. However, there is much which a user can do to reduce risk with existing technology, reduce the true cost of risk reduction, and influence vendors to take customer interests more seriously.

What makes this so important is the way in which information affects every aspect of human activity. As long as manual methods were employed, it was possible to control the transfer of information and know who had learned what. That made the enterprise compartmentalization possible, and necessary. Electronic information systems have turned the whole environment upside down. On the one side, uncontrolled data aggregation and distribution produces a wide range of threats for which there is little legal protection, and few systems with technical protection. On the other side, intelligent communications systems offer the prospect of providing tightly integrated risk management solutions which can provide very high assurance and integrity, but also provide amazingly high levels of availability because they can operate seamlessly and invisibly. This in turn introduces new risks and challenges, because it provides the means to track

176

the activities of any individual in fine detail in a way which has never before been possible. Information gathered in this way could be used to reduce civil liberty and can be misused by unauthorized people to the injury of the individual. The situation is made worse by the fact that much information has very low integrity levels. The exchange of information, usually for a fee, between finance organizations has led to individuals and enterprises being denied credit because of inaccurate data. The data exchange industry, which is expanding rapidly, demonstrates little concern for data integrity, and makes little effort to verify original data entry. Existing data protection regulations have little power to address these issues and have virtually no control over much of the information which is not stored electronically.

In the short term, every information user can take a number of steps to reduce risk. These steps have to start at the basic level of information in the many forms in which it appears in the enterprise. Having decided how to classify data and authorize access, there are many technical solutions which can be applied to the systems in use, especially the electronic systems. In the medium and long term we all need to encourage legislatures to enact sensible and effective laws to control the potential abuses of information.

# 10 Risk management for information systems

The first stage of reducing information risk is to define the way in which the sensitivity of data is to be classified and to establish the method of granting access rights to personnel. Many organizations omit this stage of risk reduction, or operate an informal, or ill defined, methodology. Unless a formalized methodology is put in place, any technological measures will fail to achieve a reliable performance, either by over protecting, or by under protecting. Every enterprise will handle data which has a range of sensitivities and most data will not need to be available to everyone. The purpose of classification and authorization should not be seen as a method of restriction, but as a method of providing maximum availability at an acceptable risk level and, for that reason, no two enterprises will share identical policies, because the data protection methodologies must relate to the enterprise policy and that will be unique. Even divisions of the same enterprise may have different requirements and this may apply to different sites within an enterprise, or division, and within work groups on the same site.

The older communications systems were much easier to deal with than the modern electronic systems, mainly because there was less overlap. Increasingly, electronic systems are linked together at different points and these links may operate automatically. For example, a commercial organization has to operate around the customers to succeed. The contact between the customer and the enterprise is through the sales personnel and that is the primary communications link. Many enterprises then define the sales function as the sales people who visit the customer, or operate a telesales phone desk. In fact, the sales personnel are much more diverse. Any person who answers a telephone, visits a customer site, or meets a customer under any other circumstances, is a salesman for the enterprise. Therefore, the sales personnel will include sales representatives, estimators, telephonists, delivery drivers, engineers, accounts personnel and, potentially, every other employee. A sale is much easier to lose than to win, and a sale is not complete until the customer has paid his bill. As a result, many enterprises lose a vast number of opportunities at each of the stages of a sale and a primary cause of this risk is failure in availability and management of information.

Before the advent of electronic communications and data systems, the written word and the spoken word were the primary methods of communication and data handling. This included the financial aspects of business including money, because money is a form of data communication, particularly since financial tokens ceased to have a direct intrinsic value. A bank note, or a cheque, has no practical value in its own right, even coinage may no longer have a direct value which matches the face value of the coin, and it can therefore be argued that all money is simply another form of the written word.

Spoken and written words are easier to control than their electronic equivalents. Unaided, the spoken word has a very short range and it is usually easy to protect. The communicators establish their identities, and a conversation takes place. Interception by unauthorized persons can be prevented by volume control and selection of a location where it can be seen that no one else is in hearing range. To improve integrity, any conversation can be documented in words and drawings. Until recently, the methods of protecting documents and speech were mature and effective. Electronic eaves-dropping has introduced new challenges. Devices, such as rifle microphones, are now able to pick up speech at much longer ranges to allow the listeners to hide from view. They are effective not only in picking up conversations in an open public place, but can also pick up conversations taking place inside a building. Other *bugging* devices, such as miniature radio microphones, can be hidden close to where a conversation will take place and enable the eaves dropper to monitor the conversation out of sight, and at a safe distance. More recently, miniature CCTV cameras have become available for covert surveillance. As the effective range of these covert devices increases, providing effective counter measures becomes more difficult, but the general principles which have applied for centuries still provide the basis for protection. Selection of a venue which can be searched before the meeting, and guarded during it, is a risk reduction measure as old as man. Careful selection of a location and observation can be augmented by technology to introduce background noise on frequencies which impair monitoring systems, and sound barriers can be employed to block the transmission of sound. Electronic communication and data handling presents different problems.

The major obstruction to risk reduction comes from the nature of modern communications systems. The two parties to a conversation, in voice, or in digital form, can only see the equipment which they directly use. In the case of telephone communication, the instruments and cabling to the junction box can be seen and inspected for evidence of tampering. This supervision can extend to a switch board and cabling within a site, but the system of cables and switch gear which provide the connection between two sites cannot be supervised by the communicators. Although most covert monitoring of telephones may still require entry to the site, and the fitting of monitoring equipment to selected telephones, it is possible to insert a monitor device somewhere in the routing system outside the site and this reduces the risk to the eaves-dropper. In early telephone systems, the complete path of a connection could be traced from one instrument to another, because a continuous cable connection was made from one instrument to another, the junctions being made by a telephonist plugging one cable to another at each stage of the link. The low voltages used in telephony made it difficult to insert monitoring equipment into the circuit without affecting the quality of the line. Three developments have changed this situation.

Modern miniature monitoring equipment is very reliable and compact. It also requires little power and its amplifiers may be powered by its own miniature battery. This means that bugging a line may introduce no noticeable difference, or introduce any unusual sounds, to alert the communicators. The small size also makes it very much easier to conceal the device. The quality of monitoring is also very good and compares well with the audio quality of the conversation in both directions, as heard by the authorized communicators. The circuits connecting the communicators are no longer physical lengths of cable. Switch gear is now a computerized system which employs virtual circuits. Between switching centres, the transmission medium may also be in the form of virtual connections and the whole process of setting up a call is automated. Between two sites, the speech will travel as packets of data and may be carried in stages by a wide range of media, including microwave radio links and, in some cases, may travel by radio to a geostationary satellite in Earth orbit and back down to earth again.

This opens up a range of new options to anyone who wishes to listen in on someone's conversation and record the information. Government agencies routinely employ technology to do just that. Until relatively recently, the only barrier to widespread monitoring of this type was the difficulty of sifting interesting conversations out from the mass of traffic. Computers have largely solved this problem because they can search millions of conversations very quickly and pick out any which contain key words. The selected conversations can then be further screened automatically to produce a manageable number which can be listened to by a person who is better suited to final judgement than a machine. Some conversations may be stored and indexed for future use, when subsequent conversations provide the detail to make the first information useful. The monitoring techniques can be applied to any type of data transmitted over public telephone links and are not confined to speech traffic. As the cost of monitoring equipment drops, and computer performance increases, this activity comes within the reach of non government organizations and even individuals. The covert nature of the activity also means that it is impossible to know how widespread it is, who is doing it, and what they will do with the information. Probably the use is not widespread because there are often other easier ways to get the information.

The easiest way to obtain information, plant misinformation, and corrupt data, is to find someone inside the enterprise who is prepared to do the work. There is widespread abuse of police criminal intelligence computers and similar public service record systems. For very small sums of money, public employees will access computer records for people who are not authorized to access the information. In some cases, an employee is bribed to remove, or alter, information. Similar abuses occur in banking systems and it is difficult to know how widespread the abuse is.

A number of factors assist the computer criminal. Many of the lost lucrative targets will keep an detected breach of their security secret because they are afraid of the commercial and/or political implications of the attack, if it becomes public knowledge. Banks have long maintained that their electronic systems are totally secure and never suffer technical failures. Anyone who has suffered a *phantom* withdrawal of funds from their account via an Automated Teller Machine will know that banks deny the possibility of a withdrawal by anyone other than the account holder. It is only recently that public pressure has forced the banking industry to admit that errors and thefts are possible. Someone fraudulently withdrawing small sums from a number of accounts on a regular basis can amass a large sum of money with little risk of detection. This new *white collar* crime is costing billions of pounds every year and the new criminals are ordinary pleasant people who go unnoticed in a crowd, but steal much larger sums than the traditional bank raiders ever could. They are usually detected by accident and there have been many occasions when a financial institution has agreed not to press charges, and to allow the criminal to keep the proceeds of his crime, on condition that they show how the crime was committed.

A high percentage of *white collar* computer crime starts by accident. A worker finds a flaw in the system design and becomes curious, gradually becoming bolder and more deliberate and drifting into crime. This is easy

182

because many information systems are poorly designed and assembled from components which have been poorly designed and tested. The industry has been driven to ever faster development of new functionality in a race between vendors to exploit a rapidly growing market. A great many products are launched onto the market before development has really been completed, and customers have come to accept this as a way of doing business, generating considerable risk.

If an enterprise has developed an enterprise policy and fixed administrative procedures, it is possible to decide what technology is required to support the operation. A framework will exist, against which every step can be measured. This will allow any information system to be built to serve a specific purpose and offer functionality needed to support the achievement of tasks and objectives. What often happens is that a system which generally appears to address functional requirements is selected on the basis of the lowest price. Usually, security is not a standard offering and is loosely bolted on if the customer asks for some protection. In a great many cases, a technical solution is chosen without identifying that there is a risk which needs to be reduced in this way.

Today, most systems have a password and login code which is set for every user and this provides the first basic level of security in a simple system which is contained within the enterprise premises. Very few users even engage this very basic protection fully and reliably. When a new work station is connected, the system administrator assigns a default password and login which the user should change to his own choice of code. Many people do not complete this step. Once a user has selected a password and login, the password should be remembered and never written down, or passed to anyone else. If it becomes necessary, in an emergency, to give someone the password to allow them to login to the user's account, the password should be changed immediately afterwards. This rarely happens. Most users select a password which is a family name, or a personally significant date, because they think that they will not forget it and then, to make sure, they write it on a piece of paper which is often fixed to a desk drawer. This is rather like a home owner who hides a spare key outside his house in the happy belief that a burglar will not think to look for it. Unfortunately professional thieves and amateurs have little difficulty in finding the hidden key and this is also true of computer passwords. The only way to make a password system effective is to select a word, or number, which does not have any direct personal significance, never write it down anywhere, never give it to someone else, and change it frequently at random intervals.

A more effective system is to employ an electronic identity card which may also require a personal password and will prompt the user to change passwords after a certain number of logins, or a period of time. This will make it much more difficult for someone to gain unauthorized access, but it will also ensure that every action is identified to the operator. This requires an audit trail system which not every information system has. The audit trail is crucial to risk management in computer systems and also important for operational management. The person who manages the system should be able to see how well the system is working and performing its task. This is only possible if the system has a method of recording all events and active users. It should also have the ability to alert the manager if an unusual event has occurred. Every *secure* computerized system will have these facilities, but alarms may only be produced if an event has occurred which could be an attack of some sort. Many conditions can occur in any information system which present a threat other than an attack. If the system is working slowly, or erratically, this may be the result of a fault which has not yet developed to the point where it will stop the system, or corrupt all the data. All too often, systems develop a fault which is really a symptom of another fault but the lack of adequate alarming and auditing can result in the obvious fault being addressed without any correction of the underlying fault. It may then be that the *correction* has made the real fault even more dangerous. This may in turn open a threat window for an attacker and is often the starting point for fraud.

As this may all seem very obvious, perhaps we should ask why many systems have these weaknesses. The main reasons are ignorance and price cutting, exacerbated by rapid technological development. Early computers were built by one company which was responsible for designing hardware and software and integrating the components into a system. This produced reliable systems, but introduced delay and raised prices. It also gave the supplier a hold over his customer because the system could only be changed for a complete system from a competitor. Many customers believed, with some justification, that suppliers took advantage of the situation to offer poor customer service at high prices. As a result, large customers encouraged the development of Open Systems and Portability. The idea seemed good and certainly increased the choice of supplier and functionality at, sometimes, dramatically lower prices. Without these changes it is probable that computers would be a much less common feature of life than they are, not least because fewer people would have been able to afford systems. Computerized and computer supported communications would have developed slowly because there would have been less advantage in interconnecting the smaller number of systems. Although the market changes made computers more affordable to more people, and produced the funding to develop many new aspects of computer based technology, it also introduced heavy risk.

The rich variety of technology has often been produced by very small companies which would not have survived in the market conditions which applied before Open Systems. The lack of training capabilities has also meant that most users buy technology which they do not fully understand. Today a person could buy a Personal Computer and a selection of packaged software from a shop, take it home, and start using it without any training. In one sense that is a triumph of design, but every user only takes advantage of a small part of the functionality available and teaches himself only those routines which are most valuable. Inevitably the user makes mistakes and if the system does not do what he expects it to, he usually assumes that it is his fault. That is rather like someone buying a car and teaching himself to drive round a field. Once he ventures onto the roads, he will suffer a number of accidents and failures. Some of these may not be his fault but it would be easy to assume that all errors were driver errors, simply because most of them are. A more accurate example could be where someone bought a basic vehicle and a number of components which were designed by various manufacturers to fit that type of vehicle and not only taught himself to drive, but also taught himself to assemble the vehicle. Very few people would contemplate doing that, but it does not seem to deter them when buying computers.

The basic difficulty is that Open Systems are not an exact specification. Therefore, one manufacturer designs and builds the main hardware items with sometimes considerable freedom. Other manufacturers design and build other parts which should be compatible, and yet more enterprises write software applications which are designed to work with the hardware and with software from other vendors. This is only possible because key components are designed to a basic specification and provide a broad platform. However, some products are more fully compatible than others. The definitions are primarily at the interface level so that, if one product is designed to meet an interface definition which is shared by another product, the two should match. This is rather like publishing a specification for a towing hitch for a vehicle. The vehicle manufacturer has considerable freedom in the design of the vehicle in terms of body design, engine, suspension and other important components, provided that he has allowed for a towing hitch which matches an exact specification. The manufacturer of the trailer has equal freedom. The only other condition is that the vehicle manufacturer has to state what weight of trailer can be towed safely, and the trailer manufacturer has to advise of any known towing limitations. However, one vehicle/trailer combination will be more successful than another. This is not unlike the situation which applies to information system components, where some combinations work better than others, but the information system may have a much greater combination of components

185

and each manufacturer is constantly seeking to develop a better and/or cheaper product. Unfortunately, he will not always share important information with others and various operational conflicts can develop. This has always presented problems since the introduction of Open Systems and is much greater when some types of security system are added later.

The basic challenges of standards definition and adherence is one problem area, but it is made more difficult by the nature of industry development. Information System hardware suffers less than software but, even here, shares some common problems. In the case of hardware, the challenges stem from integration levels and change control. It may also include false interpretations of particular parts of standards and testing which ignores large areas of the Standards requirements. The higher cost equipment generally undergoes an extensive development and testing phase before it reaches the market. A relatively small number of sub suppliers are selected and each receives a tight specification. If the manufacturer aims to offer a complete hardware package, every component will have been produced and tested under strict conditions and will be known to work together. Once the product has reached the market, it is a well tested and proven machine and will have been integrated with the selected operating system. In the main UNIX market, each major manufacturer offers a complete range of components and has adapted the UNIX Operating System to match the hardware. Every applications vendor who wants to sell products to the manufacturers' customers will *port* applications software to the hardware and operating system. At any one time there could be eight, or more, different versions of UNIX and only applications software developed for a specific version will run reliably. This means that a customer is not entirely free to change supplier, although several competing companies may offer close generic products and applications can be transported from one flavour of UNIX to another, so that any applications code could be largely re-used on a different UNIX and/or UNIX compatible hardware platform. There are also operating system vendors who provide a flavour of UNIX which can be loaded to machines from several different vendors who have agreed a binary compatibility standard. Therefore, UNIX Open Systems shares some of the benefits of the proprietary system market, where the vendor took full responsibility and inhibited supplier changing by customers, but with less restriction of customer choice.

The Personal Computer industry developed differently. As a result the computer processor 'chips' come mainly from one supplier and the operating system comes mainly from another single supplier. Therefore, two key elements are essentially proprietary products. Freedom of choice comes at hardware and applications software levels, resulting in a range of prices for what may seem like basically the same type of product. Inevitably, most PC purchases are of the lowest cost products but, as with any product, there is usually a reason why one product is a much higher price than a seemingly identical product. In the case of PC hardware, this usually reflects design, testing and control in setting basic price levels and then, in turn, from likely production volumes which are expected to be less for a higher priced product. The customer often has difficulty in understanding what he is really buying because even high cost products may use the same plastic cases as the low cost alternatives so that, externally, the machines look identical. Even with the casings removed, there may not be much visible difference.

Products designed for the more discerning customer are under a firm change control system and there are usually very few alternate component suppliers who each have to submit to the change control procedures. This means that the product is much closer to something produced by one enterprise on a single site. There may also be greater use of higher specification components, but this is not necessarily so. The strict change control procedures, together with careful selection and control of suppliers can add appreciably to product costs. Suppliers taking this level of care to control the quality of their product will also make advanced information available to those companies writing software applications to run on the machine. This again adds to the cost of machine production, although it may not affect the price of applications software. When risk reduction measures are to be added, this manufacturing approach is important and, in some cases, essential to the efficient operation of the measures.

Unfortunately, most manufacturers do not operate in this way. They source components from the lowest cost supplier, depending on interface standards to ensure reliable operation with other components. A Personal Computer is a relatively simple machine to assemble, using ordinary hand tools. This, together with a large number of component suppliers, makes it possible for almost any enterprise to establish itself as a *computer manufacturer* by shopping around for sub assemblies and then bolting them together. The typical customer does not open every machine to check who manufactured which component and when. Therefore, all the enterprise needs to do is to select a plastic case and attach a brand label. From then on what goes inside the box does not matter greatly. Sub assemblies which were *end of run* surplus equipment can be bought for the lowest prices and mixed on the assembly line with items from many different manufacturers. It is possible for a customer to buy ten PCs and find that all of them contain different components, sharing only a common case design. This does not necessarily mean that a PC produced and sold in this way will not function reliably, or even that it may not provide as long a life as the highest priced machines. If a PC is purchased for a single purpose, and is used on its own, it may perform reasonably reliably. However, more complex operation increases the risk of errors and failures. As each sub-assembly has been designed and tested to an interface definition which allows considerable scope for detailed internal design, the potential for unpredictable behaviour is high. As typical PC users employ their machines as simple tools, there is little likelihood that all faults will be known and investigated. The result is that numerous small errors and failures can occur and information may not be accurate but, provided that the level of inaccuracy is small, the problems will go unnoticed, starting an error process which can build like a snowball as error gathers error. The ability of PCs to link with other PCs, and much larger machines, creates a major potential risk, the size of which is impossible to estimate.

If information, such as a spreadsheet, contains errors it is unlikely that they will be noticed because most readers will assume that the person who created the spreadsheet has carefully checked the figures. A more demanding reader may check some columns at random, and most readers will check figures which are noticeably different from the anticipated values. People who produce spreadsheets often check in the same way, but the level of checking is much less when the spreadsheet is calculated automatically by a computer. When spreadsheets had to be calculated manually, aided only by a calculator, they were not a very popular method of presenting information. Now that a calculation is performed automatically, the spreadsheet has become a popular management tool, used to lend authority to a report. The widespread use of word processing and desk top publishing has made the production of lengthy and complex documents very easy. This has led to an increase in the size of report and the inclusion of large volumes of supporting information. As the recipient does not have the time to read large complex reports, many management decisions are taken on the basis of the summary information. It is dangerously easy to adopt a habit of relying on a computer to function faultlessly when this may not be the case. If most decisions are based on information containing many small errors, the composite effect may be unpleasant. Sometimes, deliberately misleading reports are produced, taking advantage of the computer's ability to produce large volumes of data. A writer can produce summary sections to support his position and then expand the report with sheets of figures and comments to support the summaries, knowing that most readers do not have time to carefully check all the supporting information. Readers are becoming educated to expect voluminous reports and judge a report more for its size and weight, than for its content. This ignores the ancient wisdom that the best place to hide a pebble is on a stony beach. Someone who wishes to mislead can produce a positive summary and bury some unpleasant truths in the body of supporting charts and tables. This is ingenious because he can always claim that the supporting proofs included the bad news.

The use of computerized systems can be improved by training but, however well a person is trained, there is always the possibility that heavy pressure, or a lapse in attention, will result in computer generated information going unchecked. Therefore the reliable performance of equipment is an important risk management factor. Automatic selection of the most expensive equipment may be just as much an error as the automatic selection of the cheapest. A long life is not necessarily an advantage because of the speed of introduction of technology changes, and a machine designed and tested for long life will cost more to produce. Essentially, it is a question of customer competence and cost of time. If a customer is technically competent and is prepared to spend time testing equipment, it may be possible to identify low cost equipment which is entirely satisfactory. When the cost of dedicating this skill to the procurement process is measured, it may actually cost more than selecting equipment from a smaller circle of higher priced vendors where knowledge of the companies and their records provides assurance.

Applications software is a different proposition. Any mechanical component can be tested under simulated operational conditions to find out how many operations can be carried out before the item fails. Electrical and electronic components can also be tested for a number of hours of operation before a failure. Software cannot be tested in exactly the same way. When hardware and operating system have been selected and application software is written specifically to meet a unique specification, it is possible to test every component of the resulting system, including the administrative and personnel interfaces.

An enterprise policy would provide a tested picture of the tasks and processes as they applied to the achievement of the enterprise objective. If this policy was contained in an electronic system with a series of appropriate methodologies, all applications software could be produced in a largely automated way. When any changes are to be made to the policy, it will be possible to model those changes and identify what changes will be needed in each task, process, or tool. This environment is theoretically practical, but it is likely that systems with higher levels of human activity and responsibility will be employed and that automated systems will be providing assistance in sections of the programme to produce and maintain an enterprise policy. The essence of the approach is to take a carefully tailored selection of systems to support objectives achievement. This is similar to the approach in the early days of computing.

There are two differences. In the early days nothing existed and therefore every new system was to a large extent unique and pioneering. There was also little system support for the design programme. As early computers were large, costly, virtually unique, and dedicated to number processing and analysis report generation, they did not lend themselves to supporting the design of new systems in the way that modern processors can be employed. However, the production of applications software followed a methodology. For each new machine, a team of analysts investigated the requirements and then began to chart out the complex series of steps which characterize every human activity, but of which we are generally not conscious. This chart was then carefully translated into instruction steps for the machine. As a skilled and labour intensive operation, it was costly and much effort was expended in attempting to reduce cost. The result has been the Commercial Off The Shelf applications package and its ultimate development, *shrink wrapped* software.

The COTS package in its most complete form is the *shrink-wrapped* software sold for use on PCs. A range of common functions are combined into a single set of code which can be loaded into the host machine with very little requirement for skill. The typical package is demonstrated by the word processor which combines a range of functions from which any one user will choose to regularly use only a small proportion. Equally, no word processor will meet every possible requirement of every possible user. Probably 85% of what every user wants the system to do will be done by the standard package. The 15% deficit may be handled by adding commercially available products, such as additional fonts, or by working within the constraints of the basic package. Some COTS packages contain configurable features. By selecting options, the user can modify the functionality available to more closely meet his requirements. The standard package with its default settings may meet 60-70% of any individual user's requirements and the configurable features may extend the capability to achieve almost everything which the user needs. Any remaining deficit is accepted by the user, but it may be reduced further by buying a selection of packages from one vendor who has built in commands and links between these package to form an Office environment.

The alternative is the package which includes a development language and has to be modified, possibly considerably modified. The final system is not truly a COTS package because the user has had to employ his own skill to produce a working application, but this is produced within the framework of the base package. In all cases, another enterprise has produced a package without detailed knowledge of the specific requirements of any one individual user and, therefore, the system is to some degree a compromise. The benefits are in cost and time savings and the reduced need for highly specialized skills. The disadvantage is that the resulting system may contain elements which introduce risk and require the user to compromise.

The acceptance of COTS packages is in part a necessity for many enterprises and in part a result of the considerable achievement of applications developers. Every package can introduce some risk and this is most noticeable when it becomes necessary to introduce secure functionality. Any developer with skill, adequate development equipment, and an innovative approach, can produce an applications package which offers attractive features. An individual working alone, possibly at home, can develop computer software which works, and works well. If his product meets a significant need, he can expect volume orders and his product may become a leader in its field. When he produced the initial package he might not have employed any specific design methodology and some of the features of the product might never be exploited by any user. As a result, large parts of his product may not be documented in any way. This may not be a major risk initially because the creator will still remember want he has done and why he considered it necessary. As he continues to develop the product to maintain his market position, he will add new functionality and correct faults which have come to light, possibly identified by users rather than the developer. Business is becoming brisk and he limits documentation to the minimum as he strives to keep up with demand. The enterprise grows and more people are employed to develop, test and manufacture the product. As this process continues, it becomes necessary to introduce various methodologies to maintain business and product control. Much of the original product code probably continues in the latest version of the product, even though some of it may be completely redundant. The original developer may have sold his stock and moved on, or he may now be either the senior executive, or hold a figurehead position. The people who are now doing the work on the product have no knowledge of the how and why of earlier coding. The product is patched and layered so many times that early code is hidden away and no one can remember what it was originally expected to do. The original author may now have ceased to be connected with the enterprise and several generations of developers may have come and gone, so that no one can remember who was responsible for writing particular parts of the package. This may provide windows of opportunity for an attacker to slip through and it may also provide the basis for failure when a particular user tries to use the product in a particular way. Adding secure functionality can be very difficult and risky because of the fact that large parts of the coding may be an unknown quantity, but no one wishes to start with a new product because of the delay and cost.

The development of standards has always been a painful process. Vendors would prefer customers to accept their products as *standards* because this provides a commercial advantage. The vendor either establishes a monopoly, or is able to license technology to other vendors and receive royalties without having to put in much additional work. The objective of the defacto standard is to create a situation where everything else revolves around the product which is under the full and direct control of the vendor. The defacto standard has become an important part of the Information Systems industry. Once established, the standard prevents other vendors from introducing alternative approaches because the cost of development against the marketing risks does not make it a viable commercial prospect.

The industry standard is also important and usually implies some degree of co-operation between vendors. It is mainly produced to enable more effective integration of products from different vendors and may originate from a defacto standard, or become a new defacto standard. Where the defacto standard may involve customers and other vendors learning to work around the standard, an industry standard is more likely to be an interface definition. It may be a specification for a physical product such as a connector, or it may be a compatibility agreement which enables a group of hardware from different vendors to work with an operating system from one or more vendors, to run software applications from many different vendors. The risk with this type of standard is that it may not be complete and fixed. One example is cable connectors, where people will talk about an RS232 as a standard connector, when the only thing which is really standard is the number of pins/sockets and the physical shape of plugs and sockets. Particular vendors connect cables to the plugs and sockets in different ways, so that a printer can physically connect with a computer, but will not operate because the wiring inside the plugs and sockets is different. There is also additional risk for users in the early days of the *standard* development, which also applies to standards produced by international and independent bodies. There is no guarantee that the standard will survive marketing.

One example of great potential undelivered, is the 88 Open Consortium. This group of vendors was assembled around the Motorola 88000 series of processor *chips*. The group developed its own binary compatibility standard and attempted to produce an environment similar to that created around IBM *clone* Personal Computers, but with much more powerful systems using a flavour of UNIX. In the early days a long list of companies queued to join the consortium. It was a well balanced list which included many market leaders and substantial corporations. It also attracted many small and innovative enterprises, particularly software developers. From this promising start, the programme began to lose momentum and members withdrew. As result the original rich variety of products, which had been expected by users, did not appear. This means that some users who chose products from 88 Open members may never realize their expectations and this is a risk run whenever a major new product offering comes onto the market. It may fail because either customers or fellow vendors fail to support it. Alternatively, it may continue, but never deliver all that was expected. Any enterprise which decided to switch to the new product may find that their plans are severely damaged by any such market failure. It has been claimed that the way to avoid these risks is to adopt independent Open Systems Standards.

In an attempt to introduce some sanity, various organizations have attempted to produce independent open standards. In some case, the organizations have been vendor federations of some type, possibility with users included, but in many cases, the organizations have been promoted by governments and academia. The ultimate goal is to produce international standards which every vendor and user can subscribe to. Unfortunately, this is a difficult objective to achieve. Getting a small group of people to agree on a specification can be difficult and time consuming. As that group grows, it becomes increasingly difficult to reach agreement. Once several natural languages are introduced, it becomes very difficult to agree. The Information Systems industry has attempted to reduce difficulties by adopting international English as a discussion language. This is not without risk. People from English speaking countries have some advantage because international English is similar to their first language, although misunderstanding is still possible. Others, who do not have English as a first language, have a much greater potential for misunderstanding and this potential often increases as they approach fluency.

In spite of all the difficulties, remarkable progress has been made in the definition of standards. Unfortunately, it is still not good enough. There are two major weaknesses. Time is the main enemy. With major new technology developments taking place every few months, standards are inevitably out dated by the time that they are agreed. This means that many users ignore open standards because the technology does not offer the same functionality as in products which have not been constrained by the standards process. There is also the matter of approach. Open standards have tended to be driven by governments to benefit their procurement systems with a strong contribution from academia. This assumes that industry operates in the same way as government and academic organizations, which it does not.

Results can sometimes be very disappointing. The OSI work to provide a Standards based communications environment has met with success and failure. Although X.25 networks have been available for many years and governments applied pressure by demanding vendors compliance with their GOSIP flavour of protocols, the use of X.25 has been slow to grow. In contrast, the US based Internet, with its reliance on the TCP-IP protocol has enjoyed explosive growth. There are a number of factors in this growth and there are those who will argue that the alternative ISO and ISDN network environments are superior and will eventually triumph, but the reality is that the market follows success and vendors prefer to put their development investment where the commercial return is, however good or bad the technical specification.

What has slowed the progress of ISO is the time it takes to agree elements which make up a standard, against the amazing pace of development of information systems technology. Commerce tends to look for a *quick fix*, academia tends to look for proven perfection, and governments tend to look for ease of procurement. For computer manufacturers, TCP-IP was already being addressed and products were available. The data communications vendors were producing gateway products which connected between computers and X.25 networks, and therefore serious investment by hardware vendors tended to go into TCP-IP for local networking requirements. Several governments, particularly the United Kingdom and the United States of America, started to pressure industry to produce their flavours of OSI. As most production was based on development by enterprises headquartered in the United States, any real work tended to be on the US flavour of GOSIP. Once the US Government moved away from firm mandates, industry closed down what development programmes existed for US GOSIP and concentrated effort on TCP-IP. It is difficult to see where the process will eventually lead, but it demonstrates a swing back from independent standards and assessments.

The differences have been most marked in the matter of security functionality. The United States led the way with a group of documents which became known as the *Rainbow Series* because of the coloured jackets used for each book. The most famous book was the *Orange Book*, which defined the criteria for evaluation of secure information technology products. The primary objective was to put in place a system for the evaluation of secure products which could be mandated by government departments when procuring systems for their own use. In the early days, the motivation was probably broader and inclining towards the development of national Standards for computer security. However, the interests of select areas of government came to the fore and it was intended that these secure systems would provide protection against attack by hostile intelligence agencies and be related to the established systems of classification and authorization. This led to the main criteria concentration being placed on assurance. The programme has been run by the National Computer Security Centre, NCSC, which decides whether it is in the US national interest for particular products to be evaluated. Although the evaluation is free to a vendor, the cost of preparing a product for evaluation and supporting it through the evaluation process can be considerable. Other countries have also produced their own systems of evaluation, but the Orange Book has been the common basis for evaluation of secure products for the US and friendly powers.

All these government programmes have been developed on the assumption that government agencies will be the customers and that systems will be developed to meet the detailed specifications produced by government project teams. As a result, the systems neither meet the needs of other enterprises for secure products, nor match the way in which industry develops products. This has meant that secure products have been produced for small production runs and the cost has been correspondingly high, which reduces the attraction of the products to other users. Further, the basis of evaluation does not cater for the enhancement of existing popular products to incorporate secure functionality.

In the United Kingdom, the Department of Trade and Industry produced the Green Book, not to be confused with the US Green Book, or the German Green Book, in an attempt to register secure products which would be suitable for commercial users. The programme was not very successful, but influenced the joint work of the UK, Dutch, German and French Governments to produce a Harmonized Criteria for Information Technology Security. This programme has resulted in the Information Technology Secure Evaluation Criteria, ITSEC, which aimed to produce a method of evaluating products which could be used by both government and commercial enterprises. ITSEC has met with some success and encouraged the development by the United States of the Federal Criteria-Federal Information Processing Standard, FC-FIPS as a replacement for the Orange Book programme. More recently, attempts have been made to combine ITSEC and FC-FIPS as the foundation of a programme to produce an international Common Criteria. This programme includes the Governments of the United States and Canada and the European Union. Although it is to early to say how the Common Criteria will develop, it is following the traditional path of development by governments and academia with little participation by industry, and therefore runs the risk of producing a system which is described in bureaucratic language to meet the particular needs of governments. It also overlaps work by a variety of standards bodies and industrial special interests groups in the development of security technology.

Non government enterprises have therefore been poorly served by security criteria. Even if they attempt to apply products to meet their own needs, they face an additional challenge. Secure products typically follow on from the development of standard products. This means that they not only cost more, but they can be several generations behind their standard parents in functionality. Even government users are resistant to foregoing functionality which they have become accustomed to, just to introduce security.

It can be very difficult for an enterprise to deal with this situation adequately. The only way to manage risk is to build information systems which directly meet the needs of the enterprise policy. This may not be a practical proposition for most enterprises because they cannot fully employ adequately skilled personnel and there is always a shortage of suitable people who are prepared to work on a consultancy basis. In addition to this, the growing requirement to interlink systems owned by different enterprises, in an ad hoc manner, forces the use of common elements and the easiest way to do this is to purchase the same COTS applications packages. In the longer term, the answer will probably come from the creation of more detailed standards which cover both the technical detail of the product, and the method of design, manufacture and testing. This will inevitably raise costs and reduce choice, but still provide a wider choice and greater competition than would be possible by returning to proprietary systems, or relying on custom development of systems.

The real answer must be a method of testing and describing product functionality in a standard way and to assure users that any claims are well founded. That was the original intention behind all the different evaluation criteria. When the Orange Book was written, it contained much of the Mil-Std 2167A methodology, even including common verbiage. That made a great deal of sense to government procurement officers and much more fairly reflected the operational methods of vendors all those years ago. Mil-Std 2167A was a project management/quality management system, intended to assist government procurement teams to measure bids and then measure performance against contract by the vendor. It may be argued that some of the precepts of government procurement have never been achieved in reality. It is certainly true that not every government project group is effective, or even correctly staffed. Some areas are better served than others. An army intending to procure new boots has considerable experience of this operation. There are generations of designs, against which to compare any new specification. Over this long period of time, procurement officers have devised all sorts of ingenious tests to ensure that a contract will be awarded to the bidder who offer the best value against the specification. After award of contract, samples will be tested to destruction to ensure that the vendor is meeting all requirements. The cost of one pair of boots is trivial against the millions which may be ordered. Vendors can afford to fabricate prototypes for demonstration and evaluation during the procurement cycle, and it is entirely acceptable to include the cost of destructive testing of samples during the production cycle. Therefore, the procurement team are well place to produce the criteria and evaluation process, and also to devise a specification in very fine detail, even to the point of which stitching pattern should be used. This ability can also be extended to large and sophisticated items of equipment. Years of operational experience allows aircraft and ships to be procured in this way. Producing a formal military standard was therefore a logical step. Applying it to computer security may be questionable.

In the early days of computer procurement, military users were driving development in many respects. Theirs was the large budget and the need to develop a range of computer systems to guide rockets, manage radar and weapons systems, analyze vast quantities of data. Academia had similar needs and the embryo state of the industry both needed and wanted this interest. In some cases, it was a question of finding ways of applying technology which already existed, but in many other cases, it was a question of developing new technologies to meet identified operational needs. Much of the miniaturization of computer components came from a need to fit them into missiles and military aircraft, where size and weight were very important. Similar needs drove the search to reduce power requirements, reduce heat output, tolerate wider temperature ranges, and withstand shock and vibration. In this market environment, Mil-Std 2167A was appropriate and, when the security requirements came to be drawn, it was perhaps natural that it should be used as an essential base for the wording of the Orange Book. Unfortunately for security criteria, so much has changed in the years since. Even more unfortunately, the Orange Book has been used as a basis for all the criteria which have followed.

Today, the majority of information systems products are initially produced for the commercial market. The major budget reductions in government budgets, caused by changing international situations and a movement to privatize many government services, have reduced the power of governments to fund specific custom development to meet their requirements. There is also some difficulty in persuading vendors to run the huge commercial risks inherent in government procurement. The result has been that government procurement agencies have discovered COTS as a solution to the lack of funds, the reduced vendor interests in project bidding, the availability of rich ranges of functionality and the desire of government officials to have something now, which works.

Unfortunately, all this has coincided with a substantial increase in information risks and made improved levels of trust very important. Government agencies are now routinely asking for secure functionality in information systems required by military and civil departments alike. These needs are expressed in terms of one, or more, established criteria. If the procurement mandates products which have been certified under a particular criteria, there may be no bidders who can respond. This has led to a requirement for *designed to meet* products, or the requirement for certification being a desirable factor. At face value, that looks like a realistic and pragmatic approach, but it may be increasing a number of risks for all users.

When a vendor first looks at secure functionality, he regards it as just another range of functionality to be built into the product. It does not look like much of a challenge. However, when the vendor submits his secure product for evaluation, he suffers a severe culture shock. What he has now is a partial product because the criteria requires him to present his product as a piece of custom engineering, designed to meet a detailed specification produced over several years by a government project team, rather than the mature commercial product, with added functionality, which it is. The vendor cannot afford to go back and produce a completely new product and the government procurement team cannot afford to draft a detailed specification for a trusted database, or word processor. The only way forward is for the vendor to claim *designed to meet*, without continuing in evaluation, or to continue with the evaluation and use some highly creative presentations to the evaluators to postulate a product status which is not reflected in reality. Some might say that the vendor is being forced to lie through his teeth to have his product certified. Certainly, he is being very creative with the truth. One has to ask what benefit is being served in maintaining an evaluation system which requires certificates to be issued on inaccurate evaluations.

In a pure world, the criteria would be changed and nothing could be evaluated until the new criteria was in place. From a risk management perspective, the continuance of the existing criteria should be regarded more pragmatically. Risk management is, after all, not a method of creating a new totally safe world, but of reducing all risk to the lowest level which can be achieved practically against a specific justification. Therefore, a criteria against which vendors may specify their product claims is better than no criteria. A certification system is generally better than depending only on *designed to meet* claims from vendors who have a vested interest. Therefore, on balance, there is merit in maintaining the existing systems until something better can be developed.

The basic problems will remain. The time for evaluation will result in an obsolescent product. This may be a major consideration, or a minor irritation. If the only limitation is that a word processor does not have all the functionality of its untrusted brother, that may not present a major problem, because the product will still work well as a word processor and if state of the art functionality is of key importance, it may mean switching to a different vendor. That does not happen generally in the untrusted world. Most users will stay with a particular vendor and wait to up grade when he can supply the next version, even if a competitor has introduced exciting new functionality several months before. In that respect, trusted software is

198

little different, other than the functionality gap is wider and the gap will always be there, possibly growing wider over a period. Equally, there will be occasions when the trusted version has almost caught up with its untrusted stablemate. However, some trusted products can present significant problems as a result of the age of their base elements. Operating Systems will fall into this category. The problem is most acute when the operating system is designed to mount on *clone* hardware, particularly IBM PC clones. A trusted UNIX may be based on a very old untrusted UNIX operating system. The result is that the system either has to be built on some very old hardware, or additional work is carried out to ensure that the hardware components and drivers will support the trusted operating system reliably. This can be a major challenge and in some cases may result in failure. It is less of a problem where the trusted UNIX is part of the product offering of a hardware supplier. In this situation the vendor will make some provision for maintaining a working match between the trusted operating system and the hardware platform. However, the penalty may well be a much higher price. This may dictate a more pragmatic approach to evaluation status of products.

Where an enterprise has most control over risk is in the integration, training, and deployment phases of the cycle. It is possible to add a number of robust and secure elements to any system, and to avoid the elementary errors which many enterprises accept. The main danger is in not employing analysis and evaluation adequately. Very few people have developed good analytical security skills in computing and communications. Most of those who have gained security experience, learned those skills on specialized government projects where the environment has a number of differences from other enterprise environments. Therefore, the pool of labour is small and the pool of suitable labour may be even smaller. Against this, there are a number of very visible risks, such as hackers, and a number of packaged solutions which address very visible risks in limited areas of modern information systems. As a result, it is common practice in many enterprises to select a type of solution without finding out if it addresses the specific risk management needs of the enterprise. Having selected a solution without identifying the problem, implementation becomes a process of buying a particular flavour of stock solution and trying to make it work, usually with very limited success, and at a considerable expenditure of funds.

For the majority of enterprises, the major risks will largely come from inside the enterprise. This does not mean that external threats should be ignored but, by attending to internal risks, several external risks will also be reduced and, at the same time, some external risks will increase. For example, an enterprise which has valuable information may be the subject of indirect external attack because employees are bribed to get the information. If this security hole is plugged, the attacker will need to find another more direct way of breaking into the information. If the quality of the information improves, as a result of improved data integrity, its value will increase. If several groups of information can be added together, their composite value may be greatly increased. This may make the particular information source much more attractive to an attacker. One interesting factor of Criminal Intelligence Computer systems is that they often contain a great deal of very inaccurate data. Complaints about unauthorized access to these records often come because an individual suffered loss more because the information was inaccurate than because an unauthorized person gained access to sensitive personal data. In some cases, the victim is actually complaining about losses which can now be explained, as a result of identifying that inaccurate data is being circulated in an authorized manner, but this only came to light as a result of the unauthorized access.

Therefore, it can be seen that the reduction of one set of risks may ironically increase the probability of other risks. If the low level of data integrity of some systems was fully known, no self respecting hacker would waste effort forcing access. Poor management of data can result in any system becoming clogged with data which has no positive value to the owner of the system, greatly reducing the benefits of having the system in the first place. From this it could be argued that every system owner should take every possible step to make the contents of his system attractive to attackers, because that will make the contents valuable to the owner. In addressing integrity and availability issues, the assurance of the system may have to be increased.

The strict use of the AIA, Assurance, Integrity, Availability, diagram to express the relationship of the three basic elements of trust can become misleading. There is no reason why a measure introduced to increase availability cannot also increase integrity, or for that matter increase assurance. If an identity card is introduced to enable a user to open any workstation on a network, and any application running in the network, or any database contained on any part of the network, all three elements would be increased for authorized users. Every time a user logs on to a workstation, he is checked out as an authorized user before he has any form of access to the system. During the check, his authorization is checked and he can only see, or access, applications and information to which he is entitled. That produces an increase in assurance. It also increases integrity if the security profile is related to an audit trail because every action by the user, once the system has allowed him in, will be recorded so that it will be known who has accessed any information, who has changed it in any way, and what information has been copied electronically or by printing hard copy. Assurance, integrity and availability would be further improved because it would be possible to grant read only access to some users. For example, a logistics system holds information which a number of employees need to access but might not be authorized to alter. Availability may also have been increased because the authorization process may make it acceptable to link several systems together which would otherwise have had to remain separate, or to mount several groups of information on a single machine instead of distributing them across several machines. The ability to control access reliably and to audit all activities means that it is much easier to grant access rights to any individual.

Information Super Highways offer new opportunities and present new challenges. Just as the introduction of data communications within an enterprise opened new risk levels, Information Super Highways increase the potential risks because they depend on opening private enterprise systems to individuals and other enterprises outside. The main challenge is in balancing availability with assurance. If the access is designed to support electronic trading, integrity may be the primary challenge. Information Super Highways provide the data equivalent to a public telephone network but, where a telephone network connects people who can decide what information can be exchanged, these decisions have to be automated in an open data network. Where no hacker can go through a telephone network and extract information from the human brain, he can go through the ISH and empty the computer brain of private networks. The enormous attractions and benefits of rapid access to vast quantities of information and the ability for data communication directly with other enterprises can all too easily blind users to the dangers.

There is also a serious risk of an over supply of information. The Internet is a particular example of a citizens band information environment with a considerable element of folk law. The academic community has been a major beneficiary of the Internet because a path has been opened to considerable stores of information and technology completely free of charge. This is wonderful for an academic researcher and can allow a project to be completed very much faster than would otherwise be possible. It also opens information sources which would otherwise have required expenses beyond the academic research budget. The environment benefits greatly from free and easy access for people who are prepared to spend time searching for the information they need. There are the electronic communities of bulletin boards which provide a forum for debate of almost every human condition and interest. The contribution which this will make to human development will be immense. The complication is that all of the attractions to academic development require a free commune and risk management does not seem to have a high priority. Unfortunately, this level of freedom can be destroyed if risks are not managed. It is a difficult balance, made more difficult as commercial and government enterprises begin to make significant use of the Internet.

These new users have a different agenda and different needs. In particular, they want a level of robust managed risk and are not interested in the folk culture of the Internet. They are attracted by the very low cost structure, but they are prepared to spend more to ensure a satisfactory level of service. They also expect a different level of behaviour from their personnel. One area of concern is the wide range of facilities available to users. A commercial enterprise expects its staff to focus their time and effort directly to task achievement. They are not keen to have personnel roaming the Internet in the way that an academic researcher would. They also become nervous about the amount of paid company time employees may spend playing computer games, or accessing pornographic material. Therefore many enterprises will want to heavily restrict the way in which their people access the ISH. To this is added the commercial cost factors. Where an academic researcher needs to get to source material, a business user is much happier with digest information. It can prove cheaper to buy information from a commercial information researcher than to spend time accessing free information and turning it into a usable report document. Therefore freedom of access to a rich ISH environment may introduce unacceptable commercial risks.

The risk which is most frequently appreciated is of hackers and crackers gaining unauthorized access to private information systems from the Information Super Highway. Again, this appreciation is the result of news stories which often create the impression of a much wider threat than actually exists. This fear then focuses on the connection point between the ISH and the private network. The popular solution is a barrier system usually referred to as a firewall, or a bastion firewall, which acts as a valve. The system concept is easy to understand and this has done much to popularize it. However, it is a long way short of a total solution for most systems and has the unfortunate effect of reducing many of the benefits which attracted the user to connect with the ISH in the first place.

A typical implementation path is to connect first to the ISH without any protection and users become familiar with the way that the fully open system operates. Then fear of attack results in the implementation of a barrier system. When it is initially installed, it may be configured to provide an audit facility but not prevent many categories of linkage. As the system is used, the configuration is progressively changed as fear of attack increases, until many of the advantages of ISH linkage are lost. One of the reasons for this is that the audit trail will identify a number of *attacks* which are not necessarily intentional attacks, or if they are intentional, they pose little real threat to the enterprise. This can lead very easily to over reaction to risk and the simplest path is to progressively remove interconnection facilities until the ISH becomes a carrier for limited electronic mail. Even then, the ISH may be providing a very valuable benefit.

ISH systems, such as the Internet, provide a very low cost method of electronic data communication. Two private networks in different countries could be connected via the Internet for an access charge as low as £20,000 per year, but allow unlimited usage. To provide adequate capacity for current private communications, by hiring dedicated private circuits, might cost £100,000 per year and this could increase if further bandwidth was needed to meet growing data volumes. Therefore, the enterprise would be saving a considerable sum each year by using an ISH, without making or accepting calls from any other enterprise. If the enterprise had a number of enterprises which it regularly traded with, the barrier could be set to permit communication via the ISH with those enterprises. It might not be practical to use any other form of data communication. The ISH would be accessible by even very small enterprises and by individuals at very low costs. A typical access might only cost £10 per month, plus the cost of local telephone calls from a PC to the local access point. This could represent a considerably lower cost than telefax and permit a much wider range of data to be transmitted reliably. Given these simple economic benefits, the case for ISH connection is overwhelming. Placing a very restrictive barrier between a private network and the ISH would not prevent these benefits from being obtained, but it would prevent access to many other benefits. As the typical implementation path runs from unrestricted two way access, to heavily restricted access, users will complain when they find that they can no longer access some facilities which they have found useful.

Although a barrier system may cause considerable reduction in availability, it may not necessarily produce a risk solution. It will provide no protection of information as it transits the ISH. This can only be provided by techniques, such as encryption, which provide protection for each packet of information. Without this protection, an attacker could intercept data in transit, read it, alter it, or just prevent it from reaching its destination. The attacker could *spoof* the sender. *Spoofing* is a technique where an attacker assumes the identity of an authorized user and then passes messages which purport to come from the authorized user. This can cause many problems, because the recipient of the forged messages may act on their contents, believing that they have been sent by the person whose identity is being used, or erroneous data may be included in a database and damage its integrity. It might appear that spoofing is an act perpetrated primarily by some hostile person outside the enterprise. This may not be so. For example, a senior manager was forced out of his job as the result of another employee spoofing his mail. The attack was ingenious. The perpetrator wrote a mail

203

message which was addressed to another employee and purporting to come from the junior vice president. It appeared initially that this was a genuine mail note which had been accidentally copied to every employee connected to the system. The perpetrator had faithfully copied his victim's style of writing, included some views of which the victim was suspected and gave every impression of authenticity. The company president, who was one person attacked in the mail note, accepted that this was a clever fraud, but the perpetrator was never identified because the network had no means to support the investigation adequately. The junior vice president found that he could not longer do his work because of the loss of credibility he had suffered and he had no option but to resign.

The other critical weakness of the barrier system is that it provides no protection for the private systems, except in relation to the direct ISH connection point. A false sense of security can result. It is not unusual to find that the person who is responsible for managing the ISH connection, and the barrier system between the ISH and the private networks, has no control over, or knowledge of, the private network connections. An extensive private network may exist with direct private links to other networks within the enterprise, and even links to the networks of other enterprises. Within this environment, there are probably banks of modems, permanently connected to public telephone exchange lines. An attacker will probably look for these entry points, particularly if he finds that a barrier is in place at the ISH linkage point. The modems may automatically answer any incoming call and allow the caller inside the network, from where he can break into particular parts of it, or use it as a base to attack other connected facilities. Most users hope that this type of attack will be defeated by not publishing the modems' numbers but any experienced attacker will have little difficulty in finding the numbers. The only way to effectively deal with this form of attack is to protect the modems and this can be done through techniques such as encryption, access control identity systems, and by installing dial back modems.

Dial back modems are an effective and relatively low cost solution to implement and operate by preventing any incoming call from reaching the private network. They are a simple barrier system which stores the identities and telephone numbers of authorized users. When an incoming call is received, the dial back system checks the identity of the caller and the number he is expected to be calling from. It may also check to see if the authorized user is limited to access during certain times. If the identity and permitted access time is valid, the connection is broken and the dial back system calls the user back. It then checks that the identity is valid and connects the call to the private network. This has two disadvantages. The first is that every call is paid for by the owner of the dial back system which may not present any difficulty if the callers are employees who could claim the cost back anyway. The second disadvantage is that many dial in services are provided to enable workers to access the private network while they are away from their normal place of work, or from home. The dial back system stops this use because it is not able to hold all the telephone numbers which any user might call from, and would not know how to find the right number anyway. A partial solution is to require the caller to index both his normal number and the number he wants the return call to be made to. Even if communication is encrypted, it is always possible for an attacker to masquerade as an authorized user, and add insult to injury by making the victim pay the cost of the attacking call.

An alternative approach may be to equip remote employees with a cellular telephone which is capable of data transmission. The mobile telephone number can then provide a single known number to which dial-back connections can be made. It does introduce the risk of an unauthorized person gaining access to the telephone and portable computer, but this is a lower risk which can be addressed with conventional physical security, such as the remote user always being in possession of the equipment, or locking it up when that is not possible. These simple precautions can be further improved by using a mobile phone which requires the insertion of a token and the indexing of a Personal Identity Number, PIN.

The use of over restrictive IS barriers may also increase risk, particularly if they are fitted to an existing open access system and then progressively reduce accessibility. The cost of high capacity connections to the ISH requires a funding approval within the enterprise, but very low cost connections are also possible. This places ISH connection within the reach of employees without the need to seek fund approval. Any employee with a PC could purchase a low cost connection, using his PC and its modem. The same PC may have a network card and the modem only requires a normal telephone line. It is therefore possible for the employee to bypass the barrier on the main *official* ISH link and connect the private network to the ISH through his PC, so subverting the security system without anyone being aware that this breach has occurred. An attacker may then enter the private network via this back door. Ironically, the breach may have been encouraged by over zealous use of barrier restrictions at the main access point which have reduced availability to unacceptable levels for a particular employee.

The only way of preventing these dangers is to operate an enterprise wide security policy which meets the needs of the enterprise policy, and is capable of enforcement. Most of the steps necessary to achieve this are simple good housekeeping measures. Any well run enterprise should know what equipment exists, what it does, who controls it and what purpose it serves. The low cost of powerful PC equipment has often resulted in enterprises having large numbers of units which are not fully identified on the asset register and are largely uncontrolled. Where a computer centre manager was responsible for high cost mainframe computer equipment, every purchase went through a rigorous funding approval process, was physically located in a controlled location, and was operated by clearly identified staff. This meant that the equipment met a specific agreed requirement and all aspects of its operation and capabilities were known to the enterprise managers. As PC workstations dropped in price, they came to be purchased in a much less formal manner, often as replacements for what would have been a typewriter or a calculator. However, the equipment was potentially capable of much greater use. The reduction in the cost of local area networks allowed these inexpensive powerful machines to be networked in groups which often do not correspond to the organizational charts of the enterprise. A small number of PCs networked together have a considerable capability which may exceed the sum of the individual machines. Collectively, this low cost equipment may represent a sizeable investment. In larger organizations, the combined capability of existing mainframe computers and departmental mini computers may be less than the combined capability of all the PCs and PC networks, but this capacity is unknown because it is invisible to the enterprise, even though it forms a significant part of the work capability. As management of these assets is informal, they are open to a wide range of risks which they can then introduce into the rest of the enterprise and a very important part of the financial strength of the enterprise is not under any real control. Attempts to bring these resources under control, and make them and their users accountable, are frequently thwarted because users have grown accustomed to a freedom which they are loath to loose.

Getting to grips with the situation and reducing the potential risks can be fairly simple. Again, transparency of management tends to be much more effective than heavy controls. One method of introducing this necessary control with minimum resistance is to allow relative purchasing freedom, but to identify accurately every purchase which is made and relate it to the enterprise plan. If personnel are still free to select low cost equipment, there will be no encouragement for them to find creative ways around the system of procurement and there will be no risk generated because necessary equipment has been delayed by bureaucratic control. If all communications and computing equipment is identified, it is possible to calculate the total information systems capability of the enterprise and to plan for contingencies. It is also possible to identify all the links internally and the connections with the world outside. Beyond that, it is possible to introduce reasonable controls to ensure that best value is obtained from what will cumulatively be a significant investment.

Once the extent of the capability is known, co-ordinated risk reduction and management is possible. Many organizations pay for facilities which are no longer used, or are no longer appropriate. This can be a major area of waste, particularly in large organizations. The cost savings obtained from regulating assets often proves greater than the cost of introducing sound risk management policies. In the case of information systems, it will also ensure that the enterprise is not open to action for illegal and unauthorized use of software. For whatever reason, many enterprises breech the copyrights of software authors and the size of this problem is encouraging the authors to take action to reduce this loss of income. In most cases, enterprises are not aware that they are at fault because they have insufficient knowledge and control of software used. Reasonable regulation of assets can remove existing misuse and prevent further breeches. At the same time, a more effective system can be created. It is not unusual for even small enterprises to have many different applications from different sources, all addressing a common group of requirements. As many of these applications are unique, this can cause disaster and make contingency planning very difficult. A new enterprise can avoid these difficulties by making strategic decisions on the applications and standardize, but an existing enterprise will experience user resistance.

In the same way that software authors regard the compartmentalization, necessary to trusted systems design and engineering, as an infringement of their creativity, users regard software standardization as an infringement of their freedom of choice. In both cases, these attitudes have been developed because they have been allowed to develop as a result of enterprises failing to understand the rapidly developing technologies and their implications. However, this diversity constitutes a major percentage of actual information risk. Most enterprises do not even register the software in use on their sites. It would not be unusual to find an enterprise which spent considerable time, effort, and money, on acquiring applications to run on hosts and servers, but make no effort to control, or even identify, the software and clients which will connect with it. Time and money is spent on making back up tapes of data held on servers, without knowing what the data is, its relative importance, or what copies may exist on other servers and workstation clients.

When governments began to fund networks, such as the Internet, the motives were not altruistic. One strong motivation was to create a highly resilient information network which would be able to survive a nuclear war sufficiently to maintain some level of information services for the survivors. In the early days, the computers which connected to these networks were mainly departmental and mainframe computers in government installations and universities. How effective the network would have been in a post nuclear war environment is debatable because of the diverse nature of some of the software applications. However, the concept was sound and today's international networks are potentially able to survive major disasters and still maintain some level of service. This has significant implications to mankind because it potentially avoids the risks of history, where large sections of human information have been wiped out by a natural disaster or by war. In the same way, public networks provide a means for an enterprise to survive a major disaster. However, this makes it even more important to understand what systems the enterprise owns and has access to, and that again highlights the importance of some enterprise policy on software acquisition and use.

One popular wordprocessor is much like another. Each will have a different feel and unique features, but they basically do the same job. Most of them will have conversion capabilities to enable them to read other wordprocessors. However, once someone has become familiar with a particular package, he is reluctant to change. Even if the conversion facilities originally worked well with other products, after a period of time they may not work with later versions of competitive software. As a result, it is possible that large sections of an enterprise are unable to communicate reliably because of software incompatibility. This makes the case for some level of standardization much more important. There will also be the issue of trusted systems. Although untrusted software, particularly for PC workstations, is widely available at low prices, trusted software is not, and is unlikely to be for some time. Therefore, full access to corporate resources will only be possible through the use of compatible trusted clients. Various bolt on products may be applied to provide some level of risk reduction at the PC, but these products do not lend themselves well to effective corporate trusted networks because they are fairly primitive barriers which do little to provide for the needs of networked systems. The main reason for this is that they have been designed to be added to untrusted hardware and operating systems because the manufacturers of those products are not prepared to provide adequate design access to what are their proprietary products. It is therefore probable that enterprises will have to introduce a trusted infrastructure and then work through the workstation population to introduce reliable and appropriate levels of trust by replacing workstations, operating systems and software applications. Until this process has been completed, some users may not be able to access data in the same way as they have become used to doing. This may cause some disruption, but the eventual result will be a much more efficient system which reduces risk to an acceptable level and provides the maximum levels of access to those employees who really need it. In the process, the information contained in the systems will develop a high level of integrity and increase in value as a result.

Once a reasonable level of standardization has been achieved, and the enterprise knows what assets are owned, and where they are located, contingency planning becomes much easier. When the mainframe was the primary corporate computing asset, contingency planning was easy to achieve in part. All the enterprise needed was an agreement with someone who owned a similar machine and was prepared to accept punched cards for processing. For a large corporation this might not represent much disruption because punched cards might have been transported some distance to the mainframe and the distance to the alternate system was probably no greater. There was also the option of processing records manually and this was often viable because much of the processing of a transaction was already done manually with the mainframe only producing reports and bulk documents like invoices, statements and payroll slips. If the contingency was minor, such as a fire in the print room, or a power failure, there might be little disruption. The power would normally have been backed up by standby generators, so that a mains failure would not affect the mainframe for some time. If necessary, the generators could run for several days and large installations even protected themselves to the extent that there was even spare capacity in the generator room, so that a generator could be taken out of service for repairs without the generation capacity falling to critical levels. As the generators were normally powered by diesel engines, fed from a bulk diesel tank, more fuel could be delivered and the mainframe could operate almost indefinitely on local power generation.

As computers became more tolerant of their working environment, enterprises lost the habit of providing back up power systems. In part this was a result of the sales presentation, when the departmental computer vendor stressed the cost savings against a mainframe and, in particular, the substantial savings from not providing standby power and special rooms with costly environmental control systems. Since then, powerful file servers and workstations have become commodity items where few people give any thought to the potential for failures. However, every computer system requires power, and mains power failures can occur. Even small power fluctuations can result in lost work and may even damage the processor. Therefore every enterprise should consider a suitable form of power backup. It might prove desirable to install large diesel generators which have the power to take over all site functions, including lighting, heating, air-conditioning and lift motors. That level of sophistication may not be necessary, although it would provide the independence to continue operation for long periods and could be valuable if the emergency was caused by a

209

serious natural disaster. However, most enterprises will find that compact Uninterruptable Power Supply, UPS, systems will be entirely suitable. They could be large units to protect all information assets in a building, smaller units to provide protection at departmental level, or very compact units for workgroups, or individual workstations.

If an enterprise standardizes on software applications and hardware, it is always possible to replace systems and, provided that back up copies of data have been regularly made and stored elsewhere, the level of disruption should be low, even in the event of a major incident. Accommodation of staff may prove a greater challenge. Provided the site condition permits, portable buildings can be acquired until the facilities are rebuilt. Communications and power links will need to be connected and that could prove to be a problem if the disaster has not been internal to the enterprise. This may be the point where trusted use of an ISH may pay dividends. The work force could be distributed over several temporary locations outside the effected area and still function as a unit through the medium of the ISH, and that is essentially what the ISH concept was originally hoped to achieve after a nuclear war.

If an enterprise reviews its information assets in this light, it may be considered necessary to replan systems to introduce a larger number of smaller components to assist distributed operation after a disaster. Software standardization becomes essential to the plan because it is impossible to forecast which human and material resources may be affected by the disaster. One employee may prefer to use a particular wordprocessor, or spreadsheet, but he may be disabled in the disaster and a colleague then has to cover his work. Equally, it may be that the machine is destroyed and the only machine available has a different software package. There may also be a need to exchange files more frequently via the ISH and again the use of standard applications makes this process much easier and faster. The other aspect is that any enterprise which has previously depended on simple barrier systems, such as firewalls, will now be very exposed to risk across the ISH. In risk management terms, it may be justifiable to run these higher risks, in the interests of maintaining the enterprise operation, in much the same way that classified military data has been transmitted across the Internet in time of war without any protection, simply because it was the only way of getting the information where it was needed, and the risk of not communicating was greater than the risk of hostile interception. However, adequate earlier planning will have created a multilevel trusted environment which will provide the same trust levels at any point on a network. This allows some major changes in network topology without impacting the risk reduction and management.

In looking at the standardization and control of software, this should not be confined to *shrink wrapped* workstation applications. What bedevils the development of trusted systems and the maintenance of untrusted applications, is the poor level of documentation and the inconsistent approaches of developers. The way to reduce this risk, which can represent considerable financial overhead, is to ensure that a Structured Method is employed for all software applications developments. Which Structured Method is employed is perhaps less important than actually choosing one. Some enterprises already employ structured methods, but unfortunately employ many different methods across the enterprise. A level of standardization is important. If the Structured Method is contained in a metaCASE tool, considerable savings are possible in development costs and products are built more rapidly at lower risk. The metaCASE tool provides the ability to work through a method, such as SSADM, and automatically produces code and documentation. When the final product is worked on later, it is usually possible to work only on one part of the code without having to work back through the complete product. If it becomes desirable to change methodologies at a later date, a metaCASE tool will permit engineering of existing products. However, developing applications outside a trusted environment introduces a number of serious potential risks. For this reason, it is highly desirable to employ a trusted development environment. This will also provide the means to re engineer untrusted products to elevate them to trusted capability. Beyond that, a trusted metaCASE environment may provide the automated enterprise and risk policy system and offer modelling ability.

In looking at information risk management, the examples have primarily been based on the assumption that enterprises will continue in their traditional form. This follows a pattern where large corporations are formed as a centre for wealth creation and ownership. The high probability is that traditional corporate structures will continue for some years, but there are already signs of a new revolution starting. This revolution comes partly from political actions, and partly from the Information Revolution. The growth of ISH facilities offers choice. Traditional enterprise structures can communicate more efficiently and at lower cost, or the flexibility of the ISH can create new opportunities and result in new enterprise structures and methods. If that was the only influence, any change is more likely to be evolutionary because of the vast wealth, information and power still locked in proprietary monolithic corporations. What is coinciding with these new opportunities created by information technology is change in political postures. Over the last three hundred years, there has been a political move to central control, most marked in socialist states, where the state assumes responsibility for virtually every aspect of human existence. This central

211

control has proved very costly and created armies of government employees and huge waste. It has also threatened communal life and the family unit and in the process introduced the need for yet more funding to replace these ancient and flexible structures. During the closing decades of the Twentieth Century, there is a trend back to decentralization. It may be a natural political backlash to a long period of movement in one direction, but it has begun during a period when technology is potentially able to support a return to a largely decentralized society, based on relatively small units, without losing some of the best features of the monolithic corporation. At present the one noticeable deficiency is a new method of money supply and control. That may evolve naturally as it becomes more profitable to support new enterprise structures than old structures.

# 11 The future and SOHO

Early societies were based on agriculture and were largely self supporting. Travel between communities was limited, and industry was woven into the community. Some people specialized in crafts, but based mainly on the family unit, and many would be activities for the winter months when work outside became difficult as daylight hours reduced. Urban Communities still maintained the links with the countryside and were more trading centre than industrial site. That began to change dramatically with the Industrial Revolution of the Eighteenth and Nineteenth Centuries. Industrial centres were built close to sources of power and raw materials and drew workers in from the countryside. Trading and administrative centres also developed, but workers housing tended to be built around the enterprises of those communities. Work patterns still largely followed the hours of daylight although, for many industrial workers, hours were longer than the period of daylight.

The development of electric power for lighting, and to drive machines, provided the means to work through the night, although work patterns still largely followed the daylight periods and shift working was confined to relatively small sections of heavy industry, and to mining. Large conurbations developed and the wealthier workers sought to find housing in more pleasant conditions away from the dirt and noise of production. By the early Twentieth Century, the commuter was well established and mass transit systems, such as railways, underground railways, and buses, were soon moving large sections of the communities back and forth between home and work. That pattern has continued through the Twentieth Century and become a growing problem by increasing pollution, consumption of raw materials, and the creation of largely unproductive periods which are neither available for leisure, nor for work.

213

The first electronic telecommunications produced a series of modest revolutions. The telegraph and the railway went neatly together, and were responsible for opening up large land areas for the first time. The colonists from developed countries took with them their familiar attitudes and although the first waves were interested in old crafts of hunting and agriculture, industrialization swiftly followed. The telephone began to replace the telegraph as a major form of business communication, but commerce was still tied to relatively slow forms of transport, much of it waterborne. The main revolution of the mid Twentieth Century was in new forms of transport. The motor vehicle has changed short and medium land transport patterns, allowing great mobility, and challenging mass transport systems such as railways. Air transport has revolutionized medium and long distance travel, although marine transport still caters for the transport of goods and for leisure transport. These systems have enabled greater beneficial use to be made of telephone communications, but are still significantly slower than electronic communication. There has been a dramatic increase in media entertainment and information services. The cinema brought video entertainment to the masses, but is functionally similar to the theatre. The real revolution was in combining video and sound in broadcast systems, which could span national boundaries beyond the full control of national legislation, making traditional forms of information control difficult or impossible. Television introduced social change by bringing entertainment into the home and exporting attitudes and values rapidly across the world.

As cinema brought richer information to a traditional audience, early computer based information systems brought richer information to the work place. This enhanced established systems, rather than replacing them, and introduced new concepts within an established framework. Information Super Highways are now revolutionizing information exchange and access in much the same way as radio and television have revolutionized entertainment. As with any revolution, this introduces a period of instability during which there are many new opportunities and many new risks. Any attempt to accurately predict the outcome of this latest revolution is likely to be flawed because the final result will depend heavily on which opportunities we try to seize, and how well we manage to reduce the risks. What can be predicted with some certainty is that the changes taking place in the closing years of the Twentieth Century will pave the way for major social change during the next century.

The *paperless office* has been forecast for twenty years, but has still not arrived. At a time when more information is processed, stored, and transmitted electronically, the production of paper documents is still increasing. The Information Super Highway promises to change this, but the

214

real significance may be far greater. So far, forecasts have tended to address business and private use of ISH as separate issues and assumes that business will continue in much the same structures which were established over a hundred years ago, and assumes that the domestic use of ISH will be for entertainment and domestic activities. From this basis, two specifications develop. The business specification assumes price tolerance similar to that already established for information systems. The domestic specification assumes that widespread use of the new technologies will depend on drastic cost reduction. It is possible that both estimates are wrong.

The strict divisions between workplace and home are beginning to weaken. Creative and administrative tasks do not have to involve moving people to a work site, provided that they have access to all appropriate records and can communicate with colleagues. The ISH provides the means of both communication and information access. As a result, many workers could operate from any location which allows them to access the ISH. This ability is not new and has been available to some extent for more than a decade. The first work groups to benefit from remote working have been sales and creative personnel, such as designers and writers.

The nature of sales lends itself particularly well to remote working because the salesman, by definition, is travelling to visit customers, and any visit to his employer's office will be taking him away from the customer. He will either return to his home each day, or stay in a hotel, so that any method which allows him to operate from customer sites, or from his accommodation, will improve his efficiency. He is also used to working on his own initiative and taking responsibility for managing his time. Historically, the main limitation of his freedom came from the methods of communication available to him which increased the need for periodic visits to his employer's sites. A common work pattern for a salesman has been to travel to customers for meetings during the day and then to attend to administration at the end of each day, completing documents and posting them to the office. Where there is an urgent need to quickly deliver documents, this has required a special trip to the office. New forms of data capture and data communication reduce, or remove, the need for such journeys. Communication can be via radio link, or by dial access from a fixed telephone line. Therefore, a range of administrative duties which were carried out at the end of the day can now be completed as the day progresses. Pen-based computers, voice based systems and automated data capture make it possible to build documentation during a meeting and the result could be transmitted automatically while the salesman is travelling to the next location, making considerable savings of time, and speeding the process of responding to the customer's needs. The ISH could potentially remove the need to ever visit a sales office. Of course, in the case of repeat business sales as to retail outlets, this technology could also remove the need for salesmen, or certainly reduce the numbers required.

As computer systems have spread within the traditional office, the need for personal contact has reduced. One consequence of this has been centralization of administration personnel, and greater use of telephone communication and computerization. In the process, the number of administrative workers has reduced. High street banks have found that most functions, which were previously based on personal contact, can now be conducted by telephone and that customers appreciate longer opening hours, including night and evening working. This is leading to a reduction in the number of branches and the number of counters, which also produces major cost savings, even after the cost of introducing new technology. It has also pointed up some of the significant risks which can attend the new technologies and the changing patterns of risks.

When cash was used for transactions, robbery was a major risk. Often this involved violence, but physical security reduced the risks and both the policing and judicial systems were designed to deal with this form of crime. Fraud was also catered for through established book keeping systems which had been refined over many years. This did not eliminate crime, but it did contain it, and make conviction more certain. Electronic systems have reduced physical crime by replacing cash with paper and electronic transactions, but they have created new classes of crime which involve much larger values and are both more difficult to detect, and more difficult to bring to a successful conviction. Apart from the fact that the legislation has failed to keep up with technology, and the judicial process is not able to deal with the complexity of information presented in evidence, electronic financing has introduced new factors. The electronic criminal is more widely distributed and anonymous. He is able to commit crime remotely, and in random patterns, with many small raids which collectively represent substantial values, all without the criminal coming into contact directly with the victims, and where he has the opportunity to remove any evidence which might convict him. This creates 'clean' crime where the criminal can more easily avoid the psychological factors associated with physical crime. Violently assaulting another person as part of a theft requires a very different level of commitment to that required for mugging a computer system., which is much akin to the national sport of tax evasion, where there is no obvious victim to feel guilty about.

As we come to depend ever more heavily on electronic systems, these issues must be addressed. New policing, legislation and judicial systems, are needed to deal with the new forms of crime. Although that may seem an obvious approach, it is even more important that users take electronic crime seriously and take adequate risk reduction measures. Much existing electronic crime can be prevented by good system design, which will also reduce system and operator faults, and identify where and how the fault developed. This becomes an increasingly pressing need as systems become truly distributed through the ISH communications networks. The technology and techniques for this risk reduction are already available and should be applied to all existing systems, not just to ISH linked systems. However, technology alone does not solve every problem.

Potentially, ISH introduces the ability to reduce the size of existing offices and to distribute workers geographically. Part of the growth in office building was driven by the need to group workers together into administrative units which could economically use early computers and other earlier types of office equipment. As computers developed in power, and communications capability, enterprises did not fully appreciate the options for redistributing the work force. When the London Stock Exchange was refurbished in preparation for deregulation, the planning was based on the assumption that business would still be conducted on the floor of the exchange and that the new electronic systems being installed would simply assist the established way of doing business. What actually happened was that business transferred to dealers' offices away from a Stock Exchange which became largely deserted. This business was conducted electronically and location of personnel on the floor of the Exchange became much less important. What the ISH offers is the ability for workers to operate from their homes, which may be hundreds of miles from the current centres of business, creating opportunities to substantially reduce operating costs and improve life styles. Against this, there are risks, and fear of the risks has contributed to slower change in business patterns.

Some enterprises fear that they cannot control their workers if they cannot see them. As senior managers are generally much older than their workforces, many have still not appreciated the benefits and challenges of new technology, and operate on experience which developed before the changes. As a result, it is very easy for them to fear change which they do not understand. They are not assisted by their younger employees, who see the benefits, but do not understand the challenges and threats. The only way to remove this difficulty is to improve training and ensure that older workers overcome their fear of the unknown. A senior manager who resists change today, and fails to take advantage of new opportunities through ignorance, can learn to adapt, and then use his wider experience to ensure that change is made for the right reasons, controlling the wilder enthusiasms of the young technologists who often fail to see beyond the technical aspects.

A part of the challenge is how to train people to develop an overview. Before computerization, a worker could evolve through experience of work at different levels of an enterprise. A tradition of Nineteenth Century business was that every employee started at the bottom of the organization. The future senior managers might have been the sons and daughters of the owners and they may have achieved management positions early in their careers, but they were expected to work in each part of the enterprise, however briefly, to gain direct experience of the conditions which the workforce had to operate within. That meant that every manager had some knowledge of what changes would mean to the people, and how much could be expected of them. An accelerating aspect of the Twentieth Century has been the acceptance that specialization is essential and that theoretical training can replace direct experience. Unfortunately, this produces managers who have no direct experience of the problems which their workers face, and no real knowledge of what other parts of the enterprise do, or why they do it. This produces elitists who have considerable detailed knowledge of a narrow aspect of the enterprise and a theoretical knowledge of some of the more closely related areas of the organization, much of the general knowledge having been provided in the classroom. The danger of classroom knowledge is that it can very easily be outdated, based on the narrow, and possibly theoretical, experience of tutors gained several years before. When experience is transferred in this way, it becomes easy for people to immerse themselves in the comforting familiarity of their specialization, ignoring the needs and challenges of others. The result has been a series of flawed decisions and the blind adoption of technology without full regard for the consequences. As these managers are divorced from the rest of the work force, they are dealing with numbers rather than people. It is always much easier to take unpopular choices which affect numbers and not people. Unfortunately, the numbers are people who have their own responsibilities, desires, fears, loyalties and objectives. When they feel aggrieved, and devalued, they can strike back, and do great damage in the process.

The new ISH environment is no different from any earlier technology in that it can be applied wisely, or unwisely. It has great potential for providing an environment where geographic location of users is largely unimportant, at least theoretically. Enterprises are beginning to see that it has a potential for major cost reduction, adopting technology without adequate planning and appreciation of the risks. Workers are accepting, or resisting, new working practices without understanding the benefits and risks.

For the enterprise, ISH provides the means to distribute its workforce geographically, reversing years of centralization. This may mean that groups of workers can be located in smaller buildings, sited in lower cost areas. An enterprise operating in a major city has to pay high costs for the real estate, but most of the workforce can now be located in low cost areas, resulting in substantial savings. This does not mean that workers will operate from home, and therefore does not require a major change in risk reduction procedures for sites and buildings. However, it can reduce the cost of risk reduction because some risks will be greatly reduced. A fire, or some other major incident, has a less serious effect on an enterprise if it is only able to remove a small part of the capacity for business. A major incident in a large central building will seriously disrupt business, and contingency planning will be costly but only partially effective. If a small unit is completely disabled, the effect on the enterprise may hardly be noticed. Other sites will be able to provide replacement capacity and provide temporary accommodation for workers from the affected site. If a large centralized facility suffers a major incident, loss of production will be immediate, and possibly total. Finding temporary accommodation will be very difficult and expensive. Obtaining rapid replacement equipment, particularly computers and communications, is difficult, but duplicating original facilities can be impossible unless contingency planning has already included standby facilities. Therefore distributed facilities offer much higher resilience and ISH makes it practical to link them to produce a capability which was previously only possible by centralization of resources.

To move to the logical conclusion may seem but a small step. SOHO, Small Office Home Office, is that conclusion. Taking the step to the Small Office for a large corporation is straight forward, even if it is a reversal of policy away from centralization. The basic forms of risk reduction still apply, although the Small Office is more likely to be a part of shared accommodation. There is the question of real estate values and this is a area of significant risk. Most large corporations depend upon the asset value of real estate, which generally appreciates over a period of years. Much of the borrowing requirement is underwritten by these asset values and therefore enterprises are at risk if a rapid and widespread trend to SOHO was established, reducing the demand for, and therefore the value of, prime site real estate. One approach which has potential is to turn private sites into shared sites, renting out space to smaller corporations.

A number of large corporations have moved to a half way position. They still maintain large offices, but no longer allocate specific desks to workers. Each work position is equipped with docking equipment for portable computer workstations. When workers need to visit an office, they occupy the first available work area and plug their portable computer into the docking station, which automatically connects them into the office network. This allows greater mobility, but still offers the benefits of meeting rooms and other facilities which can best be provided in an office facility. The fact that a smaller number of people will be using the facilities at any one time means that greater space can be allocated to each person. It is possible that commercial organizations will take over existing offices and provide these services to anyone who needs them on an ad hoc basis. This trend is already establishing and hotels are beginning to offer business suites, so that guests can conduct business from the hotel, removing the need for small branch offices. There may be an opportunity for enterprises providing hotel space to develop new types of facility where the primary business is renting out office suites and meeting rooms on half day and day bookings, with accommodation forming a minor part of the business. This would probably require a different type of structure, and there would be a need to urgently address risk management because at least part of the site would be open to the public.

The most exciting potential is for the true SOHO. Although large corporations attract the headlines, the vibrancy of any economy comes from the small enterprise which is able to introduce innovation and flexibility. Two factors have hampered small businesses since the industrial revolution. Financing has been a key factor, but what hampers a small enterprise most is access to, and management of, communications. A very small enterprise, of less than five people, is able to offer specialist services cost effectively if most of the output is channelled into the service offered. Unfortunately, a high percentage of effort is diverted into the marketing of the service, and the administration of the business. Communication makes up a significant part of this effort, especially if the work of the business takes place away from a fixed site. The availability of Information Super Highways and mobile communications offers a method of reducing effort and cost, while improving communication. Existing technology provides the means to complete estimates away from a base, as part of the survey work. Keyboard and pen based portable computers are now small enough to be carried safely, and used in much the same way as notebooks have been used in the past. Applications software provides the means to automate large parts of the process and prompts the surveyor to complete all necessary actions. Data capture devices provide the means to collect information more easily, by reading bar codes, taking electronic measurements, recording images, scanning documents, and fixing geographic locations. Voice based computers are becoming viable systems, and this opens the possibility of wearing a voice-based portable computer, with headset for hands-free operation. If these facilities are integrated, and linked by radio to the ISH, it becomes possible to reduce the time taken to carryout surveys, largely automates the process of preparing quotations, and updates all appropriate office systems. If the primary data capture system is a voice based computer, a seamless integration of voice communication and data becomes practical. For many small enterprises, this can reduce the amount of time spent in administrative and communications tasks from 60% per man to as low as 5%. Reductions of this size can produce significant productivity gains and enable small enterprises to focus their main effort into revenue earning.

It is possible to dispense entirely with the conventional office. For many small enterprises, the office serves as a store and a place to run the administration from. The need to devote a significant percentage of available effort to administrative functions has historically encouraged office space requirements to grow with the business. Once the first employees are taken on, the office and workshop start to grow, and soon become an important investment and overhead. Over a period of time, the successful enterprise continues to expand and the fixed facilities take progressively more of the available resources. There are only two factors which can break this cycle. A number of enterprises will continue to expand until they are forced to contract. If they have sufficient time, they will dispose of assets such as business premises and dismiss their personnel. If they survive the trauma, they will start to expand again at the first opportunity, repeating their previous behaviour. Not every enterprise is able to move fast enough and the business fails. The only other way to avoid the process is to find an alternative early in the life of the enterprise. ISH provides the means to automate processes and avoid the need for offices.

There are two basic options. An enterprise could rent data storage and processing space on the network, and it would then only be necessary to buy portable equipment to link to the ISH. The portable equipment could be very compact because it would need to store very little data. This would increase the use of communications bandwidth because the portable equipment would be functioning as an intelligent remote job entry terminal for an important part of the time. At present, the main risk of this form of working is that legislation does not adequately protect the data stored at a shared facility, and early service providers offer very little effective security. It is therefore likely that the small enterprise will wish to buy its own data processing and storage systems, linking to the ISH only for communications. However, the equipment needed would not represent significant cost, and would require very little space, so that it could be sited in the home. This would represent a valuable asset and require risk management to protect it, but considerable expansion in capacity would not entail significant expansion of space requirements. In many respects, this potentially offers a return to pre industrial revolution structures, with work centred on the family unit. If this structure was widely applied, most large enterprises would have to evolve new structures to compete. Rapid change could follow. Once small, low overhead, enterprises begin to compete for business which was previously beyond their reach, some large enterprises will be forced to dramatically reduce overheads. That would start a chain reaction and could even precipitate a world-wide recession because it would

221

destabilize a number of major markets, while the new markets being created have not yet established.

Much of commerce is based on real estate values. Any sudden reduction in demand would cause prices to slump. Much of industry will be operating on loans which have been secured against the real estate values. If those values drop, banks will panic and start calling in loans. There will also be a greatly reduced demand for transportation and other associated services. It is possible that the process has already begun and will consist of a series market distortions which could become progressively more severe, unless the new markets are able to rapidly establish. Certainly, the last decade of the Twentieth Century has already seen substantial reductions in administrative jobs, with the banking industry being hit particularly hard. There has also been substantial growth in very small service businesses. What is not yet obvious is how well the small enterprises will survive, and if they will eventually repeat the traditional pattern of expansion. Early indications are that a new class of worker is emerging, operating from his home, but carrying out at least part of his work on traditional business sites operated by his customers. Some enterprises are self supporting businesses with a broad customer base, but a growing number are based on the skills of an individual who is selling parts of his time to a number of customers who previously employed full time workers. An increasing proportion of contract working is being carried out from home, rather than from the customer's site. This is allowing special groups to find work which would otherwise not be available. Mothers with young children, people nursing sick relatives, those with disabilities, all benefit potentially from the new opportunities, and help to make up the deficit which is being created by falling birthrates, reduced working hours, and early retirement. However, an increasing proportion of these contract workers are not from special groups, but are people who previously would have sought full time employment with a single employer.

It can be argued that a move to home working will bring enormous benefits ultimately, even if it causes instability in the short term. Any reduction in business travel is potentially beneficial because it reduces cost, pollution, and use of non-renewable resources. It is also possible that leisure travel will also reduce. What has always made the Home Office impractical for most people has been limited communications bandwidth, because the only telecommunications links were low capacity copper cable for analogue voice communications. The capacity of these circuits has increased significantly, as modem technology has improved, but the major breakthrough is widespread availability of high capacity fibre optic links, and radio links for more isolated locations. Once these links are available to the home, growing use of available bandwidth becomes relatively inexpensive. The result may be that integrated home systems become available to provide a comprehensive range of communications and data for both business and domestic use. This could replace all the familiar home systems, such as telephones, television sets, burglar alarms, heating control systems, etc. It would therefore be possible to use Personal Stations which would be audio visual devices capable of voice, pen, and keyboard operation, and available for business and leisure purposes. The cost of such equipment could stand existing market costings on their head. The market, even in the early days, would be very large, and therefore economy of production scale would allow lowest cost for given quality. One device would replace a number of business and domestic devices, which would substantially reduce true cost, and make considerable resilience economically practical. Against this, the quality of design, manufacture, and quality management, would generally be a higher requirement than is traditional for domestic products, because a part of the use would be business.

All of the technical elements are available now and many of them have been available for a number of years, so that future possibilities explored above are for application of existing technology. That application could take the dual forms of large enterprises employing technology to cut costs and change structures, and small enterprises being able to operate more successfully and productively without having to become larger units. There is a further possibility which could change the whole business structure. What impedes small enterprises, and provides large enterprises with very dangerous levels of power, is funding. The amazing growth of communications facilities only partially addresses this subject, in that it makes facilities available which would previously have been prohibitively expensive. Financing may be eased because the enterprises will be more productive and profitable enterprises better able to raise additional funds. What could be the major economic product of the Cyber Age may be the Virtual Corporation.

The concept of the business cooperative is very old. It has been strongest in the retail and agricultural industries where there have always been naturally occurring small enterprises. The idea of banding together to market effectively against large competitors, and buy more effectively through combined purchasing power, is an attractive concept. Where the concept has most frequently failed is that poor communications have led to the need to establish a central body, and that body has developed progressively to resemble a conventional large corporation. In the process, it has become more monolithic and inflexible, losing most of the original advantages, without necessarily finding new benefits. The Information Super Highway does provide the means to create a new form of cooperative group as a

Virtual Corporation which operates through shared skills and time but does not require a large central corporate building and formal structure. In the process, it could develop all the advantages of group buying, marketing, and investment, without losing the benefits of a flexible association of innovative small enterprises.

What may take the ISH much further forward is Virtual Reality. Early ISH facilities offer all the administrative and creative facilities which were previously available only on purpose built sites. Virtual Reality opens up the possibility of controlling an activity remotely, via the ISH. Surgeons could operate on patients who were thousands of miles away. This would allow a patient to be treated by the most skilled surgeon, without the trauma of transportation. Aircraft, ships and production systems could be remotely piloted. This would allow a smaller number of people to operate equipment, which is capable of automatic operation for most of the time, and really only requires a pilot or operator to handle anomalies, and to instruct changes. Some tasks, such as deep water mining, would be become practical for the first time, because the operator would have all the benefits of being on the sea bed, without the problems and dangers. Amazing benefits are potentially available, but all introduce new risks.

The major risk is that people are removed from direct contact. The growth of corporations has created situations where personnel take unreasonable actions, which they would not otherwise consider, because they are divorced from the object of the action, and insulated from the consequences. The smaller the enterprise, the more human it becomes, and the more personal the actions. In the same way, people are less likely to attack close neighbours and friends, but might feel no compunction in attacking a large faceless corporation which *can afford it and deserves it.* ISH and Virtual Reality could simply increase the incidence of this behaviour, because people are removed from that direct personal contact, identity and human responsibility. We will only know that as the development takes place, and we can measure performance. Early signs from the Internet, which is the largest and longest established ISH, are not encouraging. The Internet has produced a new phenomena, *flame mail.* Electronic discussion degenerates rapidly into verbal violence and intemperance. People who are otherwise rational, polite, and considerate, become verbal warriors trampling on the feelings of others. This is not unlike the behavioural change which comes over many people when they start driving a car. The common factor is also an insulation from the outside world, and a reduction in perceptions of reality. The growth of *white collar* crime is not an encouraging precedent. At this stage, we must assume that attacks on ISH linked resources will increase and, particularly, increase in sophistication. Therefore, we should address these potential risks effectively, both with risk reducing measures and with adequate legislation. As electronic systems perform ever more tasks, we must pay much closer attention to the quality of design and construction, and also to the management of implemented technology. We must recognize our increasing dependence on electronic and, particularly, automated systems, to know that they are working, rather than to hope that they function correctly. We must also remember that the systems are there to serve people, and not other systems. If we address these risks, and seize the benefits of ISH, and the related systems, we will enter a new age of opportunity.